Understanding Local Area Networks

Third Edition

Sams
Understanding
Series

Understanding Local Area Networks

Third Edition

Stan Schatt

SAMS

A Division of Prentice Hall Computer Publishing

11711 North College, Carmel, Indiana 46032 USA

This third edition is dedicated to my wife, Jane, who I hope will always understand why all of my books are dedicated to her.

Publisher
Richard K. Swadley

Associate Publisher
Marie Butler-Knight

Managing Editor
Liz Keaffaber

Acquisitions Editor
Charlie Dresser

Development Editor
Faithe Wempen

Manuscript Editor
Barry Childs-Helton

Production Editor
Linda Hawkins

Editorial Assistant
Hilary Adams

Cover Designer
Tim Amrhein

Cover Photography
David Kadlec

Designers
Scott Cook, Michele Laseau

Indexer
Jeanne Clark

Production Team
*Brook Farling, Keith Davenport, Dennis Clay Hager, Laurie Lee,
Cindy L. Phipps, Kevin Spear, Lisa Wilson, Phil Worthington*

*Special thanks to James P. McCarter for ensuring the technical
accuracy of this book.*

DAVID C. WEST

Understanding
Local Area
Networks | # Contents

Chapter 3 Bridges, Routers, and Gateways *67*

Chapter 4 Microsoft's LAN Manager and IBM's LANs *103*

Chapter 5 Novell's NetWare *147*

Introduction

Over the last 10 years, the DOS-based microcomputer has become a fixture in the business world, dramatically changing nearly every industry it has touched. Until recently, however, we lacked the technology to connect these units so that companies could share expensive resources and ensure data integrity. With the release of MS-DOS 3.1 a few years ago (with its network features) and the development of faster microprocessors (such as the Intel 80386 and 80486) to serve as the workhorses of network file servers, we now have the necessary software and hardware to implement cost-effective, efficient *local area networks (LANs)*.

About This Book

This book is intended to explain how LANs and their various hardware and software components work. It will provide you with an understanding of the theory behind the various kinds of network architecture (the different forms networks take) and data transmission methods (how information is sent through a network). It will also provide you with an understanding of the major LANs currently on the market, as well as the degree of compatibility among these networks. Finally, the book should serve as a way for a potential network administrator to develop an understanding of whether or not a LAN is really a viable solution for his or her particular office.

In order to understand the benefits of a local area network—and what greater connectivity can mean for a company—you need to understand the basic building blocks of a LAN. The first two chapters of this book cover the hardware and software fundamentals of a LAN.

Chapter 3 examines how bridges, routers, and gateways can be used to connect networks and exchange information with mainframes and microcomputers. The micro-mainframe connection is increasingly important, since we now have the software to transfer mainframe data to a LAN, and to manipulate this data within the programs. Because the telecommunications industry now has the ability to transmit voice and data simultaneously, we will also examine how some companies are using their telephone systems as LANs. The networking world has also become increasingly complex over the past few years because it is not always easy to link different networks; they might be running incompatible software on computers with incompatible hardware.

The next four chapters apply this network theory to major LANs from IBM, Novell, Microsoft, and AT&T, as well as several different LANs running on Macintosh computers. The Macintosh has often been shortchanged in LAN books, so I have tried to balance its coverage by providing an in-depth look at NetWare, TOPS, and AppleShare AppleTalk networks.

The last five chapters provide a chance to examine some significant management issues associated with LANs. Chapter 8 covers four networks that are becoming increasingly popular: Vines, 10Net, ARCnet, and Artisoft's LANtastic. With Vines we have the opportunity to see how a universal naming service works to simplify internetwork connectivity—while 10Net and LANtastic provide examples of peer-to-peer networks in which individual workstations have the opportunity to share resources with the network.

Chapter 9 provides an in-depth look at electronic mail on a network—with "hands-on" tours of several major software packages, as well as an examination of the theory behind the X.400 electronic mail standard. Chapter 10 provides a survey of the major issues associated with network management and control. It examines several major functions that every network manager must perform.

Chapter 11 provides a guide to networkable software. It examines how network software functions, and discusses the trend toward client-server programs. Finally, Chapter 12 provides detailed advice on how to select a LAN—including information on how to write a good RFP (request for proposals) and how to evaluate the vendors' proposals when they respond to the RFP.

This book is arranged somewhat like a textbook, with quizzes following each chapter. Each chapter builds on the previous chapter's information. Try to master a chapter before moving on. If you wish to explore the data communications topics in even more depth, a companion book in this series, *Understanding Data Communications*, should prove useful. If you wish more information on Novell's NetWare (the LAN operating system with the major market share), my book *Understanding NetWare* will provide you with a much more detailed description.

I hope this book will help you understand why local area networks are destined to become an important part of our lives. I hope it will also prove valuable if you are considering the purchase of a local area network.

Acknowledgments

I wish to acknowledge the technical expertise and generous help of Marc Covitt of Hewlett-Packard; Steven Fox, David Guerro, and Randy Sprinkle of AT&T; Orval Luckey of IBM; and Bob Schulte of 3Com. I want to thank Sams for permission to reprint portions of *Understanding NetWare*.

Trademark Acknowledgments

All terms mentioned in this book that are known to be trademarks or service marks are listed below. In addition, terms suspected of being trademarks or service marks have been appropriately capitalized. Sams cannot attest to the accuracy of this information. Use of a term in this book should not be regarded as affecting the validity of any trademark or service mark.

AppleShare, AppleTalk, LaserWriter, LocalTalk, ImageWriter, and Macintosh are registered trademarks of Apple Computer, Inc.

ARCnet is a registered trademark of Datapoint Corporation.

cc:Mail and Lotus 1-2-3 are trademarks of the Lotus Development Corporation.

COMPAQ is a registered trademark of Compaq Computer Corporation.

TOPS is a trademark of Sun Microsystems, Inc.

TYMNET is a trademark of Tymnet, Inc.

UNIX is a registered trademark of AT&T.

Ventura Publisher is a registered trademark of Ventura Software, Inc.

Vines and StreetTalk are registered trademarks of Banyan Systems, Inc.

WordPerfect is a registered trademark of WordPerfect Corporation.

1 | An Overview of Microcomputers and Local Area Networks

About This Chapter

Understanding the personal computer that serves as a *network work-station* is essential before studying the theory behind contemporary LANs. In this chapter, we will discuss how an IBM microcomputer processes information. If you are already familiar with this subject, you may wish to skip to the second half of the chapter; there we review the history of LANs and observe the way a typical company uses network technology to handle a wide range of office functions. By the time you finish reading this book, you should have a good understanding of how to achieve a high level of network integration (which the "Widget Company" in this chapter illustrates).

The IBM Personal Computer: A Tutorial

Because so many businesses have selected IBM personal computers— or computers designed to run IBM PC programs (known as *compatibles* or "clones")—these machines have become the building blocks of LANs. Figure 1.1 shows an IBM PS/2 Model 70, an example of the second generation of IBM's microcomputers.

Figure 1.1 An IBM PS/2 Model 70 (Courtesy of IBM Corporation)

Later in the book you will learn how dozens (in some cases, hundreds) of these computers—linked together by network software, network hardware, and cabling—can share information and resources. In a LAN, each user has his or her own personal computer, often an IBM PC or compatible. Before looking at how the network functions, however, you need to understand how information is processed by the personal computers that comprise it.

Bits and Bytes

A computer can help accomplish many complex tasks, but its processor actually performs only one function: it keeps track of whether a wire has current flowing through it (1) or no current flowing through it (0). We refer to each of these binary digits of information as a *bit*. The American Standard Code for Information Interchange (*ASCII*) specifies that each character of the alphabet requires seven bits of information, with an eighth *parity bit* as insurance that the information has not been garbled. To an IBM microcomputer, the binary combination 10000010 represents the letter *a*. This 8-bit unit of information is known as a *byte*.

The original IBM PC contained an Intel 8088 microprocessor, a microcomputer chip that served as the *central processing unit (CPU),* or "brains," of the computer. This chip was capable of processing 16 bits (two bytes) of information at one time. The CPU had a clock speed of 4.77 MHz (megahertz), which means that the microprocessor produced 4.77 million pulses each second. (Processors schedule their work based on these pulses.) Later microprocessors had faster clock speeds, and thus could perform tasks such as mathematical operations faster. The IBM AT (Advanced Technology), for example, used an Intel 80286 microprocessor, and had a clock speed of 8.0 MHz.

Today, computer CPUs run at speeds many times that of the original IBM PC. The IBM PS/2 Model 70, for example, uses a 32-bit Intel 80386 microprocessor, and is capable of a clock speed of 25 MHz. The Intel 80486 microprocessors already are approaching 50 MHz, while the Intel 80586 microprocessor waits in the wings with even greater speed potential. Since a LAN generally uses its fastest, most powerful computer to service network workstations, clock speed is a significant factor in a LAN's overall efficiency.

In addition to performing mathematical operations, a PC's CPU processes information from a variety of sources, such as the keyboard, the I/O ports (parallel and serial), and the monitor. It needs a workspace area in which to store some of its calculations temporarily; this need for temporary workspace is satisfied by using some of the computer's *memory*.

RAM and ROM

There are two types of memory associated with microcomputers: *read-only memory (ROM)* and *random-access memory (RAM)*. ROM is permanent memory that retains information even when the computer is turned off. Microcomputers store their most critical programs in ROM, including a program that checks the computer when it is turned on to ensure that all components are working properly. A computer also stores its *bootstrap* program in ROM; this program provides the computer with enough knowledge to load information from a disk.

Unlike the ROM, RAM is temporary memory; it retains information only while the computer is on. It is measured in *kilobytes* (thousands of bytes of storage). The original IBM generally came with 256K (256 kilobytes) of RAM on its system board (*motherboard*), but its memory could be expanded to 640K by inserting a *memory circuit card* into one of the motherboard's expansion slots. Using the original IBM PC as an example, Figure 1.2 illustrates the location of both ROM and RAM on the motherboard.

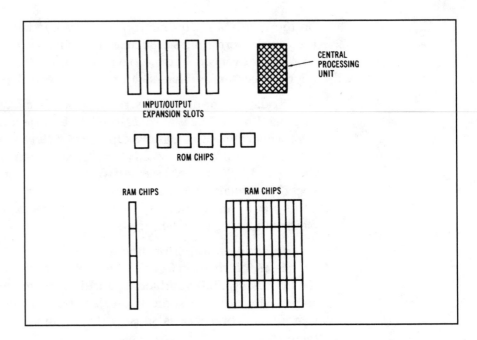

Figure 1.2 An IBM PC Motherboard

Expansion Slots

The expansion slots illustrated in Figure 1.2 are sometimes known as *peripheral slots,* or as input/output expansion slots, since they serve as the way to link the computer's CPU with external devices, or *peripherals.* One slot might be used for a *disk controller* card, which will link the computer to a disk drive capable of reading information on disks. A second slot might contain a *printer interface* card that connects the computer to a printer. A third slot might contain a card which has a built-in *modem* able to transmit information from the computer over a telephone line to a computer in another city.

Monitors and Video Adapters

Unlike today's second generation of IBM PS/2 microcomputers (which have built-in video interfaces), the original IBM PC used one of its expansion slots for a *video adapter*, a circuit card that sent video signals to a monochrome or color computer monitor. Today, most IBM PC compatibles do not have built-in video cards. Many customers prefer the flexibility offered by expansion slots.

A *monochrome* monitor is capable of displaying one color in addition to black (amber, green, and white are common). A monochrome monitor is adequate for word processing, spreadsheet analysis, and database management—tasks that do not require color. A monitor's screen contains a number of small, block-like picture elements (*pixels*); these are either lit or unlit to form characters. The number of pixels that can be displayed horizontally and vertically is a function of both the monitor and its video adapter card. IBM offered the Monochrome Display Adapter (MDA) card for the original IBM PC. MDA could display 720 horizontal pixels by 350 vertical pixels, which is still considered fairly high resolution.

A monochrome monitor requires a monochrome adapter card or a color adapter card capable of supporting monochrome modes. Many computer users with monochrome monitors want to see graphs displayed on their screens; this is possible only if the adapter card is capable of displaying graphics. While IBM's own MDA card does not permit graphics to be displayed, several companies offer video adapters (such as the Monochrome Graphics Card from Hercules Technology) that can display graphics at the same resolution as text.

Users of the original IBM PC who wished to display color graphics usually selected a Color Graphics Adapter (CGA) or an Enhanced Graphics Adapter (EGA), along with a monitor capable of displaying the appropriate level of resolution. The CGA cards are capable of providing a monitor with 640 x 200 resolution. CGA cards are also capable of displaying 16 colors, only 4 of which can be displayed at any given time. The EGA cards, on the other hand, are capable of 640 x 350 resolution, and can display 64 colors, 16 of which can be displayed at any given time. Table 1.1 summarizes the different standards IBM has used over the years for monochrome, CGA, and EGA cards, as well as the standards associated with IBM's second generation of microcomputers.

Table 1.1. IBM Video Adapter Card Standards

Standard	Resolution Pixels	Total Colors	Colors/Screen
Hercules MDA	720 x 348	N/A	N/A
CGA	640 x 200	16	4
EGA	640 x 350	64	16
PGA	640 x 480	4096	256
MCGA			
CGA Mode	640 x 200	4096	256
Text Mode	640 x 480	16	2
VGA			
CGA Mode	640 x 200	4096	256
Text Mode	720 x 400	16	2

Most programs require a user to indicate specifically which type of video adapter card will be used, so the program will send the proper signal to the card. You will discover (later in this book) that this requirement can present some problems when a program is used on a LAN; different workstations may contain different video adapter cards.

Disk Drives and Disk Storage

The term "diskette" is often used to refer to a floppy disk, such as the 3½-inch or 5¼-inch disks used in PC disk drives. The term "diskette" is not used to refer to fixed (or "hard") drives.

Since the random-access memory retains information only while the computer is turned on, a *disk drive* serves as the permanent storage device. A disk (such as the floppy disk shown in Figure 1.3) must be prepared to handle information sent from an IBM or compatible PC; the preparation procedure is called *formatting*.

A 5¼-inch double-density disk, when formatted, contains 40 concentric circles (or *tracks*). Each track contains a number of 512-byte *sectors;* these are blocks where data can be stored (see Figure 1.3). The computer maps the sectors so it can keep track of precisely where on a disk specific information is stored. IBM PC and compatibles with low-density drives generally format a disk so that it is *double-sided double-density (DSDD)* and holds approximately 360K of data. High-density drives format a DSDD diskette to hold approximately 1.2 megabytes of data.

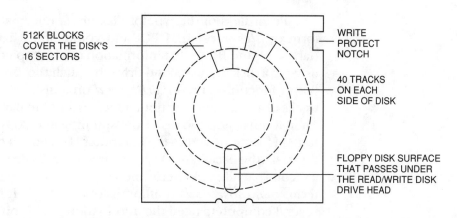

512K BLOCKS
COVER THE DISK'S
16 SECTORS

WRITE
PROTECT
NOTCH

40 TRACKS
ON EACH
SIDE OF DISK

FLOPPY DISK SURFACE
THAT PASSES UNDER
THE READ/WRITE DISK
DRIVE HEAD

Figure 1.3 Floppy Disk for an IBM PC or Compatible

There are nine sectors per track and 40 tracks on each side of a low-density disk. Simple mathematics reveals what each formatted DSDD disk can hold:

40 tracks per side

x 9 sectors per track

x 512 bytes per sector

x 2 sides per disk

or a total of 368,640 bytes per disk.

Since ASCII requires one byte per character (seven bits to represent a character, with one additional bit as a parity bit), a DSDD disk can hold 368,640 characters.

For many years, the IBM-compatible standard disk was a 5¼-inch DSDD disk, and the majority of IBM PCs and compatibles found on networks still use these. However, today's IBM and compatible PCs also support double-sided high-density (DSHD) 5¼-inch disks, which hold approximately 1.2 megabytes of data. In addition, 3½-inch diskette drives are now becoming common in IBM and compatible PCs, which hold 720K (double-density) or 1.44 megabytes (high-density). High-density disk drives can write data closer together, so that a disk can contain more tracks.

Regardless of the type of disk drive, information is saved in the form of *files*. Most IBM PCs and compatibles have two disk drives (labeled A and B), so that information can be copied from a disk in one drive to a disk in the second drive. In much the same way that a record player functions, a *read/write head* on a disk drive moves across the tracks of a spinning disk until it locates a particular file of information. Then it must stop the disk from spinning and copy the pattern of bits to RAM locations within the computer. The time it takes to accomplish this task (the *access time*) is measured in *milliseconds* (thousandths of a second), while tasks performed by the CPU are measured generally in terms of *nanoseconds* (millionths of a second). It is easy to see that if several computers need the information stored on a particular disk—and if this disk access procedure must be repeated a number of times—there will be a measurable slowdown in computer operations. In later chapters we will discuss this problem, along with the methods several LAN manufacturers have developed for speeding up the access procedure.

Hard Disk Drives

It is much faster and more efficient to load all programs and data files onto one hard disk drive rather than to use several dozen floppy disks. A computer user can place all information on a single hard-disk-drive unit capable of holding anywhere from 10 megabytes (10 million bytes) to several hundred megabytes of information. As Figure 1.4 illustrates, a *hard disk* is actually a rigid platter coated with a metal oxide material. It looks very much like a record. In the *sealed hard disk* unit, the read/write head travels rapidly (around 3,600 rpm) on a very thin cushion of air that separates it from the magnetic surface of the hard disk—at a distance that varies from 1 millionth of an inch to 1/2 millionth of an inch, depending upon the brand of hard disk. It might take approximately 15 milliseconds (ms) access time for the hard disk to locate and load a file on a hard disk, compared to 90 ms with a floppy disk drive. (You will learn in the next chapter how this speed allows one hard disk drive to serve several different personal computers in a network environment.)

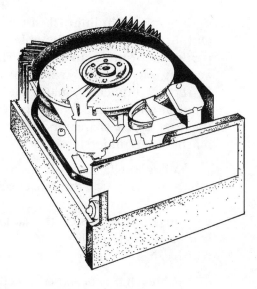

Figure 1.4 A Hard Disk

The Disk Operating System (DOS)

With the IBM PC and compatibles, a series of programs handles such "housekeeping" tasks as loading programs into the computer from a disk, saving information to a disk, and translating typed keyboard characters into a numeric language the computer can understand. These programs collectively make up the *Disk Operating System (DOS)*. The IBM PC version, licensed from Microsoft Corporation, is known as *PC DOS;* the identical program used by IBM compatibles is known as *MS-DOS* (Microsoft Disk Operating System). Some routine tasks that DOS helps users perform include formatting a disk, copying a file from one disk to another, and deleting a file from a disk.

DOS's internal operations can be divided into four basic functions: the Supervisor, the Input/Output Manager, the File Manager, and the Command Processor. The *Supervisor* is responsible for coordinating all the activities of the other programs. If certain programs must be run sequentially, the Supervisor ensures that these programs are coordinated. The *Input/Output Manager* is responsible for ensuring that the computer is able to communicate effectively with a wide range of peripherals, including disk drives and printers. For example, the Input/Output Manager must be able to translate data into a form that a particular printer can accept. The *File Manager* is responsible for keeping track of exactly where all information is stored on disk, so it can be retrieved quickly. Finally, the *Command Processor* provides communication between the computer user and the computer itself. When the user types characters, they are converted into a language the machine can understand.

Microsoft has published several different versions of PC DOS and MS-DOS, which for the most part are *upwardly compatible.* Under most conditions, it is not wise (or even possible) to mix different DOS versions of programs on the same disk, but later in this book you will learn how some LANs divide a hard disk into various sections, each of which can contain programs running under a different version of DOS.

While DOS is designed specifically to coordinate the communication between a computer and the rest of its world (including disk drives, printers, and keyboard input), some LAN programs superimpose a "shell" around the DOS programs and intercept commands normally handled by DOS. When we discuss the Novell NetWare software in Chapter 5, you will learn how such an approach can provide a number of advantages. One of these is the capability of allowing several people to use a program designed originally for only one user—without ruining the program or the information (data files) associated with it.

The OS/2 Operating System

PC DOS was designed for the original IBM PC at a time when hardware resources were far more limited than they are today. Since the IBM PC usually replaced microcomputers containing 64K to 128K of RAM, 640K (the maximum amount of RAM that PC DOS could address) seemed more than anyone could possibly need. Similarly, the operating system's ability to address up to 32 megabytes of secondary storage seemed more than enough, in an era when 10-megabyte hard disk drives were a luxury. PC DOS was adequate, though, for running a single program as long as it did not require very much RAM.

Whereas PC DOS was designed as a single-user, *single-tasking* operating system, OS/2 is a single-user, *multitasking* operating system. It is able to address a maximum of 16 megabytes of RAM, as well as manage a virtually unlimited amount of secondary storage. This powerful operating system has become the basis of two key LANs that will be discussed in Chapter 4: Microsoft's LAN Manager and IBM's LAN Server.

Microsoft Windows

Microsoft's Windows program is not an operating system, but rather, a companion program to DOS. It is a *graphical user interface (GUI)* which enables users to view applications in various "windows" on their screens. Because Windows is a single-user, single-tasking program, only one program can actually be actively running at any given time. It is possible to have a window for the network, so that a user can view network programs from this window, or even to run multiple network programs in multiple windows. The Windows program switches from one active program to another program giving the appearance that more than one program is active at a time.

Parallel and Serial Transmission

As indicated earlier, a microcomputer's expansion slots allow it to communicate with peripherals such as disk drives and printers. A *parallel printer adapter* (also known simply as a printer interface) fits in an expansion slot, and connects to a printer by a cable. Eight bits of data travel in parallel, along eight separate wires, from the PC to the printer. This method of transmission is relatively fast, but of limited range (25 feet) before data is lost.

Some printers (and virtually all modems) require a particular circuit card to convert data from the parallel form (found within the PC) to *serial* form (bits traveling sequentially, in single file, along the same wire). An *asynchronous communications adapter* (usually known as a *serial port*) serves this function. While serial transmission is often not as fast as parallel transmission, it is capable of transmitting data reliably over longer distances. Most PC's come configured with at least one built-in parallel and one serial port.

A 25-pin *serial cable* contains 25 wires, while a 9-pin serial cable contains 9 wires. Normally the data is transmitted along one wire, while other information is sent along other wires. (This practice is consistent with the Electronic Industries Association's (EIA) RS-232C standard for serial transmission.) *Parallel* and *serial printers,* as well as *serial modems*, are critical elements of most LANs.

Now that we have discussed the major features of the IBM PC and compatibles, let's take a brief look at the evolution of the PC.

A Brief History of Distributed Processing and Networks

In three decades, we have seen the computer industry evolve. Initially, all processing was performed on mainframe computers using a batch approach. Time-sharing (using public telephone lines) was an improvement, but the concept of distributed processing with minicomputers provided a quantum leap in computer affordability and convenience. Many companies replaced their mainframes and minicomputers (gradually) with microcomputers and a LAN.

While it is only with the arrival of the microcomputer that companies have been able to implement LANs, the concept itself is not new. It represents a logical development and evolution of computer technology. The first computers in the 1950s were *mainframes*. Large, expensive, and reserved for a very few select users, these monsters occupied entire buildings.

These first computers were not designed for on-line response to a user's commands. They used a *batch* approach. Users submitted coded cards containing their data and program commands. Computer professionals fed these cards into the computer, and usually sent the printed results to the users the next day. A miscoded card usually meant that the user would have to resubmit the entire program the following day.

At this time there was little need to share computer resources such as printers and modems. Computers were so few (and so costly) that the average office could not afford one. One solution to this expense problem was *time-sharing*. During the 1960s it became possible for an office to use a "dumb" terminal, modem, and card reader to connect through a telephone line with a mainframe computer. By leasing (or "sharing") time on this computer, the user was able to enjoy the benefits of computerization without massive capital expenditure.

The major problem with time-sharing was the slowness of sending information over telephone lines. During the early 1970s, the production of the *minicomputer* (so called because it was smaller than a mainframe, though it worked in much the same way) avoided this problem. Because of the dramatic drop in prices, departments were able to have their own computers. All a new user needed to become operational was a terminal—and the cabling between it and the minicomputer. As Figure 1.5 illustrates, several users were able to use the same computer, and much higher speeds were possible than under time-sharing. The concept of distributing computer resources throughout a company—by providing different departments with their own computers, rather than using one central computer for everybody—became known as *distributed processing*. But even though several departments in a company might have their own minicomputers, providing communications among these computers still posed a problem. Therefore, companies began cabling these computers together, and writing the software necessary for the units to communicate with each other.

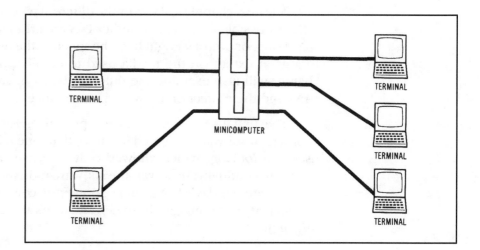

Figure 1.5 Distributed Processing with a Minicomputer

As microcomputers became much more powerful (and much less expensive) during the 1980s, companies began to take a second look at their minicomputers. Costing hundreds of thousands of dollars, these larger computers were not able to run the newer, more sophisticated business programs that were coming out for IBM PCs and compatibles.

By the mid-1980s, thousands of office workers began bringing their own personal computers to work, in order to use the new business software written for PCs. As employees began exchanging floppy disks and keeping their own databases, companies began to have serious problems with maintaining the integrity of their data. LANs offered a solution to such problems.

What Is a LAN?

A LAN covers a limited distance and facilitates information and resource sharing.

Distributed processing, taken to its logical conclusion, came to mean linking microcomputers together so they could share information and peripherals. This was the idea behind the first local area networks. The broadest possible definition of a *LAN* is: a communication network used by a single organization over a limited distance which permits users to share information and resources.

The next chapter will survey the different types of physical configurations possible for a LAN. Whether PCs are arranged in the form of a star, a ring, or even a straight line, the speed of the network will depend to a great extent on the media used to connect the units. The next chapter will also examine the different types of cabling available for LANs and their effect on network performance.

The first LANs were relatively primitive. Faced with a serious shortage of software designed for more than one user, these first LANs used *file locking,* which allowed only one user at a time to use a program. Gradually, however, the software industry has become more sophisticated; today's LANs can use powerful, complex accounting and productivity programs, usable by several users at the same time (*record locking*).

Widget's LAN

The savings a company such as Widget can realize by sharing hardware and software resources is staggering. Equally important is the increase in productivity that comes as the company runs more efficiently.

Now we'll take a look at a hypothetical company which has linked its PCs together to form a LAN with which to share information and printers. (Virtually all the applications used in this example will be explained in much greater detail in subsequent chapters, when we take a closer look at specific brands of LANs.)

Widget's LAN enables company employees to share data and peripherals (hard disk drives, printers, plotters, etc.). The Widget network enables dozens of workstations to share a variety of printers—including laser, daisywheel, and dot-matrix—instead of each personal computer workstation having its own dot-matrix printer. Instead of buying dozens of copies of a word processing program, Widget buys a special network version of the program; this enables dozens of network users to share the program—and, more importantly, one another's documents.

A single computer's hard disk serves as the storage area for a *network file server;* it acts very much like a waiter in a busy restaurant, serving up the items requested by the customers. Widget can keep dozens of varying standard contracts on its network file server; individual workstations can load these documents, make whatever changes are necessary to individualize the contracts, and then save them under appropriate names. The cost savings from these and other communal uses are impressive. A file server should be dedicated to this function and not used for any other purpose to prevent degradation in a network's performance.

Using Word Processing, Graphics, and Electronic Mail on a LAN

Widget's LAN makes it easy to produce an annual report. Several people can write different portions, and then revise and combine them using the network's electronic mail.

Every year Widget is required to produce an annual report that is printed and sent to stockholders. Since the company connected all departments with its LAN, that job has become much easier. Widget's LAN contains a number of IBM PC, IBM PS/2, and Macintosh computers that are able to communicate with one another and exchange data over the network.

Since the Accounting Department's general ledger, accounts payable, accounts receivable, inventory, purchase order-and-receiving, and payroll programs are already installed on the network, its audited balance sheet is already available—through the network—for the annual report. The Comptroller prints a copy of the balance sheet to disk (rather than sending it to the printer), and then uses a word processing program to comment on several aspects of the company's financial position before saving the entire document on the company's file server.

Since many stockholders prefer to view financial information in graphic format, the company President asks two graphic artists in the Marketing Department to develop appropriate pie charts and bar charts to show the company's growth over the past few years. The artists use a graphics program on a Macintosh workstation to develop their charts based on a computer file from the researchers. Then they send the information to a plotter on the LAN.

The President receives a hard copy from the artists. The researchers receive the President's comments by electronic mail over the network, revise the charts, and save the files on the file server.

Everyone at Widget with a workstation connected to the LAN can receive and send mail electronically. As users enter the network ("log on"), the network alerts them if they have mail, so Widget employees cannot use the excuse that they never saw a memo because it was lost in the mail. The electronic mail program also lets the sender know when a message has been read. It permits users to send blind copies (*bcc*) to other network users, and to send letters (even reports) to distribution lists. Secretaries who used to spend hours photocopying reports for distribution to managers now simply use the electronic mail to send a copy of each report to each manager's workstation.

Since Widget manufactures four different products designed for four very different markets, the President asks each of the four product managers to write a description of his or her product's current status and future plans. Each product manager saves his or her comments in a word processing file on the file server.

Meanwhile, the President is busy writing a letter to the stockholders—analyzing Widget's performance and indicating the direction the company will take in the upcoming year. The researcher prints the requested material from the Marketing and Accounting Departments; the President reads the documents, and then sends electronic mail to other employees, requesting material to fill in the remaining gaps in the corporate report. After another round of revisions, the annual report is finished, printed with a laser printer that provides letter-quality text and crisp graphics, and sent to the print shop for reproduction. The whole process is faster—and far more efficient—because the company's LAN permits an almost-instant sharing of information.

Connecting a LAN to the Rest of the World

By using a remote bridge to connect the LAN to the outside world, Widget salespeople are able to enter orders from remote customer locations. They also are able to update current inventory levels on-line. Another major tool used by the entire company is the customer database. Salespeople can use the remote bridge to connect to the LAN and use its word processing and database programs to generate personalized sales letters.

The ability to share information is particularly valuable in a competitive sales environment. Each of Widget's outside salespeople has a portable computer with a built-in modem, able to access the LAN over a phone line. Widgets come in an assortment of colors and configurations, and the company used to lose several thousand dollars' worth of orders each year through cancellations. A salesperson would take a large order, drive to Widget headquarters, and submit the order to the sales manager. Only after the order was input into Widget's mainframe computer would the salesperson learn that several of the ordered items were backordered. When customers were informed that there would be a substantial delay before delivery, they usually cancelled the entire order.

Now the situation has changed dramatically. Widget's LAN contains a *remote bridge,* a communications link between the network and the outside world. The salespeople use their portable computers to connect to the network using their customers' regular telephone lines. They enter an order while talking with the customer. If an item is backordered, the computer indicates a possible alternative: The yellow widgets are backordered two weeks, but green is very popular this time of year, and it is available immediately. Since the customer is in a buying mood, and the salesperson is present (and very persuasive), it is not surprising that many customers choose an alternative or agree to wait for a backordered item.

Whenever a customer's order is entered into the computer, a file is established for that customer. Salespeople find this information invaluable, since they are able to determine buying trends and preferences. Frequently they will send out individualized form letters to announce new product releases, or to indicate that the old widget might need an overhaul.

Because the customer list is integrated with the company's accounting programs—including accounts receivable—occasionally the Accounting Department will ask a salesperson to contact a delinquent customer about an overdue account. The receivables clerk simply sends the account information by electronic mail to the salesperson. Widget's accounting program on the LAN contains one useful safeguard to keep its receivables low. When a salesperson inputs an order from a customer site, the order entry program will flash a message on the screen if the customer has an overdue account. Frequently the salesperson can collect a check and then override the message to enter the new order.

Sharing Database Information on a LAN

A common database is particularly valuable for marketing functions. Researchers are able to download network information into Lotus 1-2-3 spreadsheets, analyze the data, and then save these spreadsheets on the network file server for later consolidation into one report.

While Widget's salespeople are transmitting orders from customer locations, the Marketing Department's researchers and analysts are busy sifting through sales reports to discover trends and develop market forecasts. The department's personnel share all their data on the LAN. Three analysts, for example, have used a Lotus 1-2-3 spreadsheet program to analyze the buying patterns of the company's major distributors. Traditionally, Widget has offered volume discounts to encourage large purchases, but now it is considering offering monthly sales specials to help balance its inventory. By identifying specific items and the month when major customers purchase them, the marketing analysts will develop a 12-month sales plan.

Because the analysts are using the same Lotus 1-2-3 program—and then saving their spreadsheet data on the network file server—the information can be shared among them. This means that after the researchers develop an item-by-item sales analysis, one researcher can access all three spreadsheets to develop a composite report that summarizes the information by product group. Using the Lotus 1-2-3 spreadsheet and the LAN, the researcher commands the six-pen plotter in the sales office to print a series of detailed graphs.

Accounting on a LAN

The Accounting Department's use of the LAN illustrates the flexibility that a LAN provides. Since programs contain record locking, it is possible for several employees to use the same program during peak periods.

The Widget Company's accounting information is on the LAN, but many of the programs have *password security* beyond the usual network level of security. For example, only a few employees in the Accounting and Personnel Departments have access to payroll records. The information on customer orders and inventory usage is available only to certain employees in Marketing, Sales, and Manufacturing.

The marketing analysts were able to use a special *interface program* to take information on sales orders and customers from the accounting programs, and convert this data into a form that could be used in a Lotus 1-2-3 program. Note that while a copy of this valuable accounting information can be moved to another program, the original accounting data is protected from tampering or change. This is necessary in order to ensure that the Accounting Department maintains a clear *audit trail,* which means that all changes and/or additions to accounting program data must be done by the Accounting Department, using a journal entry. This method leaves a permanent record that can be traced to answer future questions.

The Comptroller has been delighted with the advantages of having all accounting programs available on the company LAN. During peak periods, accounting clerks can be shifted from doing payables to doing receivables. Each workstation in the department can access any accounting program, assuming the user has the proper level of password security. Most of the clerks only have the network security level that permits them to perform routine tasks. Payroll clerks, for example, cannot change employee salaries, though they can prepare the monthly printing of salary checks.

Every LAN requires a *network administrator,* who is responsible for the network's overall management. The Comptroller must consult the LAN administrator before providing newly hired accounting clerks with new workstations. The administrator's tasks include adding new users and providing them with new passwords. If a department wants to add a new program to the LAN, the network administrator will analyze the effect of the program on the network as a whole, making sure (prior to approving it) that the new program will integrate completely with the other programs already present.

Using Printers on a LAN

Word processing on a LAN provides the user with a number of advantages, including print spooling and the choice of several different kinds of printers.

Perhaps the major use of the LAN requires the least amount of the network administrator's time. Secretaries, administrative assistants, and managers use the network's powerful word processing program every day. All Widget's form letters— including direct sales solicitations, requests for additional warranty information, notification that service contracts are about to expire, and the actual service contracts—are printed. The LAN contains a couple of laser printers with triple-bin cut-sheet feeders. This means it is possible to print a cover letter on

Widget Company stationery, a second sheet on normal bond paper, and the corresponding envelope—all automatically.

The company LAN has what is known as *print spooling software,* which enables a user to specify a specific printer for a job, and then "spool" the file to a storage area where it will be held until its turn comes to be printed. The LAN administrator can specify that a job requiring immediate attention exchange places with another file in the spooler in order to be printed immediately. The LAN is able to print several documents simultaneously on its various letter-quality and dot-matrix printers, without slowing down the network's performance significantly.

The most sophisticated word processing is handled by the Technical Publications Department, which supports Sales, Marketing, and Service, and works on special projects for the President's office. Four technical writers use many of the more advanced features of the word processing program, such as the ability to create multiple columns, indexes, and tables of contents. These materials require feedback from several individuals, including engineers, programmers, and trainers. Before beginning the revision stage, the technical writers use the LAN's electronic mail to send their rough drafts to appropriate departments for comments. Because they don't have to take the time to mail copies of the manuscript to the various departments, the technical writers have increased their productivity substantially. Now when the writers receive electronic mail informing them that a section has been read and revised for technical accuracy by an engineer, they simply load the revised section from the Engineering Department and then proofread for grammar and spelling.

A technical writer and illustrator are assigned to support the Marketing Department; they develop brochures and other sales materials. Since it is absolutely necessary for all sales materials to reflect the products accurately, the two send manuscript sections and illustration files to appropriate technical personnel for comments and corrections before moving on to the finished product.

Communications Between a LAN and a Mainframe Computer

The Manufacturing Department's use of the LAN illustrates how LANs can communicate with mainframe computers to share information.

The Manufacturing Department was the only department not to leave its mainframe environment. Located at the manufacturing facility, the mainframe computer runs a very sophisticated program for planning manufacturing resources. This program controls manufacturing costs by making sure the plant runs at maximum efficiency. The computer makes sure the assembly line will not run out of key raw materials, and that all standing orders will be filled on time.

Since Accounting now runs all its programs on microcomputers as part of the LAN, Manufacturing needs access to all sales data now at the company headquarters. It needs to know what has been sold, in order to update its inventory file and revise its forecasts. This communication is accomplished using the same link to the LAN that salespeople use when communicating from customer sites.

There is one critical difference, however. While the salespeople are using microcomputers to communicate with the company's microcomputer LAN, the Manufacturing Department needs to establish communications between micro- and mainframe computers—two machines that do not even speak the same language. Widget Company's network administrator uses the LAN software interface to the accounting programs to convert the appropriate data into an ASCII format that is easily transmitted. The administrator uses another program to emulate an IBM 3270 terminal, converting the information into the synchronous form the mainframe can understand.

Every evening the LAN sends the day's sales information over a telephone line to the company's mainframe computer, which digests the data and produces a revised schedule for the next day's assembly-line work. When supervisory personnel arrive in the morning, they can use their terminals to read this information from the mainframe where it has been stored.

All the LAN activities of Widget Company described here are available today. In the next few chapters you will learn how a LAN's hardware and software work together to produce this level of information integration. We will also survey the leading LANs currently available, and discover differences that could prove significant in determining which kind of LAN would be best for your needs.

What Have You Learned?

1. A local area network (LAN) is a communications network used by a single organization over a limited distance which permits users to share information and resources.

2. Before microcomputers (personal computers), time-sharing with terminals and modems enabled companies to share mainframe resources.

3. Minicomputers were the first computers to permit distributed processing in a cost-effective way.

4. A dedicated file server is not used as a workstation because doing so impairs its efficiency.

5. Electronic mail is a major feature of many LANs.

6. Outside computers can use a remote bridge to communicate with computers on the LAN.

7. Print spooling software permits users to designate which printer will print their files.

8. Record-locking software permits simultaneous access to the same data file by multiple users.

Quiz for Chapter 1

1. Handing in program cards and receiving the results the next day is characteristic of
   a. batch processing.
   b. on-line processing.
   c. distributed processing.
   d. remote processing.

2. Time-sharing was not a very effective way for a company to do its data processing because
   a. it required a computer at every station.
   b. communication over a phone line with a modem was too slow.
   c. computers were constantly breaking down.
   d. computers do not like to share.

3. Distributed processing means
   a. computers distributed to different users and departments.
   b. computer cards distributed to different departments.
   c. a mainframe computer doing all the work.
   d. a computer doing nothing but computing.

4. The person who provides passwords for new computer users on the LAN is called
   a. the chief of security.
   b. the network administrator.
   c. the department manager.
   d. the president of the network user's group.

5. A byte is composed of
   a. 2 bits.
   b. 4 bits.
   c. 6 bits.
   d. 8 bits.

6. A 5¹/₄-inch double-sided double-density disk, formatted for the IBM PC, will be able to hold approximately

    a. 360K.

    b. 180K.

    c. 256K.

    d. 512K.

7. To attach a modem to an IBM PC or compatible, its expansion slot must contain a(n)

    a. parallel interface.

    b. synchronous communications adapter.

    c. asynchronous communications adapter.

    d. monochrome video adapter.

8. Memory which retains information even after the computer is turned off is called

    a. RAM.

    b. ROM.

    c. RIM.

    d. REM.

2 | The Basics of a Local Area Network

About This Chapter

This chapter describes the building blocks of a local area network (LAN). We will explore how computer workstations are cabled together, and how they share resources. We'll take a close look at the rules that all LANs follow to ensure that information is not garbled or lost. Finally, we'll look at a number of standards that have begun to establish some order in what has been a very chaotic field.

The Changing Focus of Local Area Networks

As indicated in Chapter 1, a "local area network" is a system which allows microcomputers to share information and resources within a limited (local) area (generally less than one mile from the file server to a workstation). A LAN requires that the individual workstations (microcomputers) be physically tied together by cabling (usually coaxial or twisted pair), and that some network software reside on the workstation's hard disk (this permits the sharing of peripherals, data, and application programs).

Until recently, sharing peripheral equipment (such as printers, hard disk drives, and plotters) was the major use of LANs. Since hardware represented the major microcomputer cost in most offices, these early, primitive networks more than justified their cost by ensuring that valuable equipment did not remain idle. Today, some networks (such as Novell's) further increase office savings by allowing "diskless" workstations; these do not have a hard disk drive or floppy disk drives. A special "autoboot" ROM chip, inserted in the network workstation, permits the computer to become part of the network, and to use the network's disk drive when it is turned on.

It is difficult to generalize about microcomputer networks; a lack of compatibility has plagued the industry, despite efforts by the Institute for Electrical and Electronics Engineers (IEEE) to standardize the ways information can be transmitted within a network. In this chapter we will look at the components that all networks require, and the various forms they can take.

The Individual Network Workstation

The individual network workstation can work independently as a personal computer, or share network information and resources through the LAN. Usually it is linked to the network's file server or disk server by a network interface card and cabling.

Most companies decide to install a LAN because they already have a major investment in microcomputers, peripherals, and software. Rather than scrap everything and start over again with a minicomputer, these companies opt to tie their existing equipment together to share hardware and software resources.

Each microcomputer attached to the network retains its ability to work as an independent personal computer running its own software. It also becomes a network workstation, capable of accessing information located on the network disk server. As Figure 2.1 illustrates, this ability to function as a network station requires a special interface (almost always a circuit board) that plugs into one of the microcomputer's expansion slots and cables to link it to a server.

While the Apple Macintosh is used as a network workstation in a number of Fortune 1000 companies, this chapter will focus on IBM and IBM-compatible personal computers. Chapter 6 is devoted to the Macintosh and Macintosh networks.

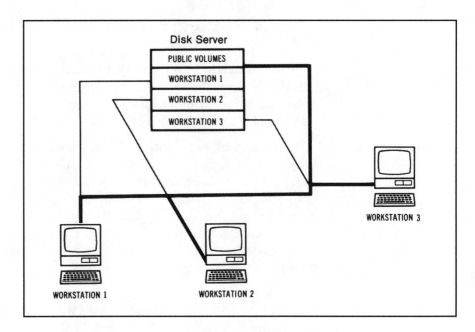

Figure 2.1 Workstations Connected with Network Interface Cards and Cabling to a Disk Server

The workstations in Figure 2.1 are IBM-compatible PCs containing network interface cards. The network program they are using works in conjunction with MS-DOS version 5.0. A cable connects each workstation (through its network interface card) to the network disk server or file server. The user can choose to use the microcomputer as an independent unit or to be part of the network. Simply by running the network software program and "logging on" (identifying oneself with a password as an authorized user), the user becomes an active part of the network.

Network Disk Servers

Some early networks used a disk server to store files and provide workstations with this information upon request.

Some early LANs used a *disk server,* a hard disk containing information that can be shared by the various workstations on the network. To the individual workstations, this disk server simply looks like another hard disk drive; if it were designated as drive E, for example, Frank Jones would save his business expense spreadsheet as `E:busexp`. The E tells

Jones's DOS software to send the data to the network hard disk for storage.

This procedure, the workstation accessing a network drive E, is identical to the way a PC accesses its own disk drives for storage of files. The procedure becomes a bit more complex, however, when a workstation wants a particular file residing on the disk server.

A file allocation table (FAT) helps the disk server keep track of where a particular file is located.

IBM and IBM-compatible PCs use a *file allocation table (FAT)* to keep track of exactly where a particular file is stored. Without seeing a copy of this valuable table, an individual workstation has no idea where its files are stored. The network disk server keeps its own FAT, and sends a copy to each workstation. Each workstation then stores the copy in RAM, which it uses as "work space" when running programs. As needed, the workstation's operating system uses the network FAT to access its files on the disk server.

Imagine what would happen if dozens of workstations received copies of the FAT and began saving documents back to the disk server. Each copy of the FAT saved back on the disk server would overwrite (and thus erase) the FAT file that existed prior to the new copy's arrival. Without a safeguard for this important table's integrity, determining which was the original FAT would prove almost impossible.

Disk servers partition their hard disk drives into separate volumes for each user. A public volume is available so that different workstations can share information.

With a simple disk server, the integrity of its FAT is maintained by dividing (partitioning) this hard disk drive into several user volumes. Each volume is reserved for a particular workstation's exclusive use, thus preserving the integrity of the FAT for that particular volume. Although certain volumes might be established as *public volumes,* usually they are classified as "read-only" to safeguard their integrity; individual workstations can view this information, but cannot change it. An example of a typical public volume use is the large customer database file for Widget Company described in Chapter 1. Several different departments might need to view this information, but the network administrator has declared the file "read-only" so that no one inadvertently changes or destroys the data.

File Servers

A file server uses software to form a shell around the computer's normal DOS. To an individual workstation, the file server simply represents a very large disk drive. Workstations do not need to be concerned with where a particular file is located.

File servers are far more efficient and sophisticated than disk servers. A file server contains special software that forms a shell around the computer's normal disk operating system. This shell software filters out commands to the file server before DOS can receive them. The file server maintains its own FAT. When a workstation demands a specific file, the file server already knows where the file is because of its FAT. It sends the file directly to the workstation. Note that the individual workstation does not designate the file server as another disk drive as is the case with a disk server. It simply requests a file, and the file server responds.

The file server is much more efficient than the disk server because there is no longer a need to send copies of the FAT to each workstation requesting a file. Also, there is no longer a need to partition the network hard disk drive into volumes, since the individual workstations no longer need to worry about where a particular file resides. As Figure 2.2 illustrates, a file server provides greater efficiency in a LAN.

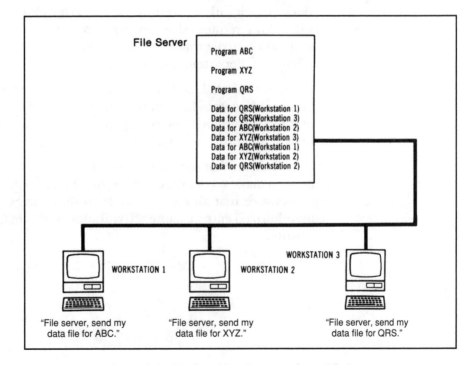

Figure 2.2 Workstations Connected to a File Server

Distributed File Servers

For most office networks, a single file server is more than adequate. This is known as a *centralized server*. It functions very much like a minicomputer; one unit handles all the file serving, with each workstation waiting its turn. If the LAN is designed to handle several different departments (as in the Widget Company example in Chapter 1), then adding more file servers to the network is usually more efficient.

These additional units are known as *distributed file servers* because they divide up (or "distribute") the file serving duties for the entire network. Since (for example) all Accounting Department workstations use the same accounting programs and access the same data, sending this information several hundred feet away to a file server is inefficient. A distributed file server, located right in the Accounting Department, can speed access time—and reduce the load on the rest of the network. This approach maintains optimum speed for other network users as well; Accounting personnel need no longer request files from a central file server that must also service other users' requests. Since the Accounting Department's distributed file server need only concern itself with accounting files, it has fewer files to search; it can find and deliver requested information much more quickly. Finally, the information arrives more promptly because the file server is located right in the department it services.

Distributed file servers have one other important advantage. If one file server becomes inoperative, the LAN is not necessarily shut down. Another distributed file server (provided it has sufficient disk space) can service the entire LAN temporarily.

While distributed file servers can provide a number of advantages, they can make security more difficult. The network administrator must now ensure that all file servers' hard disk drives are protected from unauthorized entry. Chapter 10 will address this major issue of network security.

Dedicated and Nondedicated File Servers

A dedicated file server is used only for that function, while a nondedicated file server also serves as a workstation. While more efficient, dedicated file servers are more expensive because they require a PC to be set aside for their use.

A *dedicated file server* is a microcomputer (with a hard disk drive) used exclusively as a file server. By dedicating all its memory and processing resources to file serving, the particular computer usually provides increased network speed and efficiency. In the business world, ironically, dedication is not always prized; it can be very expensive. Some LAN manufacturers brag about the price savings they offer because their file servers need not be dedicated.

When a file server is *nondedicated*, it is used as a workstation in addition to its file-serving functions. This means that RAM must be partitioned so that some of it is available for running programs. It also means that a network workstation might have to wait for a file to be sent while the file server user loads a program from memory using the machine's microprocessor. The faster the microprocessor, the faster the server can perform its tasks. Because file servers generally are the fastest and most expensive computers in the network, deciding whether to dedicate the unit is difficult. Money that might be saved by making the machine nondedicated will be lost many times over by the degradation of the entire LAN; the time lost by users of all the other workstations in the network soon shows the folly of trying to economize on this very critical network element. Generally, a centralized file server for more than three or four workstations should be dedicated.

File Servers on a Peer-to-Peer Network

Workstations on a peer-to-peer network can choose whether or not they wish to share their hard disk drives as file servers for other network users.

On a *peer-to-peer* LAN, users determine which computer resources they wish to share with other network users. A user might wish to share his or her hard disk drive as a file server for other network users. A peer-to-peer network might consist of several nondedicated file-server workstations whose resources the owners have decided to share with other network users. Similarly, other users might select their printers as resources they wish to share with network users.

Print Servers

Network print servers enable workstations to share several different printers.

Just as a network file server permits the sharing of a single network hard drive, a network *print server* can enable dozens of workstations to share various types of printers. A manager might use a letter-quality printer for his daily correspondence, but once a month he might need a wide-carriage dot-matrix printer to print a critical spreadsheet. An accountant on the very same network might use a wide-carriage dot-matrix printer daily to produce balance sheets, financial reports, and charts. Once or twice a month he might need to write a business letter using a letter-quality printer. With a LAN and its print server software, both the manager and the accountant may choose any printer on the network.

Some high-speed network printers contain their own network interface cards.

To speed up the process of heavy-duty network printing, many network managers often install printers with their own network interface circuit cards. Such printers can receive data from the network at the rate of several million bits per second; they are particularly useful for printing large graphics files (which contain so much data that they can congest other network traffic while printing).

Printers can be limited to certain users on a network. These local printers usually perform very specific tasks.

Using print server software does not mean that a network workstation cannot have its own dedicated printer. Let's say that a marketing analyst uses a thermal color printer almost exclusively to print transparencies of charts for presentations. This printer, connected by a parallel interface and cable to the analyst's workstation, can remain a dedicated *local printer* and not a network printer so it is always available to the specific user. If the analyst needs to produce a letter-quality report, he can send his word processing file over the network to a letter-quality printer.

There is a second major reason for dedicating a printer to a particular workstation and not including it as part of the network: a particular user may need to print special preprinted continuous-feed forms. A purchasing agent, for example, might need to print dozens of purchase order forms; an accounts payable clerk might need to print continuous-feed company checks. It would be a lot of trouble for these individuals to have to remove the continuous-feed forms in order to print an occasional letter.

Usually the network administrator will ensure that when a program is installed on the network, it is installed with a *default printer driver*. This means that normally the program's files will be printed on a particular printer. Word processing programs, for example, routinely might send files to the office letter-quality printer or a laser printer; spreadsheet programs might send files to a wide-carriage dot-matrix printer.

Printer sharing software should contain a *print spooler*, software that creates a buffer where print jobs can be stored while awaiting their turn to be printed. Think of this as a list of print jobs; as each file is printed, the next file in line takes its place. Sophisticated print spoolers have additional capabilities, including the ability to move a job to the front of the line if it requires immediate printing. On a large office network, time-consuming printing jobs such as daily reports often are placed in the print spooler to be printed in the evening so they do not tie up a printer during peak hours.

One occasional problem with printer server software is that some software defaults to a certain type of printer, even though there may be times when you require a different printer—a letter-quality rather than a dot-matrix, for example. The network administrator can solve this problem by creating a special batch file that automatically loads the appropriate printer driver when the program is loaded.

Print spooler software enables network users to place files in a buffer for printing at a later time.

A Guide to LAN Cabling

The LAN must have *cabling* to link the individual workstations together with the file server and other peripherals. If there were only one type of cabling available, then the decision would be simple. Unfortunately, there are a number of different types of cabling—each with its own vocal supporters. Since there is a considerable range in cost and in capability, this is not a trivial issue. This section will examine the advantages and disadvantages of twisted-pair, baseband and broadband coaxial cable, as well as fiber-optic cabling.

Twisted-Pair Cable

Twisted-pair cable is by far the least expensive type of network medium. As Figure 2.3 illustrates, this cabling consists of two insulated wires twisted together so that each wire faces the same amount of interference from the environment. This "noise" in the environment

Twisted-pair cable is inexpensive and easy to install. It is an ideal selection when interference is not a major consideration.

becomes part of the signal being transmitted. Twisting the wires together reduces (but does not eliminate) this noise. Twisted-pair wire comes in a wide range of pairs and gauges. Wires have an American Wire Gauge number (AWG) based on their diameter; 26-gauge wire, for example, has a diameter of 0.01594 inch. For network purposes, 22- and 24-gauge are the two most common types of twisted-pair cabling.

Figure 2.3   Twisted-Pair Wire (Two Pair)

Twisted-pair cable is bundled in groups of pairs. The number of twisted pairs per group can range from 2 to 3,000; many LANs use 25 pairs. Some LANs utilize the very same inexpensive, unshielded twisted-pair cable used for telephones; others require higher data-grade quality. As one option for its Token Ring Network, for example, IBM supports Type 3 unshielded twisted-pair (telephone wire) for its Token Ring Network, but requires 22 AWG or 24 AWG with a minimum of two twists per linear foot (the more twists, the less interference). It recommends four twisted pairs when new wire is installed, but existing telephone twisted-pair wire must have two spare pairs which can be dedicated to the Token Ring Network.

On the other hand, AT&T's STARLAN requires higher data-grade quality. AT&T specifies that its network requires 24-gauge *shielded* two-twisted-pair wire—one pair of wires to transmit data and one pair to receive data. Higher-grade cabling makes a difference in data transmission quality over longer distances. For example, compare AT&T's higher-grade twisted-pair standard and IBM's Type 3 twisted-pair telephone-wire standard. AT&T's workstations may be up to 990 feet from a wiring closet, while IBM's workstations must be within 330 feet.

The major limitations of twisted-pair wiring are its limited range and its sensitivity to electrical interference. When standards were first proposed for twisted-pair networks, the medium was able to handle transmission speeds of approximately one million bits per second (Mbs) over several hundred feet. Today, a new industry standard known as 10baseT reflects the technological advances that make it possible to transmit information at 10 Mbs over twisted-pair wire.

Coaxial Cable

Coaxial cable is used in both baseband and broadband networks. While more expensive than twisted-pair, it can transmit data significantly faster over a much longer distance.

Coaxial cable is almost as easy to install as twisted-pair; it is the medium of choice in many major LANs. As Figure 2.4 illustrates, "coax" is composed of a copper conductor surrounded by insulation. An outer jacket composed of copper or aluminum acts as a conductor, and also provides protection. This type of cable is commonly found in the home as an integral part of cable television.

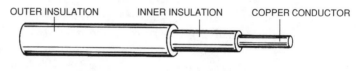

OUTER INSULATION   INNER INSULATION   COPPER CONDUCTOR

Figure 2.4   Coaxial Cable

Baseband Cable

Baseband cable can send data very fast (10–80 Mbs), but is limited to a single channel. It isn't possible to send integrated voice, data, and video signals over baseband cables.

Baseband coaxial cable has one channel that carries a single message at a time at very high speed. Its carrier wire is surrounded by a copper mesh, and usually the entire cable's diameter is approximately 3/8 inch. Digital information is sent across a baseband cable's bandwidth in serial fashion, one bit at a time. Depending upon the LAN, it is possible for baseband coaxial cable to handle a data rate of 10–80 Mbs. EtherNet (which was the first major LAN with nonproprietary communications interfaces and protocols) uses baseband coaxial cable. Since the EtherNet standard has been supported by both Xerox Corporation and Digital Equipment Corporation, baseband cabling is a popular choice for a LAN medium. Because of baseband's single channel limitation, it isn't possible to send integrated signals composed of voice, data, and even video over baseband cable. One advantage of baseband cabling is that it is easy to tap into this cable, and connect or disconnect workstations without disturbing network operations. Although the maximum recommended distance for a baseband LAN is approximately 1.8 miles (3 kilometers), 1,500 feet (500 meters) might prove to be a more realistic figure if the network is heavily used. While baseband's inability to send integrated signals—as well as its distance limitations—must be considered when configuring a network, these disadvantages may not be significant if speed of data transmission and cost are primary criteria in media selection.

Broadband Cables

Broadband cables can carry integrated voice, data, and even video signals. Because amplifiers are used, broadband has a greater range than baseband.

Unlike baseband, *broadband* coaxial cables have the capacity to carry several different signals broadcast at different frequencies at the same time. This is the approach cable television companies have taken, using 75-ohm broadband coaxial cable. Subscribers can select from several different stations, each broadcasting on its own designated frequency. All broadband systems can utilize a single cable with bidirectional amplifiers, as shown in Figure 2.5, or a dual cable system. In either case, carrier signals are sent to a central point known as the *headend*, from which they are retransmitted to all points on the network.

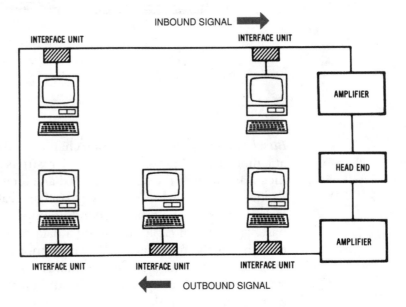

Figure 2.5   Single Broadband Coaxial Cable with Bidirectional Amplifiers

The *single-cable* approach splits a cable by frequency, in order to achieve bidirectional transmission of data. Commercial cable companies use 6-MHz channels for each communication path. Even with some frequencies designed as "guard bands" between the different channels, it is possible to allocate 346 MHz for forward communications (6 MHz/channel × 56 channels) and 25 MHz for the return data path (6 MHz/channel × 4 channels). This 25 MHz devoted to returning data can be used for several narrow-band channels.

Dual-broadband cable uses one cable for inbound data moving toward the headend, and a second cable (looped at the headend) for the outbound carriers. The full frequency spectrum is available for both inbound and outbound signals. Because of the duplication of cabling, amplifiers, and hardware, dual-broadband cable is much more expensive than the single cable approach, but it makes twice as many usable channels available, and some networks might require them. Let's take a closer look at this particular broadband approach.

With a dual-cable configuration, coaxial cable forms a two-way highway composed of two bands. Each of these bands contains several channels. Standard television channels transmit at 6 MHz. Since we have a band with a range of approximately 300 MHz, this means that it is possible to have as many as 50 channels broadcasting at a data rate of 5 Mbs. The *inbound band* carries data from the LAN's *nodes* (individual workstations) to the headend, (which is a translating and broadcasting device); the *outbound band* carries data to the network nodes, as illustrated in Figure 2.6.

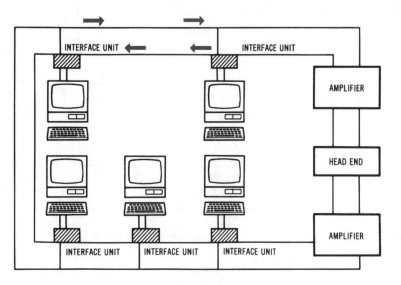

Figure 2.6 Dual-Broadband Cable Configuration

Broadband cable installation requires far more planning than baseband. Since the broadband signals are being broadcast, amplifiers need to be installed to maintain the strength of the signals. In a company with several departments (such as Widget, described in Chapter 1), each department would have a *drop line*, with *tap lines* coming off this line to each node (workstation). These taps contain resistors to ensure that all workstations receive signals at the same strength. If the Widget Company were planning to add another building in the near future, it would want to add a *splitter* (as shown in Figure 2.7), which divides the signal into two paths. Since the splitter would be added to ensure future LAN growth, the unused port would be sealed until needed. Because splitters affect transmission quality across the entire network, splitters for later use should be included in the LAN's initial plan.

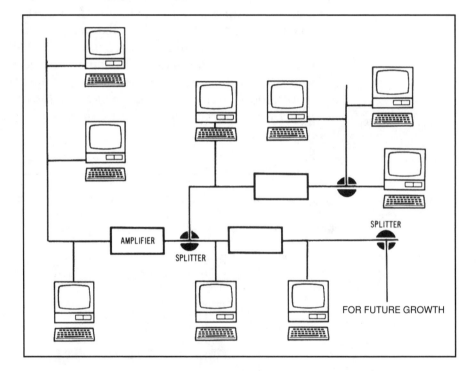

Figure 2.7   Coaxial Cable Configuration with Splitters

Fiber-Optic Cable

In recent years, one of the most exciting advances in media has been the use of fiber optics in LANs. This new type of data transmission has a number of advantages over twisted-pair and coaxial cable. Besides data transmission rates far in excess of either of these older media,

Fiber-optic technology offers immunity from electromagnetic interference and error-free transmission for several miles with the highest level of network security. Unfortunately, it currently is the most expensive medium to use for designing a LAN.

fiber-optic cabling is immune to electromagnetic or radio-frequency interference, and capable of sending signals several miles without loss. This mode of transmission is also virtually immune to unauthorized reception.

A fiber-optic cable is made of pure glass drawn into very thin fiber to form a core. As Figure 2.8 illustrates, these fibers are surrounded by *cladding,* a layer of glass with a lower refractive index than the glass in the core.

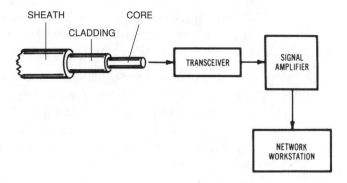

Figure 2.8   Fiber-Optic Cabling

A fiber-optic network uses a laser or LED (light-emitting diode) to send a signal through the core portion of the cable. *Optical repeaters* are often used along the path to amplify the signal, so it arrives at its destination at full strength. At the receiving end of the cable, the message is translated back into a digital or analog signal by a photo-diode. The cabling can consist of a single fiber (*monomode*), several fibers (*multimode*), or a variation of multimode (*graded index*) in which the index of refraction drops slowly from the center of the fiber towards the outside.

Monomode fiber has a very wide bandwidth, but its tiny core makes it extremely difficult to splice without special kits and technical expertise. Also, monomode requires a laser (rather than an LED) as a signaling source, which is more expensive. Multimode fiber has a smaller bandwidth but is much easier to splice. Graded-index multi-mode fiber is the most expensive medium, but it provides the highest transmission rate over the greatest distance.

Multimode fiber optics for network cabling come in groups of 2 to 24 fibers, with groups of 2 to 4 fibers being the norm. Each fiber is unidirectional, since a beam of light is transmitted in only one direction. Two-way communication requires another fiber within the cable, so that light can also travel in the opposite direction. The American National Standards Institute has established a standard for the *physical media-dependent (PMD)* layer of the *fiber data distributed interface (FDDI)* to work in conjunction with data transmission of 100 Mbs. It is possible to achieve rates up to 1 gigabit/second (Gbs).

This new fiber-optic standard is consistent with the AT&T Premises Distribution Scheme's ratio of cladding to core (62.5/125 multimode fiber). Therefore, companies that have installed AT&T fiber-optic equipment for voice transmission already are cabled for data transmission by LANs that utilize fiber-optic technology.

At present, fiber-optic cabling is too expensive for most installations, and its sophisticated technology makes it difficult to add new workstations after initial installation. If a company has a serious interference problem, however—or needs absolute network security or the capability of sending signals several miles—fiber optics might be the only solution.

Wireless Networks

In some environments, cabling is not desirable— or even possible. Wireless networks are becoming more popular.

Some environments are very difficult to cable. For instance, offices where personnel are frequently relocated might find it difficult to use conventional network cabling schemes. One solution is the "wireless" network. Microcomputers can be outfitted with small microwave transmitting circuit cards. These units transmit their network signals through the air to other network workstations (which also have microwave equipment). Token ring and EtherNet LANs are growing in popularity, but their cost is still prohibitive compared with systems using conventional cabling.

Network Architecture

Just as there are several different ways to cable a LAN, there are also several different forms a network can take. These different shapes are known as *network architecture* or *topology*. Keep in mind that the form of the LAN does not limit the media of transmission. Twisted-pair, coaxial, and fiber-optic cables all lend themselves to these different topologies.

The Star

The star topology makes it easy to add new workstations and to provide detailed network analysis.

One of the oldest types of network topologies is the *star,* which uses the same approach to sending and receiving messages as a telephone system. Just as telephone calls from one customer (workstation) to another customer (workstation) are handled by a central switching station, all messages in a LAN star topology must go through a central computer that controls the flow of data. AT&T's STARLAN is an example of a network utilizing this approach. As Figure 2.9 illustrates, this architecture makes it easy to add new workstations to the LAN; all that is needed is a cable from the central computer to each new microcomputer's network interface card.

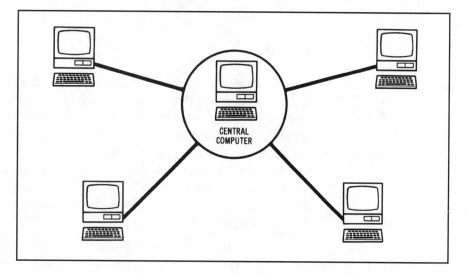

Figure 2.9 A Star Network Topology

Another advantage of star topology is that the network administrator can give certain nodes higher status than others. The central computer will then look for signals from these higher-priority workstations before recognizing other nodes. For networks where a few key users require immediate response from on-line inquiries, this feature of star topology can be extremely useful.

Finally, a star architecture makes it easier to have centralized diagnostics of all network functions. Since all messages come through the central computer, it is easy to analyze all workstation messages, and produce reports that reveal the files each node utilizes. This type of report can prove valuable as a means of ensuring network security.

The major weakness of a star architecture is that the entire LAN fails if anything happens to the central computer. This is precisely the same weakness of multiuser minicomputer systems that rely on a central processor.

The failure of the central computer results in the entire network's failure.

The Clustered Star

An alternative to the star is the clustered star topology. Several stars can be linked together.

The *clustered star* topology consists of several stars linked together. The failure of any one star does not result in the failure of the entire network, though workstations linked to the failed star will not be able to operate on the network.

The Bus

A bus topology is like a data highway. It is easy to add new workstations, but difficult to maintain network security. It requires the least amount of cabling of any topology.

Another major network topology is the *bus*, shown in Figure 2.10; think of it as a data "highway" that connects several LAN workstations. In many such networks, the workstations check whether a message is coming down the highway before sending their messages. Since all workstations share this bus, all messages pass other workstations on the way to their destinations. Each workstation checks the address on the message to see if it matches its own address. A workstation will copy a message addressed to it to the RAM on its network interface card and then process the information.

Unlike the star topology—where dozens of cables can cause logistical problems when they congregate near the central computer—bus cabling is simple. It requires the least amount of cabling of any major topology; many low-cost LANs use a bus architecture and twisted-pair wire cabling. Another advantage of the bus topology is that the failure of a single workstation will not cripple the rest of the network. EtherNet is an example of a network that uses the bus approach.

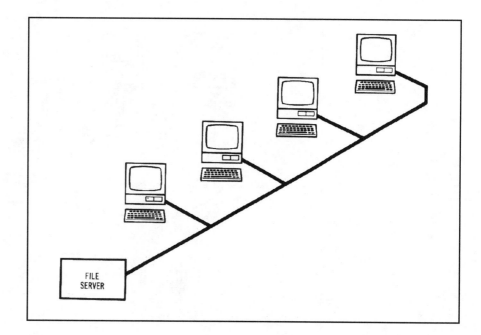

Figure 2.10   A Bus Network Topology

A disadvantage of the bus topology is that generally there must be a minimum distance between taps for workstations to avoid signal interference. Also, there is no easy way for a system administrator to run diagnostics on the entire network. Finally, a bus architecture does not have the network security features inherent in a star topology; since all messages are sent along a common data highway, security could be compromised by an unauthorized network user.

The Ring

The ring topology combines advantages of the star and the bus. A workstation assumes the role of monitoring all network functions. The failure of one workstation does not result in the failure of the entire network.

Figure 2.11 illustrates yet another major type of network architecture: the *ring*. A ring topology consists of several nodes (workstations) joined together to form a circle. Messages proceed from node to node, in one direction only. (Some ring networks are capable of sending messages bidirectionally, but still they can only send a message in one direction at a time.)

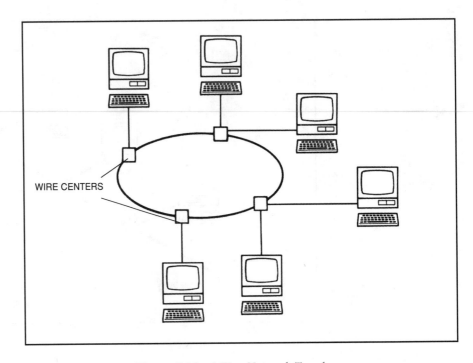

WIRE CENTERS

Figure 2.11 A Ring Network Topology

The ring topology permits verification that a message has been received. When a node receives a message addressed to itself, it copies the message and then sends the message back to the sender with a flag that indicates its receipt.

One of the major issues in a ring topology is the necessity of ensuring that all workstations have equal access to the network. In a *token ring* LAN, a data packet known as a *token* is sent from the transmitting workstation throughout the network. The token contains the address of the sender and the address of the node to receive the message. When the receiving station has copied its message, it returns the token to the originating workstation, which then sends the token on to the next workstation in the ring. If it has nothing to send, the token goes to the next workstation. (The intricacies of how a token is designed will be discussed in Chapter 4, which includes an examination of IBM's Token Ring Network.)

For system administration purposes, one workstation is designated as the *monitoring node* in the network. The monitoring node handles all diagnostic functions.

There are many advantages to a ring topology. Should the monitoring node fail, the network remains operative, since it is possible to designate another workstation for this task. With bypass software, the network may withstand the failure of various workstations by bypassing them. Additional ring networks can be linked together through *bridges* that switch data from one ring to another. (We will discuss the mechanics of how a bridge works in Chapter 3.)

If several workstations are cabled together to form a ring, it is extremely difficult to add new workstations. The entire network has to be shut down while a new node is added and the cabling reattached. There is a simple solution, however. Most token ring networks now come with connectors called *wire centers* (displayed in Figure 2.11). These enable network administrators to add and remove workstations by connecting them to (or disconnecting them from) the appropriate wire centers; the network remains intact and in operation.

Network Standards and Protocols

Over the past few years a number of network standards have been developed. Some governing organizations in this field have developed protocols, or rules, that ensure compatibility for different vendors' network hardware and software.

So far in this chapter we have examined the major components of a LAN. If the computers, application software, network software, and cabling were all manufactured by the same vendor, there would be few problems in making everything work together smoothly. Today's reality, however, is usually that network software from one LAN manufacturer will not work on a competitor's network, while application programs—and even cabling—must be selected for a specific LAN.

To provide some level of uniformity among network vendors, the International Standards Organization (ISO) has developed *Open Systems Interconnection (OSI)* standards. Different computers networked together need to know in what form they will receive information. When will a particular word begin, when will it end, and when will the next word begin? Is there a way for one computer to check whether its message was garbled in transmission? The OSI model answers these questions (and more) with a set of standards that may enable the public (in the future) to buy network products from different vendors with some assurance that they will work together.

The OSI Model

The Open Systems Interconnection (OSI) standards consist of a seven-layer model that ensures efficient communication within a LAN and among different networks.

As Figure 2.12 illustrates, the OSI model consists of seven layers of specifications which describe how data is to be handled during different stages of its transmission. Each layer provides a service for the layer immediately above it.

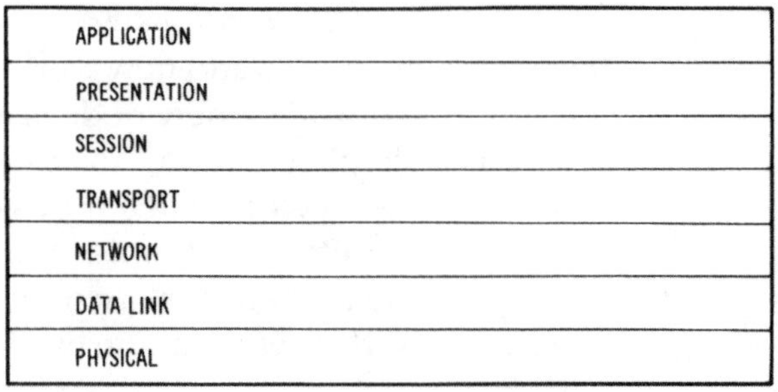

| APPLICATION |
| PRESENTATION |
| SESSION |
| TRANSPORT |
| NETWORK |
| DATA LINK |
| PHYSICAL |

Figure 2.12   The OSI Model

Perhaps an example will illustrate this principle. Whenever someone uses a citizen's band radio (CB) to communicate with another person, he or she is using a set of agreed-upon standards very much like the OSI model. Let's look more closely at how Frank's call to Betty follows a series of uniform standards.

By pressing his send button and announcing "Breaker breaker," Frank indicates that he wishes to send a message. He then uses his commonly agreed-upon nickname to identify himself before asking for his friend Betty by her particular nickname: "This is Happy Hacker, can you read me PC Woman?" After establishing communication with Betty, Frank tells her to "switch over to Channel 25 because it's clearer." Betty acknowledges her understanding of the message with a "That's 10-4, Happy Hacker."

At the physical level, Frank had to press certain buttons to broadcast a message, using radio hardware equipment which includes transistors. His use of nicknames established a concrete address for the recipient of his message, and identified him as the sender. Frank then established that his communication was being received clearly (identified the quality of transmission). After establishing an error-free channel of communication, Frank began talking (with a slight Brooklyn accent) to Betty about his new communications program. Betty was kept very busy translating Frank's technical jargon and his Brooklyn slang into standard American English. She was able to do this because Frank followed certain rules; he used American English grammatical patterns.

Frank followed a series of generally accepted standards while conversing with Betty over their CB radios. The OSI layers of standards only work when all vendors adhere to them, and do not bypass any with "shortcuts." Note that these standards are not hardware, and they are not software; they are simply a set of generally accepted conventions.

The OSI model assigns seven different layers to the complex procedures necessary for data communications along a network. The model is designed to make it easier to achieve initial agreement on the lower layers—and ultimately on the entire seven layers.

The Physical Layer

The Physical layer's standards cover the hardware standards for network compatibility. These include the voltage used, the timing of the data transmission, and handshaking requirements.

The first layer of standards—the *Physical layer*—is a set of rules regarding the hardware used to transmit data. Among the items covered at this level are the voltages used, the timing of the data transmission, and the rules for establishing the initial "handshaking" communication connection. The Physical layer establishes whether bits are going to be sent *half duplex* (very similar to the way data is sent across a CB) or *full duplex* (which requires simultaneous sending and receiving of data). (You will get a closer look at this process in the next chapter, when we examine communications between LANs and mainframe computers.)

Other hardware descriptions covered in the Physical layer standards include the acceptable connectors and interfaces to media. At this layer, the OSI model is concerned with electrical considerations and bits (1s and 0s). The bits do not really have any meaning at this level; assigning meaning is the responsibility of the next OSI layer.

The Data Link Layer

The Data Link layer is concerned with packaging data into data frames for transmission.

Earlier you saw that the OSI model has been developed so that each layer provides the layer above it with a key element. The Physical layer provides the *Data Link layer* with bits. Now it is time to give these raw bits some meaning. At this point we no longer deal with bits but with *data frames,* packets containing data as well as control information.

The Data Link layer adds flags to indicate the beginning and ending of messages. This layer's standards perform two important functions: they ensure that data is not mistaken for flags, and they check for errors within the data frame. This error-checking can take the form of sending information about a data frame to the receiving machine, and receiving an acknowledgement if everything has been received correctly.

The Network Layer

The Network layer is concerned with packet switching. It establishes virtual circuits between computers or terminals for data communication.

This third layer of the OSI model, the *Network layer,* is concerned with *packet switching*. It establishes *virtual circuits* (paths between two computers or terminals) for data communications. At the sending end, the Network layer repackages messages from the Transport layer (above it) into data packets, so that the lower two layers can transmit them. At the receiving end, the Network layer reassembles the message. To understand this use of data packets, it is necessary to look at an industry standard found at the lower three OSI model layers: the X.25 standard.

The Transport Layer

The Transport layer is primarily concerned with error recognition and recovery but also handles the multiplexing of messages and the regulating of information flow.

The *Transport layer* of the OSI model has many functions, including several orders of error recognition and recovery. At the highest order, the Transport layer can detect (and even correct) errors, identify packets that have been sent in incorrect order, and rearrange them in correct order. This layer also multiplexes several messages onto one circuit, then writes a header to indicate which message belongs to which circuit. The Transport layer also regulates information flow by controlling the messages' movement.

The Session Layer

The Session layer is concerned with network management. It handles password recognition, logon and logoff procedures, and network monitoring and reporting.

So far, you've seen that the OSI model is concerned with bits and data messages, not with recognizing particular users on the network. Think of the *Session layer* as the layer concerned with network management. It has the ability to abort a session, and controls the orderly termination of a session. The user communicates directly with this layer.

The Session layer can verify a password typed in by a user, and enable a user to switch from half-duplex transmission to full duplex. It can determine who speaks, how often, and for how long. It controls data transfers, and even handles recovery from a system crash. Finally, the Session layer can monitor system usage and bill users for their time.

The Presentation Layer

Network security, file transfers, and format functions are dealt with at the Presentation layer.

The *Presentation layer* of the OSI model is concerned with network security, file transfers, and formatting functions. At the bit level, the presentation layer is capable of encoding data in a variety of different forms, including ASCII and EBCDIC.

The American Standard Code for Information Interchange (ASCII) is a seven-bit-plus-parity-bit character code for the transmission of data. It is the convention used most universally. Many of the larger IBM computers use Extended Binary Coded Decimal Interchange Code (EBCDIC). The Presentation layer must be able to handle both of these standards for data transmission.

For true communication, both communicating computers' Presentation layers must contain the same protocols, or rules for handling data. This layer handles protocol conversion between different computers using different formats. Most word processing functions we associate with formatting text (including pagination, number of lines per screen, and even cursor movement across the screen) are also handled in the Presentation layer.

The proliferation of terminals with incompatible codes is treated at this level. A *terminal protocol* resolves these differences by enabling each data terminal to map the same virtual terminal. In effect, this procedure means that a set of translation tables exists between a local terminal and a remote terminal. The local terminal sends a data structure that defines its current screen in terms of how many characters/line will be displayed. (This number can vary considerably; many terminals display 132 characters/line, but other formats are available.) The data structure goes to the remote terminal's corresponding control object, which translates this number into a code that its terminal can understand and implement. Other codes indicate boldface, underline, graphics, etc.

The Application Layer

Network programs found at the Application layer include electronic mail, database managers, file server software, and printer server software.

The *Application layer* handles messages, remote logons, and the responsibility for network management statistics. At this level, you will find database management programs, electronic mail, file server and printer server programs, and the operating system's command and response language.

For the most part, the functions performed in this layer are user-specified. Since different user programs establish different needs, it is difficult to generalize about the protocols found here. Certain industries (such as banking) have developed sets of standards for this level.

CCITT X.25 Standard

The CCITT X.25 standard establishes rules for data packets that are to be sent to public switched networks. The X.25 set of three layers corresponds to the first three protocol layers of the OSI model.

The Consultative Committee for International Telephony and Telegraphy (CCITT) has developed a set of international telecommunications standards. As Figure 2.13 illustrates, the first three layers of the *X.25 standard* (Physical, Frame, and Packet) correspond to the OSI model's first three layers (Physical, Data Link, and Network).

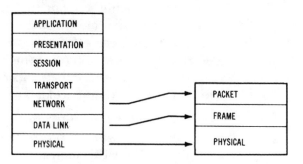

Figure 2.13 The X.25 Standard and the OSI Model

- X.25's *Physical layer* corresponds to OSI's Physical layer. It uses the CCITT's X.21 recommendation to define the RS-232 standard for asynchronous data transmission, as well as full-duplex *point-to-point synchronous transmission* between the DTE and a *public switched network.* These are communications standards discussed at length in *Understanding Data Communications,* published by Sams.

- X.25's *Frame layer* corresponds to the OSI model's Data Link layer. Here the data is actually exchanged between a DTE and the network.
- In X.25's *Packet layer* (corresponding to the OSI's Network layer), data is in packet form, which is a requirement for public switched networks. The X.25 standard ensures that information sent from *data termination equipment (DTE)* can be understood when received by a *public packet network*.

These data packets contain several discrete types of information that distinguish one message from another. A packet contains an *ADDRESS field* indicating its destination. A *CONTROL field* provides several kinds of information, including indications that a message is beginning or ending, that the message has been received successfully, or that an error has occurred and is acknowledged.

The X.25 standard is designed for packet switching; using this particular convention, the Network layer of the OSI model functions very much like a gigantic mail room. Messages from a host computer are placed in packets, addressed, and sent to the bottom two layers for transmission. Since there may be several different ways (circuits) to route a message to a particular workstation, special *routing tables* keep track of traffic in order to balance the workload. The major use of the X.25 standard is in conjunction with mainframe communications and public switched networks—a subject covered when Chapter 3 looks at communications between LANs and mainframe computers.

The Network layer contains other conventions besides X.25. There are procedures for recognizing message priorities and sending messages in proper order. Finally, this layer controls network congestion by preventing the sending computer from sending information faster than it can be received or stored.

High-Level Data Link Control Procedure (HDLC)

High-level Data Link Control procedure (HDLC) defines the standards for linking a DTE and a DCE.

The X.25 standard, found particularly at the Data Link and Network layers of the OSI model, defines the standards for linking a DTE device such as a computer and a *DCE* device such as a modem utilizing *High-level Data Link Control procedure (HDLC)*.

Under HDLC, all information is sent in frames; a *frame* consists of six fields, with flags composing the beginning and ending fields. As Figure 2.14 illustrates, the flags are identical bit patterns, characterized by six straight one-bits.

| 01111110 | ADDRESS | CONTROL | INFORMATION | FRAME-CHECK SEQUENCE | 0111110 |

Figure 2.14 An HDLC Frame's Format

The ADDRESS field consists of the destination address if the frame is a command, and a source address if the frame is a response. The CONTROL field contains information indicating whether the frame actually contains a command or a response. The INFORMATION field usually contains integral multiples of 8-bit characters, but this is not always the case. You will see in a few minutes that this is a significant difference between HDLC and the subset of it used by IBM (called SDLC).

The FRAME-CHECK SEQUENCE field is used to ensure that the receiving station can distinguish information from garbage. It is necessary to have a way to handle situations where information might contain more than five straight one-bits. How can the receiving station determine whether the data is really information or simply a flag indicating the end of a frame?

"Bit stuffing" ensures that data in a packet will not be mistaken for control bits.

The solution to this problem is called *bit stuffing*. The HDLC protocol ensures that a zero-bit is inserted in any word that contains more than five straight one-bits. The information contained in the FRAME-CHECK SEQUENCE field tells the receiving station where to eliminate the zero-bits that have been stuffed into the frame before reading the information.

The HDLC protocol is designed to handle data exchange between a controlling central computer and its secondary stations. The central computer is responsible for error checking, as well as for polling the secondary stations at designated times. When it receives a signal that a station has a message to send, it sends a *poll bit* that permits a response from that station. This mode of operation is called *Normal Response Mode (NRM)*.

A second mode of operation permits all secondary stations to send messages whenever they desire, without waiting for a poll bit from the central computer. This method is called *Asynchronous Response Mode (ARM)*.

Synchronous Data Link Control (SDLC)

Synchronous Data Link Control (SDLC) data packets contain some control codes unique to IBM.

IBM's computers that run under its Systems Network Architecture use Synchronous Data Link Control (SDLC), a subset of HDLC. While it contains the same basic HDLC frame—consisting of beginning and ending flags, with the same HDLC bit pattern—there are some differences. SDLC's information field contains data that can only be integral multiples of 8-bit characters. An equally significant difference is that SDLC contains several commands and responses not found under HDLC. (Chapter 3 will return to SDLC when it examines the link between LANs and the IBM mainframe world of Systems Network Architecture.)

IEEE Network Standards

IEEE has developed standards for a bus LAN (802.3), a token bus LAN (802.4), and a token ring LAN (802.5).

Several IEEE committees have developed standards for LAN topologies and access methods, using the OSI set of layered standards as a foundation. Three of these IEEE 802 standards are of particular interest to us: 802.3 (the CSMA/CD bus standard), 802.4 (the token bus standard), and 802.5 (the token ring standard). A fourth standard, 802.6, is concerned with standards for a metropolitan area network, a subject beyond the scope of this book. The complete set of 802 standards can be ordered directly from the IEEE, whose address is listed in the bibliography.

Why did IEEE develop four different—and even contradictory— standards? The reason is that by 1980, when the 802 committee's subcommittees first met, a wide range of incompatible LAN products already existed. Some vendors had opted for bus topologies, while others had chosen token rings or stars. The vendors had also chosen widely divergent methods of handling a very significant problem facing a LAN: avoiding data collisions among network nodes that have information to send.

So many different kinds of LANs had proliferated because no one topology or data access method is best for all LAN applications. IBM has illustrated this fact by offering a bus topology network (PC Network) as well as a token ring topology (Token Ring Network); each network was designed to meet a different set of customers' needs. (Chapter 4 will discuss IBM's networks.)

For the end user, the major advantage of the IEEE 802 standards is that they will eventually result in the standardization of the Physical and Data Link layers in the OSI model. This means different manufacturers who comply with these standards will produce hardware that can work in the same system. For network software to work, however, vendors will have to follow the standards established by the higher layers of the OSI model. This may take some time.

IEEE 802.3 and EtherNet

When the IEEE 802 committees began their deliberations, they were faced with a *de facto* standard, Xerox's EtherNet Local Area Network. By 1980, Intel and Digital Equipment Corporation had joined Xerox in indicating that all their products would be EtherNet compatible. Rather than requiring that all LANs follow the EtherNet standard, a subcommittee provided 802.3 as an acceptable EtherNet-like standard.

As discussed earlier, the IEEE 802 subcommittees developed standards based upon the first three layers of the OSI model. They developed the Data Link layer into two *sublayers:* a *Logical Link Control (LLC)* sublayer and a *Media Access Control (MAC)* sublayer. The LLC standard is very like the HDLC standard we described earlier, while the MAC sublayer is concerned with detecting data collisions.

The EtherNet Data Packet

The IEEE 802.3 committee defined an EtherNet data packet's format, the cabling to be used, and the maximum distance for the network.

The IEEE 802.3 standard describes a LAN using a bus topology. This network uses 50-ohm coaxial baseband cable, capable of sending data at 10 Mbs. As Figure 2.15 illustrates, the committee specified exactly how a frame should be composed. Notice the similarity between this frame and the HDLC protocol discussed earlier in this chapter.

PREAMBLE	DESTINATION ADDRESS	SOURCE ADDRESS	TYPE	DATA	FRAME-CHECK SEQUENCE

Figure 2.15   The EtherNet Frame Format

The EtherNet packet begins with a PREAMBLE, consisting of eight bytes, used for synchronization. The DESTINATION ADDRESS can be a single workstation's address, a group of workstations, or even several groups of workstations. The SOURCE ADDRESS is critical so that the workstation receiving the message recognizes where it came from. The TYPE field is important because there must be a way of designating which type of format the data is using. Without this information, it is impossible to decipher the packet when it arrives. The DATA field is strictly limited; it can only hold a minimum of 46 bytes and a maximum of 1,500 bytes of information. Finally, the FRAME-CHECK SEQUENCE field ensures that the data in the other fields arrives safely. In addition to specifying the type of data frames that can be packed in a packet and the type of cable that can be used to send this information, the committee also specified the maximum length of a single cable (1,500 feet), and the ways that repeaters could be used to boost the signal throughout the network.

The CSMA/CD Protocol

Carrier-Sense Multiple Access with Collision Detection (CSMA/CD) is a protocol for defining the ways that networks will avoid data collisions.

The IEEE 802.3 subcommittee specified the way a LAN using the bus topology should construct its frames of information (and send them over the network) in order to avoid collisions. The protocol is known as Carrier-Sense Multiple Access with Collision Detection (CSMA/CD).

To illustrate the CSMA portion of this protocol, imagine a network user who wishes to send a message. In terms of the OSI model (incorporated into the IEEE 802.3 standard), the Physical layer of the user's workstation model generates a signal. It listens to detect another carrier signal from another user who is about to send a message. If no other signal is detected, the first user's message is sent.

There are problems with this seemingly tidy solution to traffic control on a network. What happens if two network users are located fairly far apart? It is possible for their network interface cards to issue a carrier-sense signal, listen and hear nothing, and then send their messages—only to have the data collide. To avoid this type of accident, the committee added Collision Detection (CD) to the Carrier-Sense Multiple Access approach. This means that two users' network interface cards listen while they transmit a message. If a user detects a collision, the card listens for the other workstation to send a transmission and then transmits the message again.

There is still another problem with this approach. Imagine two drivers who arrive at the same intersection where there are four-way stop signs. Both drivers arrive simultaneously, come to a complete stop, wait a reasonable time, and then begin to move again, only to have to slam on their brakes to avoid a collision. Embarrassed by the near collision, the two drivers pause before starting again. Unfortunately, they start again at precisely the same time, and once again narrowly avoid a collision.

While the two drivers' adventure at an intersection sounds like a silent-movie comedy plot, the reality of collision after collision is certainly not funny to network administrators. To avoid this possibility, network planners have designed their CSMA/CD approach so that each workstation waits a different random amount of time after a data collision before once again transmitting a message. After a collision, a special signal called a *jam* is sent through the network. This signal ensures that all network stations—no matter how far apart—are aware there has been a collision.

After repeated collisions, the network will double its random delays before permitting stations to transmit once again. This approach does not eliminate collisions completely, since it is still theoretically possible for two well-separated workstations to wait different amounts of time and still transmit messages that collide. These accidents, however, become much less frequent, thus more manageable.

Despite the ingenuity of this approach to collision avoidance, there is one additional consideration. A heavily used bus network utilizing CSMA/CD can begin to look very much like a Los Angeles freeway during rush hour. Even though data is supposed to move at 10 Mbs, the doubling and redoubling of the delay duration after a few collisions could reduce the network's throughput to as low as 1–3 Mbs.

IEEE 802.3 10Base5

The IEEE 802.3 bus standard originally was developed for thick baseband coaxial cabling.

When the 802 committee developed its standard for a bus network, thick coaxial cabling was the norm for EtherNet. As a result, sometimes the original set of IEEE 802.3 specifications is referred to as "10Base5" because it describes a bus network with thick baseband coaxial cabling that can transmit data at 10 Mbs over a maximum distance of 500 meters.

IEEE 802.3 10Base2

The IEEE 802.3 "10Base2" standard describes a bus network that can transmit data at 10 Mbs over thin baseband coaxial cabling for a maximum distance of 200 meters.

Many network vendors have found it much easier and less expensive to use thin baseband coaxial cabling when installing an 802.3 bus network. The IEEE 802.3 "10Base2" specifications describe a bus network composed of thin coaxial cabling that can transmit data at 10 Mbs for a maximum distance of 200 meters.

The IEEE 802.3 STARLAN Standard

The 802 committee has approved an IEEE 802.3 standard that utilizes a clustered star topology, and transmits data at 1 Mbs for a maximum of 500 meters.

The IEEE 802 committee has developed a standard for a CSMA network that uses a *clustered star topology* in which stars are linked to each other. Sometimes known as "1Base5," this set of specifications describes a network that can transmit data at 1 Mbs for a distance of 500 meters using two pairs of 24-gauge twisted-pair unshielded wire.

IEEE 802.3 10BaseT

The IEEE 802.3 "10BaseT" standard describes a logical 802.3 CSMA/CD bus, physically configured as a distributed star, capable of transmitting data at 10 Mbs for maximum distance of 100 meters.

The IEEE 802.3 "10BaseT" set of specifications combines the best features of a star and a bus network. While the network is logically a bus with data being transmitted over the entire network, it is configured as a physical *distributed star,* using inexpensive twisted-pair wire. 10BaseT networks can transmit data at 10 Mbs for a maximum distance of 100 meters.

What makes 10BaseT so attractive to network managers is that workstations are linked to a hub that contains built-in diagnostics. When a hub recognizes that a workstation is faulty, it can bypass that workstation so that the entire network is not disrupted.

IEEE 802.4 Token Bus

IEEE 802.4 defines a bus topology using a data packet "token" that is passed from workstation to workstation. Since only the workstation owning the token can transmit information, this effectively eliminates the possibility of data collisions.

The IEEE 802.4 subcommittee developed a standard for a different type of bus network that does not have the contention approach of the 802.3 model. This type of network is desirable if it is absolutely necessary that there be no data collisions.

To understand how this token approach is in sharp contrast to the CSMA/CD bus approach, imagine a public forum on a very controversial issue. Under the CSMA/CD method (by analogy), several people might try to speak simultaneously—only to stop politely when they heard another speaker begin. With dozens of speakers trying to speak (but not wanting to interrupt each other), the process would become chaotic and inefficient. Under the token approach, there would be a token which serves as a symbol of authority, enabling a particular person to speak. A speaker would hold the token and make his or her speech. When finished, the speaker would pass the symbol of authority through the room to the next person who had indicated a desire to speak. No one who did not have the token physically in hand would attempt to speak. The token bus approach works in much the same way.

Figure 2.16 illustrates the token bus frame format under IEEE 802.4. The PREAMBLE field is used primarily to synchronize the signal. The START FRAME DELIMITER and END FRAME DELIMITER fields define the limits of the frame. The FRAME CONTROL field carries information from either the Logical Link Control (LLC) or Media Access Control (MAC) sublayers, while the DESTINATION and SOURCE ADDRESS fields function identically with those found in the 802.3 EtherNet frame. The DESTINATION ADDRESS field can contain a specific workstation's address, a group address for several workstations, or addresses for several different groups (a *broadcast address*). The INFORMATION field and the FRAME-CHECK SEQUENCE fields both are identical to those discussed under the 802.3 model.

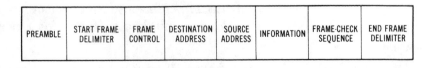

PREAMBLE	START FRAME DELIMITER	FRAME CONTROL	DESTINATION ADDRESS	SOURCE ADDRESS	INFORMATION	FRAME-CHECK SEQUENCE	END FRAME DELIMITER

Figure 2.16 The Token Bus Frame Format

The token is actually a data packet. A workstation sends the token to the address of the workstation designated to receive it. This station copies the message and then returns the token to the sending station. Figure 2.17 illustrates how a token is actually passed in a bus topology.

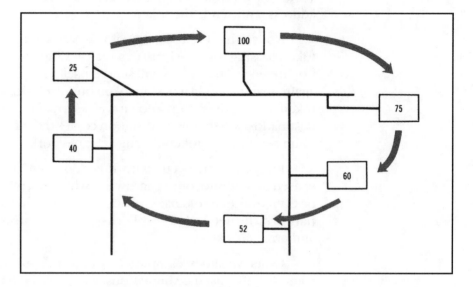

Figure 2.17 How a Token Is Passed in a Bus Topology

The network maintains a table comprised of addresses for each workstation. These addresses may bear no resemblance to the station's physical location on the bus network; they indicate the order in which each station will receive the token.

The token is passed from station to the station with the next lower address. When the station at address 100 sends the token to address 75, it listens to make sure that the token was received satisfactorily. If a workstation needs to use the network more than other workstations— and so requires the token more frequently—it can be listed several times in the network table of addresses, so it will receive the token more often.

Remember that the token is really a bit pattern. If a station does not receive a reply from the station to which it sent a token, it sends a second token. If there is still no reply, the sending station sends a special message down the network, requesting the address of the next station to receive the token by sending what is called a *"who follows" frame.* If this fails to invoke a response, it sends a general request through the network, asking any station that wants to send a message to respond to receive the token. This is known as a *"solicit successor" frame.* The sending workstation then changes the token's address to match this address, and sends the token.

Notice that the topology of this 802.4 standard is a bus, yet the token passing is in the form of a logical ring. The last address workstation to receive the token will send it back to begin the process all over again. In a smoothly working token bus, each workstation receives the token, inserts the information it wishes to send, and then sends it to its destination, where the workstation copies the information before once again sending the token through the network.

Problems can occur with this approach. The most serious are caused by malfunctioning hardware, which can result in missing tokens or even multiple tokens. To keep such a situation from crippling the network, the network controller assumes responsibility for monitoring and error checking.

Other weaknesses inherent in the token bus approach include some specific distance limitations, as well as limitations on how many new workstations can be "tapped" into the bus. Under EtherNet, for example, there are minimum distances required between individual workstations. There are also limitations on how many new workstations can be added to the bus, because each new workstation creates a certain amount of signal distortion.

IEEE 802.5 Token Ring Network

IEEE 802.5 defines a token ring network in which workstations pass a token around a physical and logical ring. The token ring uses amplifiers to boost signals, so it has a greater range than a bus network.

The IEEE 802.5 standard was developed to cover LANs with ring topologies that use a token to pass information from one workstation to another. At this point, we will examine the theory behind this set of standards; Chapter 4 will take a closer look at IBM's token ring network.

As Figure 2.18 illustrates, the sending workstation in a token ring network places a message on the token, and directs it to its destination address. The receiving workstation copies the message and then sends the token back to the originating workstation—which (in turn) removes its message and passes the token to the next station.

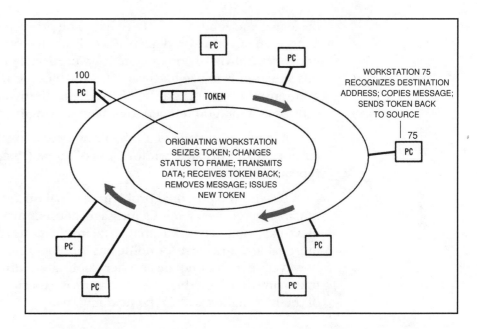

Figure 2.18 How a Token Is Transmitted on a Token Ring Network

Because it is crucial that an originating station know whether or not its message has been received, the frame format is slightly different. Figure 2.19 reveals that there is an ACCESS CONTROL field.

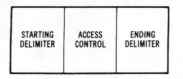

Figure 2.19 Format for a Token

This field controls the actual passing of the token. The *ENDING FRAME DELIMITER field* also contains a new wrinkle. Two bits in this frame are used to indicate whether the station receiving a message recognized the address, and whether it actually copied the message successfully.

In a smoothly running token ring network, each station receives the token and checks to see if the message address matches its own. If its address matches, it copies the message and sends the token on by repeating the signal. If the message is for another workstation, it repeats the signal and sends it on. There has to be provision in the network to handle an inactive or defective workstation; otherwise, the entire network would fail if one workstation were disabled. One way to handle this situation is to use hardware that enables the network to bypass a nontransmitting workstation. Earlier we discussed the use of wire centers as a method to keep the token moving past inactive stations.

A major advantage of a token-ring over a token bus is that it can cover a greater distance without loss of signal (since each workstation repeats the signal).

Besides the potential problem of a malfunctioning station that is not able to receive or send a message, another major negative feature of a token ring network is that large installations require significantly more cable than a corresponding bus topology. In a very large network, however, there may not be another viable alternative. Because of IBM's token ring topology, this type of network is expected to gain at least 70% of the LAN market within the next few years.

What Have You Learned?

1. File servers offer many advantages over disk servers in a LAN.
2. The major LAN media include twisted-pair wire, coaxial cable, and fiber optics.
3. Broadband coaxial cable can transmit several different messages simultaneously using different frequencies.
4. In a star topology, the entire LAN fails if the central computer fails.
5. CSMA/CD is a method for detecting and avoiding data collisions on a LAN.
6. X.25 is a standard for packet switching with layers of standards corresponding to the first three layers of the OSI model.
7. The OSI model consists of seven layers of standards designed to ensure LAN compatibility of hardware and software.
8. HDLC consists of protocols for placing a message in a packet for transmission.

Quiz for Chapter 2

1. The X.25 set of standards covers how many layers of the OSI model?

    a. One

    b. Two

    c. Three

    d. Four

2. Which OSI model layer concerns itself with hardware specifications?

    a. Data Link

    b. Network

    c. Physical

    d. Presentation

3. Bit stuffing is used to

    a. pad insufficient information.

    b. distinguish beginning and ending flags from information.

    c. convert 8-bit words into 16-bit words.

    d. fill a data turkey.

4. When a central computer polls a station to see if it has a message to send, this is an example of

    a. Asynchronous Response Mode (ARM).

    b. Normal Response Mode (NRM).

    c. Infrequent Polling Procedure (IPP).

    d. Polling by Authorization (PBA).

5. A protocol is really

    a. a set of demands.

    b. a set of rules.

    c. a translation book for diplomats.

    d. a call with very high authorization.

6. A CB radio call is very much like
    a. full-duplex transmission.
    b. half-duplex transmission.
    c. quarter-duplex transmission.
    d. no duplex transmission.

7. In the OSI model, error recognition and recovery is really the responsibility of
    a. the Physical layer.
    b. the Application layer.
    c. the Session layer.
    d. the Transport layer.

8. In the OSI model, password verification is the responsibility of
    a. the Session layer.
    b. the Physical layer.
    c. the Data Link layer.
    d. the Network layer.

9. Distributed file servers are
    a. special file servers designed for LANs.
    b. multiple file servers designed to speed up the network.
    c. inexpensive file servers.
    d. file servers also used as workstations.

10. A dedicated file server is
    a. a hard working file server.
    b. a file server used as a workstation and as a file server.
    c. a file server used only for serving files to workstations in a LAN.
    d. a file server that never breaks down.

11. A print spooler is really
    a. a buffer used to store files for printing.
    b. the central processing unit.
    c. a printer's spooling mechanism.
    d. a place for assembling and disassembling printer material.

12. To send simultaneous voice and data signals, a LAN should use
    a. twisted-pair wire.
    b. baseband coaxial cable.
    c. broadband coaxial cable.
    d. two coffee cans with lots of string.

13. A data highway is a good description of which network topology?
    a. A bus
    b. A star
    c. A ring
    d. A token ring

14. A dead workstation on a token ring network can cripple the network without
    a. special software.
    b. wire centers or special bypass hardware.
    c. extra tokens.
    d. a dead station token (DST).

15. A broadcast address enables a message to go to
    a. a single workstation.
    b. a single group of workstations.
    c. several groups of workstations.
    d. a selected peripheral.

16. A jam signal sent through a network means
    a. the network traffic is too congested.
    b. there has been a data collision.
    c. it's time to go.
    d. the printer's paper feeder is jammed.

17. The IEEE 802.3 standard is closest to
    a. IBM's Token Ring network.
    b. Xerox's EtherNet LAN.
    c. a generic star network.
    d. a generic token ring network.

18. For a relatively large network covering a long distance, probably the best network topology would be

    a. a bus.

    b. a token ring.

    c. a token bus.

    d. a superbus.

19. If interference is a major problem, a network designer should consider

    a. baseband coaxial cable.

    b. broadband coaxial cable.

    c. twisted-pair wire.

    d. fiber optics.

20. Database management software and electronic mail software would be found in which layer of the OSI model?

    a. The Application layer

    b. The Presentation layer

    c. The Data Link layer

    d. The Network layer

3 | Bridges, Routers, and Gateways

About This Chapter

The major problem many companies face is how to link their various computer networks. The Accounting Department might have an EtherNet LAN that uses thin coaxial cabling, while PCs in the corporate offices are linked via a 10BaseT LAN that uses twisted-pair wire. Manufacturing might be using an IBM mainframe computer, while Research & Development has a DEC minicomputer.

In this chapter we will examine how different LANs can be linked via *bridges* or *routers*. We will also look at how mainframes and minicomputers can communicate via *gateways* that can link together these very different worlds.

We will take a close look at this mainframe world and how information is handled there—including the most common protocols used; new standards are emerging for communications between microcomputers and mainframes. We also will examine the possible levels of communications between microcomputers and minicomputers.

Finally, we will examine how some companies are using their PBX phone systems as limited LANs, communicating over these switches with their mainframe computers—as well as with several different packet-switched networks.

Bridges

Bridges are devices that connect LANs at the Data Link layer of the OSI model. They do not concern themselves with higher-level protocols.

Bridges are devices that function at the Data Link layer of the OSI Model (a topic we discussed in Chapter 2). At this level, there is a concern with packets' source and destination addresses, but not with any higher-level protocols. Packets that have the same Data Link layer can travel through a bridge, regardless of whether they use Novell's IPX protocol or the XNS protocol (which several major network operating systems use).

The major function of a bridge is to forward and filter packets, depending upon their destination addresses.

A bridge keeps a table that lists the addresses of the microcomputers found on its LAN. It examines a packet to see if its destination address is found on this particular LAN. If the packet is addressed to a local microcomputer, the bridge *filters* it from the packets transmitted to the bridge, and redirects it to its final destination on the local LAN. Packets addressed to microcomputers not found on this local LAN are *forwarded* across the bridge, to the bridge on the other side. This bridge goes through the same process of determining whether this same packet needs to be filtered or forwarded to still another LAN.

Bridges are usually very fast because they do not need to do any reformatting. They simply read a destination address and make the decision to filter or forward the packet. Bridges can have different types of cabling interfaces so that, for example, an EtherNet LAN with thick coaxial cabling can be bridged to a second EtherNet LAN that uses twisted-pair wire.

Spanning Tree Bridges

A spanning tree approach to bridging multiple networks results in a single path from one LAN to the next.

A *spanning tree bridge* has been adopted as a standard by the IEEE 802.1 committee. The spanning tree method describes how to bridge multiple networks in which more than one loop might exist. The bridges "negotiate" among themselves to ensure that only one bridge port is available in each direction on a LAN, and that the path selected is the most efficient (given network traffic conditions). Figure 3.1 illustrates the spanning tree approach to bridging multiple networks.

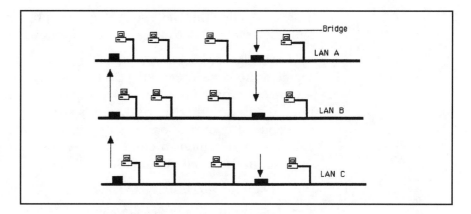

Figure 3.1   The Spanning Tree Algorithm Determines the Direction in Which Data
Will Flow to and from a Network Bridge

Source Routing Bridges

Source routing bridges are
utilized by IBM's Token Ring
Network. A workstation
determines the complete
route a packet must take, and
includes this information as
part of the packet.

IBM's Token Ring Networks use a *source routing* approach when they
are bridged. Each LAN ring is assigned a unique number. A workstation
sends out an *all-routes broadcast frame,* and requests information on
the address of the workstation that will receive the packet. Each ring
adds its number to this all-routes broadcast frame and forwards it on.
The destination workstation receives this frame and sends it back to the
transmitting microcomputer. This frame now includes a complete set
of routing directions, including which rings must be crossed to reach
the destination address.

Bridging EtherNet and Token Ring Networks

Because EtherNet and Token
Ring packets have different
structures, a bridge
connecting these two
networks must do more than
simply forward and filter
packets.

Some companies have both EtherNet and Token Ring LANs, and wish
to link the two. As discussed in Chapter 2, these two networks use very
different packet structures. An EtherNet packet has a maximum size of
only 1,500 bytes; a 4-Mbs (megabits per second) Token Ring packet
might contain 4,000 bytes, while a packet from a 16-Mbs Token Ring
Network might have close to 18,000 bytes. To make matters even more
complicated, a bridge connecting these very different environments

must reconcile EtherNet's spanning tree approach to routing packets with the Token Ring Network's source routing approach.

A bridge connecting Token Ring and EtherNet networks must segment the large Token Ring packets into several smaller packets for transmission over EtherNet networks. When source routing information crosses an EtherNet bridge, it is stripped off so that the packet resembles a conventional EtherNet packet. IBM's 8209 bridge, for example, is designed to connect these two very different worlds. It operates in three different modes:

- Token Ring to EtherNet version 2
- Token Ring to IEEE 802.3 LANs
- A mode in which the bridge detects the type of LAN, and then switches to mode 1 or mode 2

Routers

Routers function at the Network layer of the OSI model and are protocol-specific.

Routers function at the Network layer of the OSI model, and thus are protocol-specific. A router might route TCP/IP protocol packets, for example, or NetWare packets.

One major advantage of a router over a bridge is that it builds a "fire wall" that protects one network from packets generated by another network, thereby reducing message traffic at the workstation level.

Bridges connect LANs so that they form one very large network. Connecting several EtherNet LANs via bridges, for example, results in every workstation on every connected LAN receiving all packets.

Naturally, traffic is very heavy on all these connected LANs. If a network interface card goes bad on one workstation—and begins generating thousands of bad packets (a *broadcast storm*)—it can congest all the bridged LANs. A router, on the other hand, is protocol-specific; it can be programmed to permit only those packets which match certain profiles.

Routers are much more sophisticated—and much more expensive—than bridges. Before transmitting a packet to its destination, a router can analyze current traffic conditions and determine the best route for the packet to take. If traffic conditions change (for example, if a router down the road fails), the router can change its proposed route and redirect its packets over this revised path.

If it becomes necessary to link LANs that run different network operating systems which utilize different protocols, routers are required. For example, a company which has a NetWare LAN, a Vines LAN, and an IBM LAN Server network would need routers that understand these different protocols, so it could translate packets into the appropriate format before forwarding them to the destination network. Bridges operating at a far less sophisticated level would not be able to distinguish a Vines packet from a NetWare packet.

A second solution to this problem would be to have each of these three different LANs use a common protocol—such as the *Transmission Control Protocol/Internet Protocol* (known as the TCP/IP protocol)—on top of its file server protocol. Then install routers that only need to understand TCP/IP protocol.

The World of Systems Network Architecture (SNA)

IBM's SNA contains several layers of protocols which are very similar to those of the OSI model discussed in the last chapter. SNA uses SDLC, a subset of HDLC.

Any discussion of the mainframe world has to begin with IBM's set of specifications for distributed data processing networks. As Figure 3.2 illustrates, *Systems Network Architecture (SNA)* provides a model composed of network layers, very much like the OSI model we surveyed in the last chapter. The data flow through this model is virtually identical to that of the OSI model, except that the frames use the Synchronous Data Link Control format (SDLC) rather than the High-Level Data Link Control (HDLC). As pointed out in the last chapter, the SDLC frames contain some frames that are transmitted from one node to another throughout an SNA network.

TRANSACTION SERVICES	controls document exchange distributed database access
PRESENTATION SERVICES	formats data
DATA FLOW CONTROL	synchronous exchange of data
TRANSMISSION CONTROL	matches data exchange rate
PATH CONTROL	routes data packets between source and destination
DATA LINK CONTROL	transmits data between nodes
PHYSICAL	provides physical connections

Figure 3.2   Systems Network Architecture (SNA)

IBM's NewView provides a centralized management system that performs diagnostics on SNA protocols, communication sessions, and network accounting procedures. It also displays network diagnostic alerts, and determines network component failures. NetView also has the capability of monitoring X.25 traffic in the SNA environment. IBM's X.25 SNA Interconnection program allows SNA networks to carry data under X.25 packet-switching protocols.

Synchronous Versus Asynchronous Data Transmission

While asynchronous transmission sends data one byte at a time, synchronous transmission uses frames that permit a stream of data.

Data transmission in the microcomputer world has long taken the form of asynchronous transmission. Serial printers and modems are everyday reminders of how common this form of data communications really is. The SNA mainframe world uses the Synchronous Data Link Control (SDLC) protocol, a synchronous method of data transmission we discussed briefly in Chapter 2. As Figure 3.3 illustrates, asynchronous transmission is limited to sending characters a byte at a time, while the synchronous approach sends continuous information until the entire transmission is concluded.

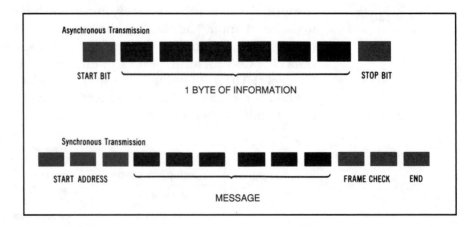

Figure 3.3   Asynchronous Versus Synchronous Transmission

Some older IBM mainframes use *Binary Synchronous Communication (BSC),* a protocol which is synchronous but is not SDLC. This protocol is character-oriented (rather than bit-oriented, as is SDLC); it assumes eight-bit characters. We will focus our efforts on SDLC protocol machines in this chapter.

Note: Several companies—including IBM—market a Binary Synchronous Communication Adapter card and Binary Synchronous 3270 Emulation program. These two items are the keys to tying a microcomputer LAN to an older IBM that uses BSC protocol.

Logical Units (LU)

Logical units (LUs) can represent end users or application programs.

Communication in an SNA network takes place between *logical units (LUs).* Logical units can represent end users (as is the case with the firmware associated with IBM 3270 terminals) or application programs (such as an accounting program or database program). The application programs do not concern themselves with where the terminals are physically located but rather with the terminal's network name. SNA is capable of translating this network name into a corresponding address.

Network-Addressable Units (NAUs)

Network-addressable units (NAUs) consist of logical units (LUs), physical units (PUs), and System Services Control Points (SSCPs).

SNA uses *network-addressable units (NAUs)* to perform a number of network management functions; these include handling the communications portions of application programs and providing network control. There are three types of network-addressable units. These NAUs can be logical units, *physical units (PUs),* and *System Services Control Points (SSCPs).* We will examine the latter two types briefly before looking at an actual SNA network in operation.

A physical unit is not actually a physical device. It represents something tangible (a terminal or an intelligent controller, for example) to Systems Network Architecture—which deals (in effect) with this PU rather than with the device itself.

Finally, a System Services Control Point (SSCP) serves as the SNA network manager for a single SNA domain. It coordinates communications among network elements, makes sure the corresponding physical devices are active when two logical units wish to converse, and provides error-checking information.

The Path Control Network

The Path Control Network is responsible for identifying the addresses of devices that wish to converse on the network, and then establishing a network path for their conversation.

Under SNA, the *Path Control Network* contains a path control layer and a data link control layer. This network is concerned with traffic flow, transmission priorities, and error recovery.

The Path Control Network is responsible for identifying the correct addresses of units that wish to converse, and then establishing a network path for their conversation.

> **Note:** Remember that all LUs, PUs, and even SSCPs have different network addresses under SNA.

Sessions

A session consists of a logical and physical path connecting two NAUs for data transmission. NAUs can have multiple sessions.

A *session* under SNA is a logical and physical path connecting two NAUs for data transmission. SNA thinks of its terminals, controllers, and front-end communication processors as *nodes*. Each of these pieces of hardware has a corresponding PU. If a terminal wishes to communicate with a front-end communication processor, for example, the SSCP would establish a session between the two nodes. Two end users would establish an LU-LU session.

The SSCP controls the activating and deactivating of a session. An application program can maintain several different sessions with different terminals simultaneously under SNA. Figure 3.4 illustrates the NAU elements found under SNA.

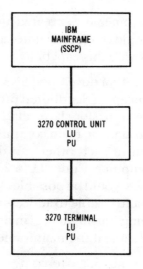

Figure 3.4 The NAU Elements Found Under SNA

LU 6.2

LU 6.2 contains specifications that ultimately will enable programs written in different languages under different operating systems to communicate with each other.

Earlier we described how it was possible to have a session between a program and a terminal; someday it will be possible to have transparent communication between two programs. IBM has added *Advanced Program-to-Program Communications (APPC)* to SNA, resulting in two new protocols (LU 6.2 and PU 2.1).

LU 6.2, when fully implemented by program developers, will enable a microcomputer running a program under an operating system such as DOS to communicate with a mainframe computer that runs under a different operating system—while still retaining full stand-alone processing capabilities. The revolutionary concept behind this protocol is that different computers running different programs (written in different languages under different operating systems) can interact with each other.

For years corporations have longed for the ability to download information from a mainframe directly into an IBM personal computer running Lotus 1-2-3. Similarly, there is a real need to be able to upload customer files created under a DOS program (such as dBASE IV or Paradox) directly into a mainframe database. LU 6.2 promises to provide this capability.

IBM developed SNA before personal computers were popular; its concept of distributed processing (which was incorporated under SNA) was a master-slave relationship. All communication under SNA goes through the main computer. Two end users who wish to send information to each other can do so only by going through the mainframe computer. Under LU 6.2, theoretically, true peer-to-peer communications would be possible. A personal computer as part of an SNA network would be able to address a second personal computer directly, without going through the mainframe. Such a path might be particularly valuable if the mainframe should fail.

LU 6.2 overcomes many of the limitations of SNA because it provides a true generic *application program interface (API)* between application programs and Systems Network Architecture. Since this interface includes hardware specifications, the network can be thought of as machine-independent—as long as all vendors adhere to these requirements. Rather than establishing a traditional master-slave relationship (the historical norm under SNA), LU 6.2 allows either node in a network session to initiate the session.

IBM has begun to provide tools that will help implement LU 6.2. The *Server/Requester Programming Interface (SRPI)* is a protocol that allows PC applications to issue requests for services and receive replies from IBM mainframe computers. This interface permits program-to-program communications under terminal emulation conditions (discussed in the next section of this chapter). SRPI is a subset of IBM's Advanced Program-to-Program Communications programming interface. IBM has upgraded its mainframe operating systems to work in conjunction with LU 6.2.

TSO/E Release 3 is an operating environment upgrade for mainframes that run under the MVS/XA TSO/E environment; this version implements SRPI, and allows the product to handle requests for data and services from PCs. IBM has also developed IBM PC Requesters, a product that runs under the new SRPI interface. With this product, an IBM PC will have a DOS menu with which to access data from databases. The workstation will be able to request data on a record-by-record basis if necessary.

The major problem with LU 6.2 is that existing software packages and hardware do not follow the APPC guidelines. It will take some time before there are enough programs available to make this new protocol a major force in the SNA world.

Micro-Mainframe Communications

Until the software and hardware that follows LU 6.2 comes along, the main method for micro-mainframe communications will continue to be the emulation of various IBM terminals.

The main areas of emphasis in this book are LANs, and how microcomputers within a network can communicate with each other (as well as with mainframes). Various important options are, however, available today—including some that are limited to a single microcomputer emulating an IBM terminal.

Despite the exciting possibilities of LU 6.2, the dearth of software written for the interface means that for the foreseeable future, microcomputers will continue to communicate with the mainframe world by *terminal emulation*. Let's examine several ways—both local and remote—of tying the two worlds together.

327X Terminal Emulation via Cluster Controller

An IBM mainframe computer can communicate with various peripherals through a 3274 or 3276 *cluster controller*. The 3274 controller can connect up to 32 terminals and/or printers to the mainframe; only seven devices can be connected to the 3276. As Figure 3.5 illustrates, an IBM PC can be connected directly to the mainframe through the cluster controller, using coaxial cable and special software and hardware for emulating the IBM 3278 terminal.

Figure 3.5 shows DCA's IRMA card, which fits into an IBM PC's full-size slot. The IRMA card contains RAM, ROM, a 3270 coaxial interface, and a high-speed processor capable of handling 4 million instructions per second. By pressing the PC's two shift keys simultaneously, a user can shift between a DOS application and 3270 terminal emulation.

Anyone who has used an IBM 3278 terminal knows that its keyboard and screen are both very different from those found on an IBM PC. Terminal emulation software allows the PC user to press standard

PC keys and have the equivalent 3278 keystrokes sent to the cluster controller. Similarly, the software "paints" the IBM monitor's screen with what appears to be an IBM 3278 display.

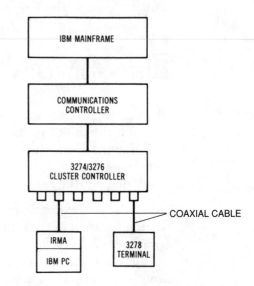

Figure 3.5 An IBM PC Connected to a Cluster Controller

While the 3278 monochrome is the terminal most commonly emulated, there is also software to emulate the 3279 color terminal. At one time, IBM even offered a 3270-PC; this PC model had a built-in 3270 terminal emulation board, and a hybrid keyboard that provided some features of these two very different keyboards.

Local LAN Gateways

A LAN gateway can be attached via coaxial cable to a 3274 cluster controller to provide a local micro-mainframe connection.

A single IBM PC in 3278 terminal emulation, connected directly to the cluster controller by coaxial cable, is using one of the controller's ports; that is a major limitation. Several PCs connected in this way would severely limit the mainframe's ability to serve all company users. Using coaxial cable, it is possible to connect an entire microcomputer LAN to an IBM cluster controller port via a gateway. As Figure 3.6 illustrates, any PC in such a network has access to 3270 terminal emulation. DCA is one of many companies that currently offer this coaxial-connect gateway.

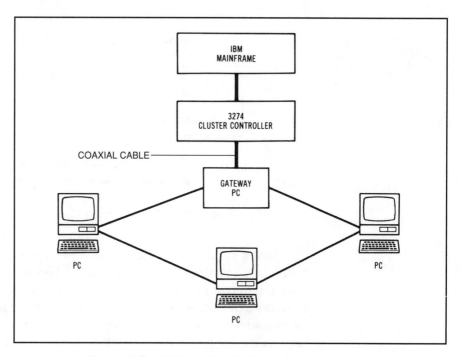

Figure 3.6 An IBM PC with 3270 Terminal Emulation

Remote Gateways

Remote gateways enable LAN
users to communicate with a
mainframe computer by
using 3278 terminal
emulation over a gateway PC.
This gateway emulates a
cluster controller and
communicates with the
mainframe computer via
modem.

Useful as coaxial-connect gateways might be, many companies have their local area microcomputer network at one location, and their mainframe facilities elsewhere. In this situation, remote LAN gateways prove particularly valuable. Widget Company (our example in Chapter 1) illustrates this likelier instance of micro-mainframe communications.

At the remote site, the designated "gateway" PC is equipped with a *gateway interface board* and special gateway software to emulate a cluster controller. As Figure 3.7 illustrates, each remote PC can emulate a 3278 terminal, using the gateway PC's synchronous modem to communicate over a phone line with a mainframe computer. This one gateway server is capable of running as many as 64 3270 emulation sessions. CXI permits 64 concurrent host sessions—and a data rate as fast as 56 Kbs (kilobits per second) via synchronous modems attached to IBM 3705 or 3725 controllers.

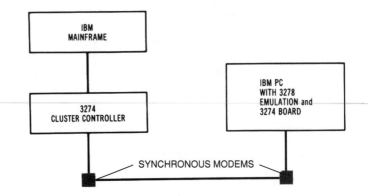

Figure 3.7   Remote 3270 Emulation with a Gateway PC

IBM's 3720 communications controller links the mainframe with LANs. IBM currently offers a special Token-Ring interface to its 3720 controller. You may recall (from our discussion of the SNA world and the nature of SNA sessions) that one user can find himself needing three or four editing sessions simultaneously. These mainframe sessions are very valuable; often the network administrator will establish some order of priority for using them.

All network users can emulate a 3278 terminal and communicate with the mainframe computer through the gateway PC (theoretically, at least)— but if several network workstations need to establish micro-mainframe communications, a traffic jam ensues quickly. A single gateway PC, processing information and transmitting it through a modem which communicates over a single telephone line, will prove inadequate for this workload. There are a number of ways to alleviate this problem.

- If the gateway PC is also being used as a workstation, it can be designated a *dedicated gateway,* to be used only for that purpose.
- If the processing speed of the dedicated gateway PC is still not adequate to handle the communications workload, a second gateway file server can be installed. (Remember, however, that these two servers will be sharing a single modem and a single telephone line.)

• If the second remedy proves inadequate, the only solution is to install a second network—complete with PC workstations, gateway PC, modem, and a second telephone line. (It is possible to connect the two networks together using a bridge, which was discussed earlier in this chapter.)

Micro-Mainframe File Transfers

Many of the micro-mainframe file transfer programs permit only bulk transfer of files. The microcomputer user is not able to select key fields from a mainframe database and retrieve only this very specific information. The more sophisticated file transfer programs permit the selective retrieval of information.

We have seen that it is possible to link workstations in a LAN to a mainframe computer by using 3270 terminal emulation and a gateway. The major limitation of this emulation is that an intelligent PC is forced to assume the role of a "dumb" terminal. The terminal emulation software normally permits on-line inquiry using the mainframe programs and has the capability to save each screen of 3270 terminal information.

Unfortunately, this is not the major reason companies want to link their microcomputers with their mainframe computer. Users want to be able to download and upload selected information, not merely dump screenfuls of information.

Since microcomputer and mainframe computer are running different programs under different operating systems, however, file transfers in both directions create enormous problems. Even more serious, the very file structure of micro and mainframe application programs usually differ. IBM mainframe computers use an EBCDIC format, while microcomputers use an ASCII format.

Also a problem is the file-size limitation of a microcomputer; there is a fundamental difference in size between a micro and a mainframe. Mainframe files may not be downloadable simply because the microcomputer does not have enough disk space to handle them; the micro's software may not be able to handle the large number of records found within a mainframe file.

Many of the leaders in micro-mainframe communications offer *file transfer programs* with their 3270 terminal emulation products. These programs do not permit a user to manipulate the data within a mainframe's application program and select certain fields; they merely enable a microcomputer user to download or upload complete files.

With DCA's IRMAlink FT/370, for example, it is possible to transfer files between an IRMA-equipped PC and an IBM mainframe running under CICS, VM/CMS, or MVS/TSO. DCA also requires that a magnetic tape be installed on the mainframe side, and that it be linked to a terminal controller. Once this is accomplished, it is possible to transfer files simply by entering the source filename and the destination filename. AST offers the AST-3270/FTS-R advanced file transfer system for the MVS/TSO and VM/CMS environments. Basically this provides bidirectional transfer of binary or text files.

Several companies have developed *intelligent links* that tie together their own mainframe computer programs with major microcomputer software. Information Builders, for example, offers FOCUS for the IBM mainframe environment and PC/FOCUS for microcomputers. Using this program, it is possible to use the mainframe data base for distributed processing. PCs tied to a LAN can be used as transaction workstations to enter data. Management Science of America offers Executive Peachpack II, for example, which ties together its mainframe MSA application programs data with Lotus 1-2-3's formats running on a PC. Several vendors offer links to spreadsheets that will accept Data Interchange Format (DIF).

Up until now, the lack of uniformity in microcomputer and mainframe software has made it necessary to purchase separate interfaces (provided they were available) for each vendor's programs. On-Line Software's OMNILINK is a micro-mainframe link that includes software for both the micro and mainframe to address this problem. It includes a file reformat utility; this program automatically converts downloaded data into formats used by Lotus 1-2-3, dBASE IV, and several other leading programs. It is possible to select criteria, and then download only those records within a file that meet the selected standards.

There are a few vendors who have begun to address the possibilities of LU 6.2 and its potential for facilitating data transfer from microcomputer to mainframe. Network Software Associates' AdaptSNA LU6.2/APPC is just what the name implies—an implementation of LU 6.2 and PU 2.1. The software enables a DOS program to communicate directly with a partner program running on a mainframe or minicomputer. This implementation does away with the traditional SNA master-slave relationship, permitting peer-to-peer communication.

PCs can also be configured to participate in IBM's Distributed Office Support System (DIOSS) or other host-based APPC system. CXI's Application Program Interface enables microcomputers to transfer data directly to a mainframe using computer-to-computer communication—and not simply "dumb" terminal emulation. Similarly, Rabbit Software has developed Program Interface Module (PIM), which also permits direct transfer of data. Microcomputer users find this process transparent; they do not have to learn mainframe computer procedures in order to use a microcomputer program.

Remote Job Entry (RJE)

There are many times when remote PCs need to send information to mainframe computers unattended in batch form. While 3270 terminal emulation has become a very popular way to communicate with mainframes, this older method is often preferable.

In many situations, micro-mainframe communications are needed primarily for uploading data after business hours. A company with several retail outlets, for example, might require each branch to upload sales figures during the evening, so the mainframe computer can digest the information and update its accounting files. As a method of transferring large amounts of data, IBM originally designed the 3270 terminal emulation protocol for on-line inquiry and RJE. RJE contains such features as data compression and compaction to minimize line charges for data transmission.

Network Software Associates' AdaptSNA RJE is a good example of an RJE SNA communications emulator. Emulating an IBM 3770 Remote Job Entry workstation, this hardware/software package offers a number of powerful features that RJE users expect. An Applications Programming interface permits unattended operation, as well as automatic error recovery. In addition to supporting LU-LU and SSCP-LU sessions, the package contains EBCDIC/ASCII conversion tables. It uses "on-the-fly" processing to reformat data received from the host computer automatically.

Clearly, 3270 terminal emulation has inherent limitations (in particular, the method of dumping one screenful of information at a time). So much effort has been expended to get around these that many people have forgotten the very useful niche RJE can fill in micro-mainframe communications.

Micro-Mini Communications

Through terminal emulation it is possible for microcomputers—individually or as part of a LAN—to communicate with minicomputers such as IBM's AS/400 (as well as its older System 34, 36, and 38 computers).

Many microcomputer users are far more anxious to communicate with their departmental minicomputer than with a corporate mainframe. This process is very similar to 3270 terminal emulation, except that the microcomputers need to be equipped with

- 5250 emulator boards.
- file transfer software to communicate with IBM minicomputers.
- corresponding software and hardware to communicate with DEC, Hewlett-Packard, and other major minicomputers.

Several major vendors offer this combination of hardware and software. AST, for example, offers the AST-5250/Local Cluster, which enables a PC to function as a local cluster controller. It provides 5250 terminal emulation for up to four clustered PCs connected serially to a "master" controller PC.

As Figure 3.8 illustrates, this controller is connected via standard twinax cable to a host minicomputer (whether AS/400, System 34, 36, or 38). This "master" PC can also be connected to a minicomputer via asynchronous modems with remote PCs. These, in turn, can also use 5250 terminal emulation; such modems are capable of supporting speeds up to 9,600 bits per second (Bps).

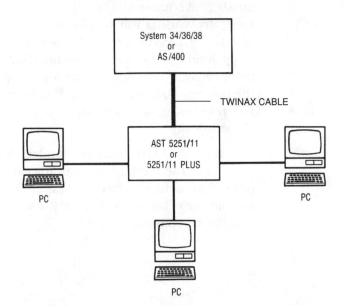

Figure 3.8 Local Microcomputers Linked to an IBM Minicomputer

Clustered PCs operate in a background mode relative to the master PC. This means that one or more clustered PCs operate in 5250 emulation mode, while the master PC is operating in DOS mode. It is also possible to have concurrent DOS and host sessions on a PC.

Many of the same file transfer limitations found in micro-mainframe communications are also present in micro-mini communications. Techland Systems addresses many of these problems with its Blue Lynx hardware and software. When this board is used with DecisionLink's file transfer software, the micro user is able to perform bidirectional file transfer. Four concurrent host sessions are supported. On-Line's OMNILINK facilitates micro-minicomputer file transfers in much the same way; key fields within a minicomputer database can be selected for downloading to a microcomputer. Even more sophisticated software (available from companies such as Fusion) permits the transfer of selected data from as many as eight different files on an IBM minicomputer.

Virtual Networking Systems

Banyan Systems has developed Vines software, which permits sharing of resources on a virtual network. PCs can actually share a mainframe or minicomputer hard disk.

On a *virtual network* all resources appear to be local so that the differences between microcomputers, minicomputers, and even mainframes are of limited importance to the end user. Banyan Systems, for example, has developed Vines software in conjunction with its family of network file servers. As Figure 3.9 illustrates, Vines permits the sharing of resources, applications, and information wherever they are located on a virtual network.

A microcomputer user can access files from a mainframe as easily as if this information were on his PC. The microcomputer can save information onto the "virtual disk" of the mainframe or minicomputer that is also attached to the Banyan file server. Since the software supports LU 6.2, it is extremely easy to communicate with other users, even if you do not know precisely where they are on the network. The software keeps track of users' addresses, and permits electronic mail transfer simply by indicating the receiver's name.

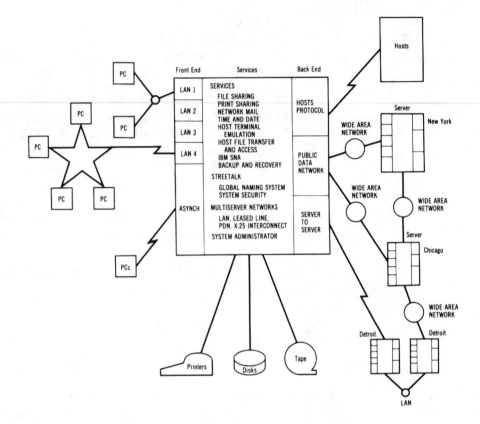

Figure 3.9 Banyan's Virtual Networking System
(Courtesy of Banyan Systems, Inc.)

The PBX

One of the major capabilities offered by Banyan's virtual network is the ability to transmit and receive information from different networks without becoming too concerned with the mechanics of the process. To the end user, this complex system seems simple, since the complexities are handled by the Vines software. For several years, data processing professionals and telecommunication managers have speculated about the possibility of using an office's telephone system—its *private branch exchange (PBX)*—to accomplish not only what Banyan has done, but also the integration of voice and data.

PBX History

The PBX has been around for approximately 80 years. The newer units are completely digital. They are distributed most commonly with twisted-pair wire but also with coaxial cable and (less frequently) fiber optics.

The PBX has a long history. To understand the concept of a PBX, imagine an office before it. As Figure 3.10 illustrates, each phone was directly connected into the trunk cable that carried the signals back to the central office exchange.

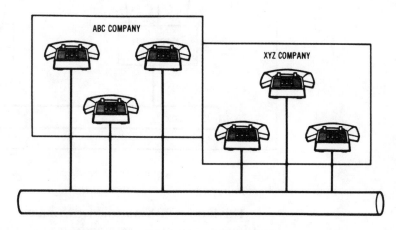

Figure 3.10 A Phone System Before the PBX

The PBX simplified this situation. As Figure 3.11 shows, only a few wires are required to connect the PBX to the trunk. In the late 1800s a first-generation PBX phone system was in operation. Bell's 701 family of PBXs (launched in 1929) represents the second generation, in which operators were no longer needed to handle outgoing calls. A third-generation PBX arrived around 1980; it featured distributed architecture, nonblocking operation, and integrated voice and data.

Note: Sometimes the term *PABX* (private automatic branch exchange) is used to differentiate a PBX in which all in-house and outgoing calls are automatically switched. To avoid confusion, we will use the generic PBX term to encompass the newer PABXs in our discussion of the newer digital switches.

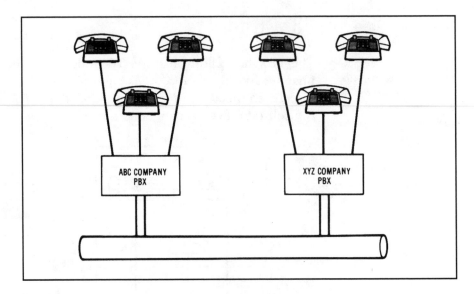

Figure 3.11 A PBX Phone System

This kind of PBX is attractive to many college administrators whose buildings are spread over a wide area. Such a system's advantage is its *distributed architecture*—which simply means that switching modules are distributed over coaxial cable or optic-fiber media.

These new systems promised that their additional channel capacity would make overloading impossible, and that they would always be able to access a call. Nonblocking operation is, however, more a promise than a reality. AT&T allows users the opportunity to select a configuration that can be blocking, nonblocking, or "essentially nonblocking" (one in one million attempts to access a call will be blocked).

Today there is some debate over whether we now have a fourth generation of PBX. AT&T points with pride to its System 85's high-speed data bus, which can handle voice and data simultaneously over the same wire. Other vendors insist that their digital switches are just as sophisticated. For our purposes, however, what really matters is how the new PBXs work—and why they are increasingly popular as alternatives to LANs.

The coder-decoder is essential to a PBX, since it converts a digital signal to analog, and an analog signal to digital.

To understand how a PBX digital switch works, it is important to remember that our telephone system sends *analog* signals (defined in the next subsection) over phone lines. A device called a coder-decoder, or *CODEC,* converts the voice analog signals into digital form. Many of the newer PBX systems place this CODEC in the telephone handset. As Figure 3.12 illustrates, this means that all communication to and from the PBX is digital.

Figure 3.12   A Digital PBX with the CODEC in the Telephone Handset

Data Switching Within the PBX

To understand how data is switched within a digital PBX switch, it is necessary to look at PAM (pulse amplitude modulation) and PCM (pulse code modulation).

The *analog transmission* of voice signals is really the transmission of audio frequency sine waves which are equal in frequency and amplitude to the original voice tones. Using *pulse amplitude modulation (PAM),* a telephone system samples the analog voice signal 8,000 times/second. This sampling produces pulses of varying amplitude; these represent the original signal. As Figure 3.13 illustrates, the switch amplifies the voice call to regenerate this original signal.

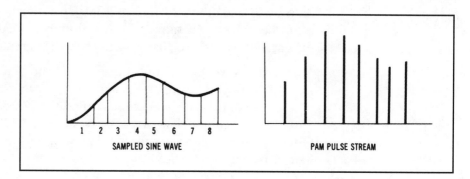

Figure 3.13   Regeneration of a Sampled Sine Wave as a PAM Pulse Stream

There is a problem with this type of signal transmission, however. It is possible to experience line noise, which can become enhanced as it is regenerated, distorting the original signal. Today, digital PBXs have moved a step beyond this method of transmission.

The newer method, *pulse code modulation (PCM)*, measures the sampled signals and then digitally encodes them. The signals are sampled at 8,000 times per second, and then translated into 8-bit words. This means PCM produces a *bit stream* (also called a data stream) of 64,000 bits/second. As Figure 3.14 illustrates, this process reproduces the voice signal very clearly.

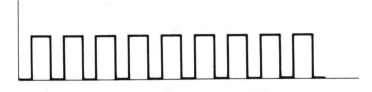

Figure 3.14   The PCM Bit Stream

Transmitting the PCM Data Stream

A PBX transmits the PCM data stream along a coaxial cable data bus. This data highway assigns the conversations to time slots using a technique known as time division multiplexing (TDM).

A PBX uses a high-speed data bus to transmit the PCM data stream. The digital switch's network controller is responsible for monitoring the data bus. Since this coaxial cable "highway" is capable of transmitting data much faster than the 64-Kbs PCM voice signal, several messages are *multiplexed* over the same path. A multiplexer is a device that transmits data at high speeds so that systems run with greater efficiency.

Each conversation multiplexed onto the data bus is given a time slot. Because this technique is known as *time division multiplexing (TDM),* the data bus is sometimes called the *TDM bus.* AT&T's System 75 PBX, for example, has two TDM buses with 512 available time slots. Since two time slots are required for a conversation—and some slots are lost in overhead considerations—it is possible to have 236 simultaneous voice conversations. (A data conversation takes up three time slots, and even more slots on some other PBXs.)

Connecting the PBX to Other PBXs and Computer Networks

PBXs can communicate over very high-speed T1 lines at 1.544 Mbs. The data is multiplexed, using either time division multiplexing (TDM) or frequency division multiplexing (FDM).

There are several different ways to connect digital PBXs to other PBXs, as well as to other computer networks. The *digital multiplex interfaces* in most of today's PBXs enable them to send data to host computers (or other PBXs) over very high-speed *T1 links* provided by common carriers. These links can handle 1.544 Mbs. Each of the 24 T1 channels can support one asynchronous connection of up to 19.2 Kbs, or a synchronous connection of up to 56 Kbs.

Time division multiplexing (TDM), discussed previously, is one way to move data through T1 lines. A second method, *frequency division multiplexing (FDM),* divides the T1 channels into subchannels by frequency (rather than assigning data specific time slots along the data highway). Voice and data can then be sent simultaneously over different frequencies. Figure 3.15 illustrates the difference between these two approaches to transmitting data.

In Chapter 2 we discussed the significance of the CCITT's X.25 protocol for communication between a computer (DTE) and a public data network (PDN). We saw that X.25 provided a standard for the packets of information that are transmitted synchronously over a network. In the example that follows, we will be transmitting information from a PBX, in X.25 packet form, to such public data networks as GTE-TYMNET and TELENET.

Assume that our microcomputer is connected to a digital PBX, and we wish to send a message to a public data network (PDN). In addition to X.25, several other CCITT standards would have to be observed for this to work:

- X.3 Packet Assembly/Disassembly facility (PAD) in a public data network
- X.25 Interface between DTE and DCE for terminals operating in the packet mode on public data networks
- X.28 DTE/DCE Interface for a start-stop mode DTE assessing the PAD in a public data network situated in the same country
- X.29 Procedures for the exchange of control information and user data between a PAD and a packet-mode DTE or another PAD

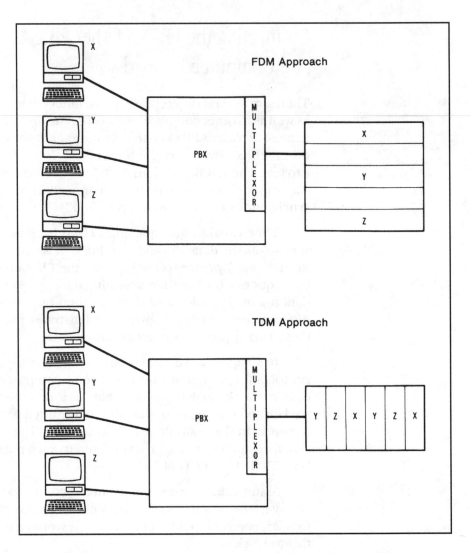

Figure 3.15   Frequency Division Multiplexing and Time Division Multiplexing

The PBX functioning as a LAN contains an X.25 gateway; our microcomputer tied to the PBX sends an asynchronous transmission (over RS-232 cable) to a PBX serial port. The PBX X.25 gateway places this information into X.25 packets and transmits them to the public data network (PDN). Packet messages received from the PDN are stripped of headers and trailers, and then transmitted to the microcomputer in asynchronous form.

One particular case we have not considered is the communication between two public data networks. The CCITT's X.75 standard handles this situation by providing a common format for communication:

• X.75 Terminal and transit call control procedures and data transfer system on international circuits between packet-switched data networks

Figure 3.16 illustrates how the CCITT standards work together to ensure effective data communications among network components, as well as between dissimilar networks.

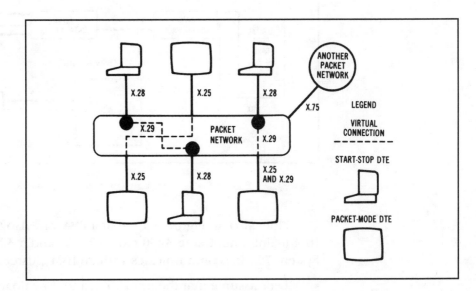

Figure 3.16   The CCITT Standards

PBX Communication with IBM Mainframe Computers

A PBX offers substantial savings for companies using it for micro-mainframe communications. Its twisted-pair wiring is much more economical than coaxial cable. It also offers protocol

Normally, when 3270 terminals (or microcomputers using 3270 terminal emulation) communicate with IBM mainframes, a principal cost is the coaxial cabling required. Using a PBX as a gateway to an IBM mainframe, on the other hand, has a major cost advantage: the terminals or microcomputers can be connected to the PBX by twisted-pair wire.

conversions from ASCII
asynchronous data to
EBCDIC synchronous data
using SDLC format.

When data from a 3270 terminal is transmitted to the PBX, a special data module converts the speed of the data stream; 2.36 Mbs (coaxial-cable speed) becomes 64 Kbs—a speed that twisted-pair wire can handle. Figure 3.17 illustrates this relationship.

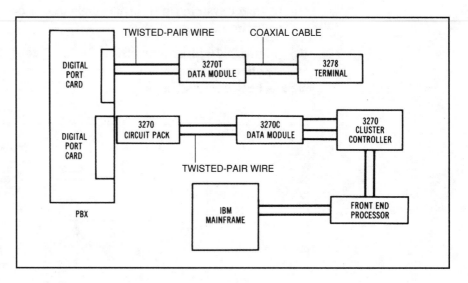

Figure 3.17   Data Can Travel from a Mainframe to a PBX

Note also, in Figure 3.17, that a PBX can also transmit data to an IBM mainframe. Using 3270 circuit packs and a 3270 data module, a System 75 PBX communicates with an IBM cluster controller.

Let's assume that the uploading and downloading of data (rather than on-line inquiry and communication with an IBM mainframe) is the primary reason many of the microcomputers linked to the PBX. In that case, the microcomputers can connect to the PBX asynchronously, through its asynchronous RS-232C ports. The PBX is capable of providing protocol conversions from the micro's ASCII data to IBM EBCDIC coded 3270 BSC, or to 3270 synchronous data using the SDLC format.

PBX resource management
tools such as modem
pooling, SMDR (Station
Message Detail Reporting)
and ARS (Automatic Route
Selection) provide effective
controls for cost-effective
management.

If the PBX is remote from the mainframe, it offers several advantages as a gateway for micro-mainframe communications. One major advantage is *modem pooling*. This PBX feature means modems can be accessed through hardware (by dialing a specific number for a specific modem) or by software (automatic selection of the fastest modem the connection between terminal and host can support).

One area where most LANs have been weak—and PBXs strong—is network record-keeping. For several years, PBXs have featured *SMDR (Station Message Detail Reporting)* software, which enables offices to track each person's phone calls. Law offices, for example, can use this software to charge each call an attorney makes to the client automatically. This same SMDR function within a PBX can monitor all microcomputer use of resources—and, if desired, record charges to various workstations or departments for usage of long-distance data lines.

Another strong PBX resource management tool is *ARS (Automatic Route Selection)*. Since so many different kinds of long distance lines are available, ARS can provide substantial savings by automatically selecting the most economical route for dial-out data calls.

Integrating Voice and Data

A digital PBX can integrate voice and data. Some are able to provide voice messages accompanying the text that flashes across a computer terminal.

Slowly the dream of integrated voice and data, long envisioned by many telecommunications pioneers, is becoming a reality. The digital PBXs are able to integrate voice and data information; some are even able to send this information simultaneously over the same line. Today a salesperson can call his sales manager using the company's PBX, leave a customer proposal drawn up on a Lotus 1-2-3 spreadsheet, and leave a voice message to accompany it. The sales manager can call up the spreadsheet on a terminal and hear the accompanying message ("This proposal looks strange because of one complication. Let me explain...").

One integrated voice/data feature that shows the utility of a PBX as a LAN is its ability to match an internal caller with a company directory. (In many large companies, a middle manager is likely to receive as many internal calls from departments as external calls from customers.) Imagine how much more efficient communication can be when a caller is greeted by name before introducing himself. The receiver's voice terminal flashed the name as it began ringing.

ISDN and the Future Office

The Integrated Services Digital Network (ISDN) is a CCITT model that provides for the integration of voice and data, as well as for a universal interface between different networks. The model consists of several channels of multiplexed information, transmitted at 64 Kbs.

Study Group XVII of the CCITT worked four years (1980–1984) to develop a set of standards for future voice and data integration. Taking a broad view of future global telecommunications, the committee planned an architecture that would provide integrated access to circuit-switched and packet-switched networks, as well as end-to-end digital transport of data. The resulting model—the *Integrated Services Digital Network (ISDN)*—represents a network of the future. It will include truly integrated voice, data, and even video, travelling smoothly (over the same pathways) from one type of network to another.

The ISDN concept of a *universal interface* means that each terminal will understand every other terminal. It will be possible to send information such as interactive videotex and facsimiles at the relatively high speed of 64 Kbs. ISDN standards define a digital interface divided into two types of channels: B channels for customer information (voice, data, and video) and D channels for sending signals and control information. These D channels utilize a packet-mode layered protocol based upon the CCITT's X.25 standard.

The two major ISDN interfaces are the Basic Rate Interface (BRI) designed for relatively small-capacity devices and the Primary Rate Interface (PRI) designed for high-capacity devices such as PBXs.

The CCITT committee defined two major interfaces that use these B and D channels. The *Basic Rate Interface (BRI)* is used to serve devices with relatively small capacity such as terminals. A second interface, *Primary Rate Interface (PRI),* is used for large-capacity devices such as PBXs. Both interfaces utilize one D channel and several B channels, transmitting at 64 Kbs.

Since the PRI channel structure represents the form most PBXs will take in the future, let's take a closer look at this model. The CCITT model consists of 24 slots, with 23 B channels and one D channel. Like the current T1, the maximum transfer rate on the PRI is 1.536 Mbs. Perhaps this ISDN framework will become clearer if we view it within the context of the AT&T 510 Personal Terminal that combines both voice and data.

As Figure 3.18 illustrates, the terminal is connected by a Basic Rate Interface (AT&T's Digital Communication Protocol) to the digital PBX (System 75). Then, through a Primary Rate Interface (AT&T's Digital Multiplexed Interface), the data is transmitted to a carrier network.

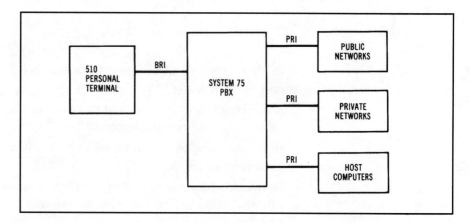

Figure 3.18 AT&T's Integration of Voice and Data

What Have You Learned?

1. Bridges connect LANs at the Data Link layer of the OSI model and filter or forward packets.

2. Routers connect networks at the Network layer of the OSI model and are protocol-specific.

3. IBM's mainframe and minicomputers utilize Systems Network Architecture (SNA).

4. Network-addressable units (NAUs) consist of logical units (LUs), physical units (PUs), and System Services Control Points (SSCPs).

5. LU 6.2 provides an application program interface (API) that will permit peer-to-peer communication.

6. With appropriate hardware and software, an IBM PC or compatible can emulate an IBM 3270 terminal and communicate with a mainframe via a 3274 or 3276 cluster controller.

7. An IBM PC or compatible can serve as a LAN gateway. The PC is connected via coaxial cable with the cluster controller and provides terminal emulation for an entire LAN.

8. From a remote site, an IBM PC or compatible can emulate a cluster controller and serve as a gateway for a LAN.

9. An IBM PC or compatible can perform remote job entry (RJE) for a LAN.

10. A private branch network (PBX) telephone system can serve as a LAN, linking together voice and data communications.

Quiz for Chapter 3

1. Which of these devices transmits packets most quickly?
   a. Gateway
   b. Bridge
   c. Router
   d. IMOK

2. A device operating at the Network layer of the OSI model is the
   a. bridge.
   b. router.
   c. gateway.
   d. repeater.

3. Under SNA, the Path Control Network is concerned with
   a. traffic flow.
   b. transmission priorities.
   c. error recovery.
   d. all of the above.

4. An IBM PC or compatible can communicate with a mainframe computer via a cluster controller if the PC is equipped with
   a. a dot-matrix printer.
   b. a 30-megabyte hard disk.
   c. 3270 terminal emulation hardware and software.
   d. a communications front-end processor.

5. Microcomputers that are part of a LAN can communicate with a mainframe located in the same building by using
   a. communications software.
   b. an IBM PC or compatible LAN gateway, connected via coaxial cable with a cluster controller.
   c. laser technology.
   d. fiber optics.

6. A gateway PC that is used only for this function is known as a
    a. gateway server.
    b. distributed server.
    c. dedicated gateway.
    d. remote job entry station.

7. A mainframe database file is likely to consist of
    a. EBCDIC characters.
    b. ASCII characters.
    c. ANSI characters.
    d. 8-bit words.

8. For the uploading of microcomputer information to a mainframe computer, a very efficient method is to have the PC emulate a
    a. 3278 monochrome terminal.
    b. 3279 color terminal.
    c. 3770 remote job entry workstation.
    d. 3705 front-end processor.

9. To communicate with an IBM System 34/36/38, the PC should emulate a
    a. 3770 remote job entry workstation.
    b. 3278 monochrome terminal.
    c. 3279 color terminal.
    d. 5250 terminal.

10. PBX stands for a
    a. public broadcasting exchange.
    b. public branch exchange.
    c. private branch exchange.
    d. preferential broadband exchange.

11. Converting analog signals to digital transmission (and digital signals back to analog) is performed by a(n)
    a. operator.
    b. transformer.
    c. coder-decoder.
    d. switchboard.

12. A digital PBX measures and samples signals 8,000 times per second, and translates these signals into 8-bit words using a process called
    a. Pulse Amplitude Modulation (PAM).
    b. Pulse Code Modulation (PCM).
    c. Public Data Network (PDN).
    d. Pulse Amplitude Authorization (PAA).

13. A technique for transmitting a data stream through a coaxial cable bus by assigning time slots is known as
    a. Pulse Code Amplification (PCA).
    b. Time Division Multiplexing (TDM).
    c. Frequency Division Multiplexing (FDM).
    d. Pulse Code Modulation (PCM).

14. A T1 high-speed link is capable of transmitting data at a maximum speed of
    a. 64 Kbs.
    b. 19.2 Kbs.
    c. 1.544 Mbs.
    d. 15 Mbs.

15. The standard used for transmitting packets of information to a public data network is
    a. 802.3.
    b. X.25.
    c. X.3.
    d. 802.6.

16. When a PBX serves as a LAN, a network manager can monitor the data usage of each network user by using the following PBX feature:
    a. ARS
    b. SMDR
    c. CCITT
    d. X.25

17. The Integrated Services Digital Network (ISDN) will provide
    a. integrated voice and data information.
    b. an interface between different networks.
    c. several channels of multiplexed information at 64 Kbs.
    d. all of the above

18. Under the ISDN model, small-capacity devices such as terminals will use the
    a. Basic Rate Interface (BRI).
    b. Primary Rate Interface (PRI).
    c. Universal Rate Interface (URI).
    d. Terminal Rate Interface (TRI).

19. The maximum transfer rate under PRI is
    a. 1.536 Mbs.
    b. 64 Kbs.
    c. 19.2 Kbs.
    d. 56 Kbs.

20. Under the ISDN model, a high-capacity device such as a PBX would use a
    a. Primary Rate Interface (PRI).
    b. Basic Rate Interface (BRI).
    c. T1 line.
    d. all B channels.

4 | Microsoft's LAN Manager and IBM's LANs

About This Chapter

Having discussed how LANs work in theory, it is time to look at how they work in actual practice. In this chapter we will look at Microsoft's LAN Manager, the leading competitor to Novell's NetWare (which dominates the network operating system market). We will also examine IBM's LAN Server—which started as a derivative of LAN Manager but has begun to differentiate itself.

We will look at IBM's DOS-based LANs, as well as its OS/2-based LAN Server. Since IBM's major LAN architecture is the token ring, we'll take a close look at how this approach transmits information.

Microsoft's LAN Manager

Microsoft's LAN Manager requires the OS/2 operating system on its file server, but network workstations can run DOS or OS/2. They also can run Microsoft Windows. LAN Manager is the first network operating system designed specifically for a *client-server* computing environment (which will be defined shortly).

Network workstations under LAN Manager run the LAN Redirector software, while the file server runs server software.

The two key components of LAN Manager are the *Redirector* and the *Server*. Each network workstation runs the Redirector software so that it can intercept and redirect input/output operating system calls to the network. This Redirector software also is responsible for configuring the individual workstation's use of network resources.

The Server portion of LAN Manager resides on a file server, where it is responsible for file management, scheduling, security, and printer services. This software also serves as a network monitor, alerting the network supervisor to any network alarms.

Microsoft has licensed its LAN Manager software to a number of companies, including 3Com, AT&T, and Hewlett-Packard. Microsoft itself has taken over responsibility for supporting 3Com's version of LAN Manager (3+ Open), because 3Com has decided to focus on internetworking products such as bridges and routers.

Advantages of OS/2

OS/2 is a true multitasking operating system. A program failing under protected mode will not disrupt other programs running.

LAN Manager comes with a version of OS/2 which is optimized for use in a network environment. Running the LAN Manager network operating system on top of the OS/2 operating system (rather than DOS) provides a number of advantages:

- OS/2 is a true multitasking operating system. Protected mode operation means that if a program fails, other applications are not affected.

- OS/2's sophisticated scheduling program ensures that all network programs receive equal access to the file server's central processor.

- Because OS/2 was developed to take advantage of 16-bit and 32-bit computers, it is able to address 16 megabytes of RAM and up to 1 gigabyte of virtual memory. This means that programs requiring very large amounts of memory can utilize secondary storage (such as disk space) as if it were a part of RAM.

LAN Manager optimizes itself to take advantage of 32-bit microprocessors. It uses the HPF386 high-performance file management system.

LAN Manager can take advantage of Intel-based 32-bit microprocessors (80386 and 80486) by configuring itself during installation, depending upon the type of server installed. For 32-bit servers, LAN Manager installs a 32-bit version of the OS/2 high-performance file system (HPF386). The HPF386 file system can optimize the file server by caching directories and data. These techniques speed up file retrieval, because the file server can examine a directory in RAM before immediately retrieving the requested file. It does not have to bring in a directory stored on disk before retrieving the desired file.

LAN Manager as a Platform

As a network operating system running on top of OS/2, LAN Manager serves as a platform for modules that provide additional network functions. As Figure 4.1 illustrates, DCA/Microsoft's Communications Server can connect LAN Manager to host as well as peer computers.

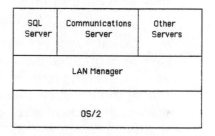

Figure 4.1   LAN Manager Is a Platform for Modules That Provide Additional Network Functions

Microsoft has also developed LAN Manager implementations for DEC's VMS operating system and for UNIX. Microsoft is currently working on LAN Manager implementations for the IBM mainframe operating systems MVS and VM.

Client-Server Computing

Client-server computing consists of a "front-end" client application program accessing a "back-end" server. While these applications can take many forms—including E-mail, spreadsheets, project management, etc., the first major client-server products have focused on database management programs. Microsoft's own SQL Server is an example of a client-server database server designed to run in conjunction with LAN Manager.

A database server running a database program provides the key records requested by a client workstation running "front-end" client-server software.

When running a client-server database management program on a LAN Manager network, a *client* workstation would request certain records from another workstation which serves as the *database server*. This database server, rather than sending the client workstation all its database records (as well as the entire program), would send the specific records requested. The client workstation would then use its "front-end" software to display these records.

The advantages of client-servers running under LAN Manager include a significant reduction in network traffic; fewer records need be transmitted, and the program itself need not be transmitted to the client workstation. Client workstations need not have powerful and expensive high-speed microprocessors (Intel 80386, 80486, etc.), because they need run only their "front-end" software, not sophisticated database programs.

LAN Manager permits an OS/2 workstation to provide *network peer services.* This means a user's workstation could also serve as a database server, printer server, or communications server. One limitation of this service is that only one other network user (besides the workstation's own user) can access the peer service for resource sharing.

LAN Manager's Network Administration Tools

LAN Manager contains a number of tools to make network administration more efficient. For example, several servers can be grouped into a single domain and treated as one server; users with proper authorization need only one password to access all these servers.

The LAN Manager Replicator service permits copying of files from one file server to multiple file servers.

The LAN Manager *Replicator service* enables a network manager to copy changes in files (or in a single server) to other servers. This service could be used, for example, to replicate a network utility running on one server to a selected group of servers. The Replication service is also useful to ensure that all file servers are running the same version of an executable file. The network supervisor can specify that certain frequently changed files must be replicated at short intervals, while files that change infrequently can be replicated each evening.

Network managers can manage a LAN Manager remotely from any OS/2 workstation. They also can assign specific duties (such as printer management, communications management, or workgroup management) to designated operators. These operators can be delegated *network supervisor rights* over these specific areas.

LAN Manager also provides *network auditing;* a network supervisor can track any network resource selectively. Because this information is stored in text files, it can be accessed by any standard network performance program.

Network Security Under LAN Manager

LAN Manager provides a high level of network security. A network supervisor can limit users to specific login times and specific workstations, specify the minimum number of characters required for a password, and prevent users from going back to previously used passwords. LAN Manager uses the U.S. government's *Data Encryption Standard (DES)* to encrypt passwords.

LAN Manager also provides a clear *audit trail* of all network transactions. A network supervisor can track what files a particular user accessed, and when these transactions took place.

A network supervisor can restrict network use of files, directories, printer queues, and named pipes. (These resources also can be allocated to specific groups.) In areas where there is public access, diskless workstations can be installed; LAN Manager's *Remote Program Loading (RPL)* feature can configure them to boot under either DOS or OS/2.

LAN Manager's *hot fix* feature prevents it from writing to a bad block; instead, it will write the data to a safe storage area if it detects a bad block. Network supervisors can add a duplicate disk drive (*disk mirroring*) so this feature can be used if the primary file server disk fails. Similarly, for additional protection, LAN Manager supports duplicate drives and controllers (*disk duplexing*). If the file server's disk controller card fails, it will switch to the duplexed controller card and duplexed drive, and continue operations.

For even greater network security, LAN Manager has a UPS service which protects the network's data. This service sends out warning messages when the UPS's battery power begins to fail, and then initiates a proper file server shutdown prior to the loss of battery power.

LAN Manager's Printer Support

LAN Manager enables a network supervisor to create several *print queues* for temporary storage of files to be printed. Several print queues can be created for the same printer; conversely, a single print queue can feed several printers. The network supervisor can specify the priority of different jobs; memos, for example, might receive a higher priority than reports. Network supervisors, as well as print queue operators, have the ability to delete, pause, or reprioritize print jobs.

LAN Manager's Optional Features

Microsoft furnishes a number of optional features for LAN Manager that provide additional connectivity, programmers' tools, and administrative utilities:

- Macintosh computer users can connect to LAN Manager networks and access file and print services by using *Services for Macintosh*. This program also permits automatic backup and restoration of AppleTalk volumes on a LAN Manager server.

- *TCP/IP protocol* is included with LAN Manager. It runs as a *demand protocol architecture,* which means users can change protocols simply by typing `Load TCP` or `Unload TCP` on the command line.

- Optional *TCP/IP Utilities* enable a user on a LAN Manager network to access networks running TCP/IP by using TCP/IP's *File Transfer Protocol (FTP)* and Telnet terminal emulation services.

- A *LAN Manager Toolkit for Visual Basic* enables programmers to develop LAN Manager applications running with Microsoft Windows' graphical user interface. The toolkit includes Windows-based network management software, as well as several utilities for monitoring network performance.

- A *General Upgrade LAN Program* provides a *migration path* for users of 3Com's 3+ and 3+ Open network operating systems. This feature allows these users to attain complete compatibility with LAN Manager, without having to rekey any data they have already created.

LAN Manager and NetWare

Since NetWare dominates the current network market, Microsoft has had to add features to LAN Manager to provide some measure of interoperability. LAN Manager 2.1, for example, enables network managers to cut and paste files from NetWare servers to LAN Manager servers—even though these two very different types of servers cannot communicate directly.

The IBM PC Network Program

For companies with small, DOS-based networks, IBM offers its IBM PC Local Area Network Program, running on Token Ring Network hardware. This powerful (yet easy-to-use) software package warrants a close look at its many features.

Note: Recently IBM changed this program's name (it was originally called the PC Network Program) to the PC Local Area Network Program. Since so much literature refers to the program by its original name, we will continue to do so, though you should be aware of this change in terminology when shopping for the system.

The program permits disk drive and printer sharing, as well as the sending and receiving of messages and files. For beginning network users, there is a series of menus within menus; more experienced users may simply use network commands to send and receive information.

There are two different installation options: *Basic Services* and *Extended Services.* Basic Services uses the command-line-and-menu-driven functions found in all earlier versions of this program. Extended Services lets you define, name, and access the resources of multiple servers as a single set of resources. A master server, known as a *domain controller,* controls security for this single set of resources. Figure 4.2 illustrates how Extended Services requires users to log in to a domain controller to gain access to the network. The remainder of the discussion will center on the Basic Services version of the program, which is still in the majority on most networks.

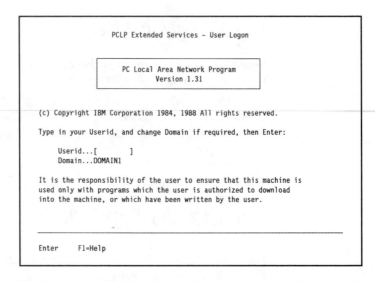

```
                    PCLP Extended Services - User Logon

                   ┌─────────────────────────────────────┐
                   │      PC Local Area Network Program    │
                   │              Version 1.31             │
                   └─────────────────────────────────────┘

        (c) Copyright IBM Corporation 1984, 1988 All rights reserved.

        Type in your Userid, and change Domain if required, then Enter:

            Userid...[        ]
            Domain...DOMAIN1

        It is the responsibility of the user to ensure that this machine is
        used only with programs which the user is authorized to download
        into the machine, or which have been written by the user.

        ───────────────────────────────────────────────────────

        Enter     F1=Help
```

Figure 4.2   Logging In Using the Extended Services Version of the PC LAN Program
(Courtesy of IBM Corporation)

PC Network Program Configurations

The PC Network Program
requires users to indicate,
when entering the network,
how they wish to configure
their workstations. The four
configuration options are
Redirector, Messenger,
Receiver, and Server.

The PC Network Program has four different configurations:

Redirector (RDR)

Messenger (MSG)

Receiver (RCV)

Server (SRV)

The *Redirector* configuration really restricts the user to certain activities; it is not recommended as a user configuration. It accepts requests for applications directed to servers, and passes these requests along to the servers. It accepts and passes along data, and it sends messages. The Redirector can be used for workstations with limited memory resources.

The *Receiver* configuration includes all Redirector activities; it also receives and logs in messages. The Receiver represents a *minimum* user configuration; a user needs to be able to receive and edit messages, as well as transmit them.

A full user would usually opt for the *Messenger* configuration—which provides full-screen message editing and message forwarding capabilities, as well as all the functions of the Redirector and Receiver.

The *Server* configuration includes all the functions of the Messenger, Redirector, and Messenger configurations, as well as the ability to control disk drives, directories, and printers.

Users can choose to go to the program's Main menu (Figure 4.3), using the normal defaults built into the network. Other users might prefer a command line, where they can issue the NET START command.

```
┌─────────────────────────────────────────────────────────┐
│                  IBM PC Local Area Network                │
│                                                           │
│    Main Menu - Task Selection                             │
│                                                           │
│      1.    Message Tasks                                  │
│                                                           │
│      2.    Printer Tasks                                  │
│                                                           │
│      3.    Disk or Directory Tasks                        │
│                                                           │
│      4.    Print Queue Tasks                              │
│                                                           │
│      5.    Network Status Tasks                           │
│                                                           │
│      6.    Pause or Cancel the Network Setup              │
│                                                           │
│    Choice                                                 │
│                                                           │
│    Enter - Continue      F1=Help                          │
│                                                           │
│    Esc - Exit                                             │
└─────────────────────────────────────────────────────────┘
```

Figure 4.3   The IBM PC Local Area Network Main Menu
(Courtesy of IBM Corporation)

Experienced users will change their network configuration based upon the amount of available memory needed to run specific application programs, the need to share additional resources, and the need for additional memory to hold long messages in a buffer.

Why would an experienced user want to reconfigure his network workstation? There are many reasons for changing the normal default values. The network default value for use of network devices, for example, is five. If you needed to use more than five network devices to perform certain operations, you would need to reconfigure your workstation. Similarly, if you needed to share more than five of your workstation devices with the network, you would also reconfigure. Finally, network default values for the size of the buffer used for printing (512 characters), the size of the buffer used for waiting messages (1,600 characters), and the number of network computers that will be using your devices (10) are also likely to need to be changed from time to time.

The RAM installed on a network workstation has certain limits on its ability to serve other network functions. To serve as a file server, for example, a network workstation needs to have at least 320K of RAM for DOS and the PC Network Program. A network user who wanted to run a program that requires 320K—while still keeping the workstation's file-server capability—would need 640K of RAM in order to serve both purposes. As a file server, this workstation could then share its disk drives, directories and printers; as a workstation, it could still share those resources found on other workstations.

Note: The PC Network Program cannot utilize extended or expanded RAM on a file server or a workstation, and the RAM allocated for the program is not available to other programs.

The Messenger configuration requires a minimum of 256K of RAM for the PC Network Program and DOS. A workstation with this configuration can send and receive messages, and transfer them to other computers. (Transfer involves saving messages directly to a file by logging them in.) We will see very shortly how easy it is to send a message on this network.

Configuring your workstation as a Receiver requires 192K of RAM for the PC Network Program and DOS. As a receiver, you can send and receive messages, save these messages by placing them into a log file (you need not view them the moment they are received), and share resources such as network disk drives, directories, and printers.

The Redirector configuration requires only 128K of RAM. It allows a workstation to send messages and to share network disk drives, directories, and printers.

Table 4.1 shows a handy summary of these different configurations and their major functions, as found in *The IBM PC Network Program User's Guide* (reprinted here courtesy of IBM Corporation):

Table 4.1. Summary of Workstation Configurations for the IBM PC Network Program

Configuration	You Can Use the PC Network Program to
SERVER (320K RAM required)	Send messages
	Use network disks, directories, and printers
	Receive messages
	Save (log) messages
	Use network request keys
	Receive messages for other names
	Transfer messages to other computers
	Share your disks, directories, and printers
MESSENGER (256K RAM required)	Send messages
	Use network disks, directories, and printers
	Receive messages
	Save (log) messages
	Use network request keys
	Receive messages for other names
	Transfer messages to other computers
RECEIVER (192K RAM required)	Send messages
	Use network disks, directories, and printers
	Receive messages
	Save (log) messages
REDIRECTOR (128K RAM required)	Send messages
	Use network disks, directories, and printers

New users first encounter the options shown in Table 4.1 in a menu format (see Figure 4.3); examining the way the configurations are presented will demonstrate why network users would choose one over another. Later in this chapter, we'll examine each of these options—and the network operations behind them. For now, notice that help is available simply by pressing the F1 key.

Let's take a look at how messages are sent and received on the network. First, it is important to realize that the PC Network keeps track of machines, not people. Each network workstation must have a name (up to 15 letters) so that other network users can address it. This is an unusual approach; in the other network operating systems we will examine, a user ID serves as a login.

Sometimes more than one person uses a workstation. The PC Network Program permits a maximum of 16 names to be assigned to a particular workstation. If five people in Accounting share a workstation, for example, it could have six names—the name "ACCOUNT" and each of the five users' names.

Message Tasks Available Under the PC Network Program

Figure 4.4 illustrates the way that messages are edited prior to being sent on the PC Network. Notice that the use of the asterisk (*) results in the message being sent to all network workstations. A message can be up to 1,600 characters in length (80 characters per line x 20 lines). The one exception is a *broadcast message.* Broadcast messages are sent to all computers on the network, and are limited to 128 characters.

```
                        Send Messages

    Send the message to: (* for all computers) Bill

    Type the message below:

    This is a test to see it work.

    Ctrl-Enter Send message         Esc- Previous menu or Exit
    Tab- cursor to next field       Ctrl-PgDn - Erase message
    Ctrl-Home - Return to Main Menu  F3 ADJUST PARAGRAPH F4 VIEW MESSAGES
    F1 - HELP   F2 - COMMAND LINE

    Message sent . . . and successfully received    Characters free 1571
```

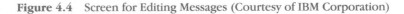

Figure 4.4   Screen for Editing Messages (Courtesy of IBM Corporation)

The *message screen editor* is capable of "word wrap," so that all lines contain complete words. Because of this feature, some messages might start to look unprofessional, interspersing short lines with long lines. Pressing the F3 key will hyphenate words, making the paragraph look more even and more professional. (Notice that the lower right corner of the screen keeps track of the number of free characters by subtracting the characters found in a message from 1,600.)

The message function of the PC Network Program is a good example of how the program uses the IBM PC's special keys and function keys:

- Use the F1 key when requesting additional information.
- Use the Tab key to move the cursor from field to field.
- Use the Esc key as a way to exit a menu, or to move backwards and view a previous menu screen.
- Press the Ctrl and Home keys simultaneously to return to the program's Main menu.
- When the editing of a message is complete, send it by pressing the Ctrl and Enter keys simultaneously.

The PC Network Program does have a number of safety features built in to help network users avoid making serious mistakes. A user who inadvertently presses the Esc key before sending the message (for example) does not lose the entire message; the program asks him to press the key again to confirm that he meant to leave the menu without sending the message.

Notice that the PC Network Program asks for a specific name for the addressee (the message's destination). Many network administrators will publish a network directory (of users and their network names) to prevent confusion when it comes to sending messages. It is very unlikely, for example, that a large company would have only one Bob; users in other departments may know Bob, but not his last name. This is why it is so practical for a workstation's network adapter card to be able to handle 16 different names. Since Bob handles payroll for the XYZ company, his workstation might have PAYROLL as one of its names.

The PC Network Program has a number of ways of handling incoming messages. These depend upon how users have configured their network workstations. Figure 4.5 illustrates the way a message's arrival is signaled.

```
MESSAGE FROM   | SALES|
_____

Press Ctrl-Break to Continue
Press Ctrl-Alt-Break to View Message
```

Figure 4.5   The PC LAN Program Signals an Incoming Message
(Courtesy of IBM Corporation)

As a user, you have several choices regarding how to handle a message once it is received:

- You could choose to erase the message and continue working; pressing Ctrl and Break will put the message into a waiting area. The message will be accessible through the Message Tasks menus at a later time. (Because buffer room is limited, however, users should view their messages frequently, and then erase them.)

- You could view the message by pressing the Ctrl-Alt-Break keys, after which, pressing the Esc key would return you to your work.

Note: Except in the instance when you receive a "message waiting" signal, these three *network-request keys* (Ctrl-Alt-Break) perform a far different function normally. Pressed simultaneously, they will interrupt whatever you are doing, and take you directly to the network menus. After making the desired network menu selections, you are returned to whatever you were doing prior to pressing the three keys.

- Your third alternative when receiving messages is to configure your workstation to save incoming messages to a "log" file automatically. Then, at your convenience, you simply use the DOS command TYPE to view your saved messages. With this option, your workstation will "beep" when a message arrives, but will not disrupt your current activities.

If you are using a Receiver configuration, messages are automatically logged to your workstation console and displayed, unless you specify another location to which they should be sent (such as a log file). Not using such a log file can result in the disruption of your current work, and you will need to refresh your screen continually to eliminate message "garbage."

Tip: It is also possible to have messages sent to a logged printer rather than a log file, but the printer would need to be dedicated to this function and could not be shared with other network users.

Figure 4.6 illustrates how messages are viewed on the PC Network. Notice that the same function keys used on the Send Messages screen are used on this View Messages screen. Two additional options (Save Message and Print Message) can also be performed by using function keys. Notice that PC Network distinguishes between *waiting messages* (those stored in memory) and *saved messages* (those already saved and logged to a file).

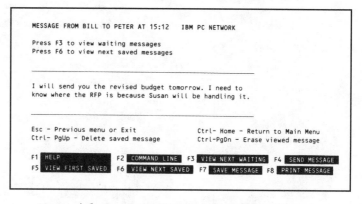

Figure 4.6   Receiving Messages on the PC LAN Program
(Courtesy of IBM Corporation)

It is possible to have the network save all incoming messages so you will not be disturbed. It is also possible to receive messages for another name assigned to the workstation. A third option permits users to forward their messages to another computer if they need to work at another network node.

Some additional message commands indicate the power of this PC Network feature. If you are faced with a deadline (for example) and do not want to be interrupted, you can tell the network to start saving messages. The network will continue to do this until told otherwise. Let's say that you expect a very important message and need to see it the instant it arrives. You may give the command to stop saving messages. At this time the network will begin displaying your messages as they are received.

Another very common need in an office is for someone to "cover" for another employee. Let's say that Bill and Susan are working on a very important project. Susan must go to a meeting, telling Bill to "cover" for her so they can act on the message as soon as it arrives. Bill can give the network the command to let him Start Receiving Messages for Another Name; then he can indicate that Susan's messages should be sent to him. When Susan returns, Bill simply selects the Message Task entitled Stop Receiving Messages for Another Name.

Many large firms have the *call forwarding option* on their PBX telephone systems. PC Network has a similar feature in its message program. If Bill needs to spend the day working in the Accounting department, he can use the Forward Messages to Another Computer option, and have all messages sent to that particular computer (ACCOUNT). Figure 4.7 illustrates the PC Network menu that would be used for this purpose. When he returns the following day, he selects Stop forwarding messages. Up to 12 names may be in use for call forwarding on a network workstation at any given time.

```
┌─────────────────────────────────────────────────────────────────┐
│                 Start or Stop Forwarding Messages                 │
│                                                                   │
│                                                                   │
│       1. Start forwarding messages                                │
│                                                                   │
│       2. Stop forwarding messages                                 │
│                                                                   │
│       1 Choice                                                    │
│                                                                   │
│       Forward messages for (name on your computer)                │
│                                                                   │
│        ┌──────┐                                                   │
│        │ Bill │                                                   │
│        └──────┘                                                   │
│       To (name on another computer)                               │
│                                                                   │
│        ┌─────────┐                                                │
│        │ Account │                                                │
│        └─────────┘                                                │
│       Tab- cursor to next field        F1 - Help                  │
│       Enter - Continue                  Ctrl - Home - Return to Main Menu │
│       Esc - Previous menu                                         │
│                                                                   │
└─────────────────────────────────────────────────────────────────┘
```

Figure 4.7   Message Forwarding with PC LAN Program
(Courtesy of IBM Corporation)

Printer Tasks Under the PC Network Program

It is possible to share up to three printers with the network. Printers may be designated as shared or as local. There are queues for each printer.

Refer again to Figure 4.3; note that the second and fourth options available from the PC Network Main Menu refer to Printer Tasks and Print Queue Tasks, respectively. Both options illustrate the degree of control over network printers available under the PC Network Program.

Every printer attached to a workstation using the PC Network has to be designated as either a *local printer* (limited to that particular workstation) or a *network printer*. Even more significant, the PC Network Program's print management functions control all printing so that network print commands must be used. A workstation user cannot simply use a PRINT command, even with his own local printer; he must use the network's NET PRINT command.

As Figure 4.8 illustrates, there are six printer options covered under the Printer Tasks Menu. A user may share up to three printers with the network. It is possible to declare a printer a shared printer without providing the name of this printer to other users. The result will be a printer that performs like a local printer, but utilizes the network's print management program.

```
                        Printer Tasks


    1. Start or stop sharing your printer

    2. Start or stop using a network printer

    3. Print a file

    4. Change the print size on a network printer

    5. Display devices you are sharing

    6. Display network devices you are using

    1 Choice

    Enter - Continue                      F1 - Help
    Ctrl-Home - Return to Main Menu       Esc - Previous menu
```

Figure 4.8   Printer Tasks Menu (Courtesy of IBM Corporation)

Why would anyone ever decide not to share a printer with the network? First, if you have a major printing job that must be completed as quickly as possible, obviously you do not want to wait your turn. Second, there is a limit to the number of devices that can be shared with the network at any given time. You might want to share a different device (such as a plotter or modem), and thus need to remove one of your printers from the network.

There are also some print server restrictions. Each server requires 256K of RAM and supports three printers. Up to 100 files can be placed in a *printer queue table*, where they will be printed in *background mode* while the computer's processor continues to perform other functions.

Network application programs are typically installed so that they send print jobs to the printer queue automatically. The new user is often unaware of this process, since (with low levels of network printing activity) the printing of a file may seem almost instantaneous.

The PC Network Program permits separate queues for each of the network printers. A user can request the status of any printer queue. As

Figure 4.9 illustrates, it is possible to check or change the print queue from a menu. Option 6 will cause the particular entry you have highlighted to Print Now (rather than waiting for its turn in the queue). The program allows users to set up a *Separator Page* that will print out between files, indicating who printed the file, the name of the file itself, and the current date and time. Files that are "spooling" are still being sent to the printer queue. Their status cannot be changed until they finish spooling.

```
                    Check or Change the Print Queue IBM PC NETWORK

        1. Update queue      ID  User Name  Size   Device  Status
                             -Start of Queue-

        2. Hold              010 FRED        16422  LPT1    Printing

        3. Release           019 PAUL        12350  LPT1    Spooling

                             020 SUSAN         546  LPT2    Waiting
        4. Cancel

                             021 FRED        20195  LPT2    Waiting
        5. Print Next

                             -End of Queue-

        6. Print now

        1 Choice
                                              PgUp and PgDn - Scroll List
        ↥ and ↧ - Select File                 F1 - Help
        Enter - Change queue                  Esc - Previous menu
        Ctrl-Home - Return to Main Menu
```

Figure 4.9 Printer Server's Print Queue
(Courtesy of IBM Corporation)

The IBM PC Network Program has a number of printer control commands. The NET PAUSE PRINT [=printdevice] pauses the network sharing of a specific printer. The NET CONTINUE PRINT [=printdevice] resumes network printing. There are companion server commands that would also cause this result, but we will look at those when we examine the Server functions found on the PC Network.

Sharing Disks and Directories with the Network

The third option under the PC Network Program's Main Menu is "Disk or directory tasks." The tasks consist of the following choices:

- Start or stop sharing your disk or directory.
- Start or stop using a network disk or directory.

- Display devices you are sharing.
- Display devices you are using.

The PC Network Program permits directory sharing, but it does not permit you to designate that a particular file is to be shared. The result of this restriction is that you will need to place a file in its own directory if you wish to share only that particular file. Your decision to share a directory is not automatically sent as a message to other network users. The PC Network Program assumes you will make the availability of this directory known to the people who need to know about its existence, and who have legitimate reasons to use it.

To share application programs with other users, IBM suggests placing these programs in one subdirectory. The PC Network Program has an Installation Aid utility; this program will create the subdirectory, install the application programs, and mark each program file as "Read Only." Because some application programs have program files that require read/write/create access, the usual practice with the PC Network Program is to create several user subdirectories, each of which contains copies of these files. The Installation Aid utility can create these private subdirectories for each computer user who wants to run these application programs.

You can establish a password for a particular directory or subdirectory that you are sharing. Let's assume that we wished to share a very sensitive directory (TOPSEC) with a remote computer user named FRANK. You have decided to use the password ABCXYZ. You would enter the following:

```
NET SHARE FRANK=C:\TOPSEC ABCXYZ
```

This information could be placed in an AUTOEXEC.BAT file with an asterisk (*) replacing the secret password. When the batch file actually runs, the network will prompt you for the password.

You can take some additional steps to increase the security found under PC Network. A file server's physical location, for example, offers some additional control. Some PCs can be locked with a key to disable startup and/or keyboard use. A Controller who has sensitive payroll records on a PC which is being used as a file server could take the simple precaution of locking the machine with the key. Some companies save sensitive data onto diskettes, which are then stored under lock and key.

Virtually all network activities under the IBM PC Network Program can be accessed by direct commands, as well as through the system of nested menus. This means that an experienced user who wished to share a directory with the network could use a command (NET SHARE) to accomplish this task. The network command structure uses the naming conventions of the DOS hierarchical file structure. This means that if Bill wished to make his budget reports (found on his drive C, in a directory named \BUD\BUDRPT) available to the entire network, he would use the following command:

```
NET SHARE C:\BUD\BUDRPT
```

The problem with this arrangement is that network users who want to access this file will have to provide its exact path. A user who wanted to treat Bill's directory as his own drive D, for example, would have to type the following:

```
NET USE D:\BILL\BUD\BUDRPT
```

Bill could make everyone else's work much easier by using a *network name* for his directory. Let's assume that the network users already refer to Bill's famous budget reports as "The '93 Budget Report." He could provide the network name BUDGET to replace the SHARE command:

```
NET USE BUDGET=C:\BUD\BUDRPT
```

Now other network users who want to access this directory (as their "D" directories, for example) could type the following:

```
NET USE D:\BILL\BUDGET
```

Users who wish to share their entire disk, rather than certain directories, can do so by sharing their root directory (C:\). Everything in this C-drive directory will then be available to other network users— including all subdirectories found on drive C. Figure 4.10 illustrates how Bill could go about sharing a customer list (found in one of his subdirectories) with the rest of the network.

As Figure 4.10 illustrates, the IBM PC Network Program permits five different combinations of user access to the directories you wish to share with the network:

Read Only

Read/Write

Write Only

Write/Create/Delete

Read/Write/Create/Delete

```
            Start Sharing Your Disk or Directory          IBM PC NETWORK


    DOS name for disk or directory
    c:\BILL\SALES\CUSLST
    _____

    Network name for your disk or directory
    CUSTMR

    Password for disk or directory (Optional)
    PROFIT

    Other users can
    1. Read only          4. Write/Create/Delete
    2. Read/Write         5. Read/Write/Create/Delete
    3. Write only

    4 Choice
         Tab - Cursor to next field        F1 - Help
         Enter - Continue                  Ctrl-Home - Return to Main Menu
         Esc - Previous menu
```

Figure 4.10 Sharing a Directory with the Network (Courtesy of IBM Corporation)

The program's default value is Read/Write/Create/Delete. A user who wanted to share a directory and simply pressed the Enter key at this point, would provide this level of access for *all* network users without realizing it. Users who need only view information can be limited to "Read Only" status, while other members of your particular project or department might require the full "Read/Write/Create/Delete" privileges.

The PC Network Program does not provide the level of security that a more sophisticated program (such as Novell's NetWare) provides. Any user who knows the password (PROFIT) for Bill's device (in this case his disk drive containing this subdirectory) will be able to access this material with the same level of access as anyone else. Of course, Bill could decide not to share this particular directory—in which case network users would not be able to access the files in the directory, even though they might have access to the disk drive.

The PC Network Program's providing the same level of security for all network users can be seen as a limitation; there is one additional way around it. It is possible to offer this same subdirectory to the network several times—with several different network names and device passwords. A company controller, for example, might want to set up his payroll subdirectory so that certain individuals would access it under one network name with "Read Only" privileges, while his payroll clerk (who needs to change the "hours worked" and "hourly rate" fields) would use a different network name and have greater privileges—including the ability to change key fields.

Saving Time When Starting the PC Network Program

The PC Network Program permits you to save your configuration values (established when you first entered the network) in an AUTOEXEC.BAT file. If you indicate you wish to save your network setup, the program saves the optional parameters you have established—including which resources you wish to share with the network and which resources you are using currently. If you are receiving messages for additional names when you save your configuration values, this will continue when you enter the network the next time.

You will need to ask yourself several questions before saving your network setup under the PC Network Program. Since memory is a very valuable resource (affecting the network's speed and its ability to respond to users' requests), you need to decide precisely what you plan to be doing the next time you enter the network. To accommodate a very important and lengthy report, for example (which will take up a large amount of memory), you might have to reduce the buffer size for your messages from 512K to 60K. This decision, in turn, may reduce your workstation's ability to run a large application program (such as Symphony) and still serve as a network server.

The IBM PC Network Program permits the user who is sharing resources to adjust the allocation of time and memory used for network functions against the amount used for local functions performed on that particular machine. The tasks the user performs on his own machine are known as *foreground tasks;* those performed by other network users are called *background tasks.* A network timer provides intervals composed of timer ticks of 18.175 milliseconds. The network's normal default value of 5/4 allocates approximately equal time to both foreground (5 intervals) and background (4 intervals) tasks. Five intervals are equivalent to 90.875 milliseconds (5 x 18.175 milliseconds). The *Time Slice Intervals (TSI)* parameter defines the way the server will divide its time. The file server performs a foreground task until it reaches the time to perform a background task. It then checks to see if there is a background task to perform. If there is, it temporarily halts what it is doing, and begins performing the background task.

While the file server is incapable of multitasking—and really only performs one task at a time—it switches back and forth so many times within a second that the results may seem to be multitasking. Despite this speed, there are some file server tasks that can cripple the entire network's speed. One example is diskette formatting. During this relatively lengthy procedure, the file server will not release DOS to enable the time slicing procedure to work. (Obviously, file servers should not be used to format diskettes.) If foreground and background tasks are allocated larger time slices, the network response will seem erratic. It may seem to take forever for certain tasks to be performed.

Other Ways to Boost Network Performance

A number of additional parameters can be adjusted to maximize PC Network performance—including the amount of memory used for disk sharing, print spooling, and background print performance. The *Receive Request Buffer (/RQB),* for example, can be adjusted on the file server to specify the maximum buffer available for file transfer between file server and network workstations. The larger the number specified for /RQB, the more data the file server can send to the workstation at any given time. The result of this larger value for /RQB is that the file server does not need to perform as many "send" operations, and thus can perform other network procedures more quickly.

The *Request Buffers (/REQ)* parameter determines how many user requests can be handled at any given time. This value can vary from 1 to 3, with 2 serving as the default figure. The larger this parameter, the more requests can be processed—and the faster the network performance. A "1" requires 8K of memory, a "2" requires 16K, and a "3" will require 48K.

Network print buffer parameters also can enhance performance under the PC Network Program. The *Print Buffer Parameter (/PRB)* specifies how much of a print file the printer server can keep in memory at any given time before it has to retrieve more of this file. The default value of 512K is sufficient, unless there is very heavy printer activity on the network. Similarly, the *Print Priority Parameter (/PRP)* is used to specify how much of the foreground task interval is used for printing files while the server computer is performing other tasks. The default value for this parameter is "3," but a network user who wants greater responsiveness from his server computer should specify a "1" or "2."

LAN Server

LAN Server runs under OS/2. This file server software provides what IBM terms "requester/server relationships" (and what the rest of the industry refers to as *client-server relationships*). Regardless of the term used, the software—when running under a truly multitasking operating system—permits distributed data bases on a LAN to become a reality. Users need only request a particular record, and the actual processing will take place elsewhere on the network. IBM offers *Extended Services (ES)* for OS/2 (which replaced its OS/2 Extended Edition). ES includes the Communications Manager and the Database Manager, but not the OS/2 software itself. The Communications Manager provides Advanced Peer-to-Peer Communications for OS/2. The Database Manager supports the ANSI SQL II standard.

LAN Server offers enhanced database access functions because of the availability of the optional Distributed Database Connections Services/2 (a component of IBM's Systems Applications Architecture). This feature permits connections between host databases and the databases on remote network client stations.

As in the case of the Extended Services version of PC LAN Program, LAN Server requires that a minimum of one domain be created, and that a server act as a domain controller. One very valuable feature of LAN Server (known as *location independence*) enables the network administrator to treat a group of network servers as a single server; in such a case, users can access files on any server, without being required to know on which server that information resides.

Figure 4.11 illustrates a typical LAN Server screen. Unlike the DOS-based PC LAN Program, this program can utilize OS/2's greater power to track network activity and issue alerts. Its graphics-oriented user interface is consistent with IBM's *Systems Application Architecture (SAA)*, the company's long-range plan for providing a uniform interface across its product line. Another SAA goal is to provide transparent movement of information across IBM's range of computers. LAN Server is preferable to LAN Manager for customers who have a heavy investment in IBM mainframe equipment; it offers enhanced micro-mainframe communications with its Communications Manager, and enhanced access to mainframe databases with its Database Manager.

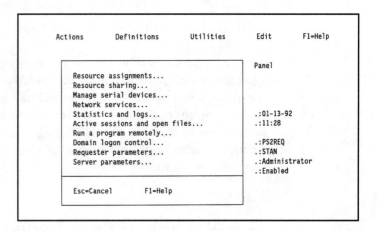

Figure 4.11   A Typical LAN Server Screen (Courtesy of IBM Corporation)

Customers can purchase an Entry Package or an Advanced Package. The Advanced Package includes such system-fault-tolerant features as disk mirroring and disk duplexing. Both versions support the Network Device Interface Specification; this means that a number of network interface cards (not just IBM hardware) can be used with this software.

LAN Server and OS/2 2.0

While Microsoft's LAN Manager and IBM's LAN Server started out as very comparable products, the two companies have chosen to go their own separate ways. When LAN Server is run in conjunction with IBM's OS/2 version 2.0, differences with LAN Manager become apparent. LAN Server can take advantage of the fact that OS/2 version 2.0 is a true 32-bit operating system. Users can run DOS, Microsoft Windows, a 16-bit version of OS/2, and the 32-bit version of OS/2 as network users. IBM does not yet offer LAN Server support for Macintosh computers.

LAN Server can generate alerts about printers, nearly full disks, and power problems. These alerts can be interpreted by LAN Server's own network management program as well as by the NetView program running on a host computer.

IBM and NetWare

While LAN Server is IBM's major network operating system, IBM has an agreement with Novell to also offer NetWare to its customers. The two companies have agreed that they will link LAN Server and NetWare more closely together so that communications between the two programs will be transparent to users. This agreement will benefit IBM's large customers who might have both LAN Server and NetWare running on LANs they wish to link.

The IBM Token Ring Network: Overview

Regardless of the network operating system software used, IBM offers a powerful, fast, LAN hardware platform that is capable of handling hundreds of workstations without degradation. The IBM Token Ring Network uses a star-wired ring topology, and follows the baseband signaling and token passing protocols of the IEEE 802.5 standard. The network utilizes unshielded twisted-pair telephone wire (designated by IBM as Type 3 cabling). It is also possible to use IBM's Type 1 or Type 2 cable, as well as fiber optics. The Token Ring Network operates at 4 megabits per second (Mbs) and supports up to 260 devices using shielded twisted pair, or 72 devices using telephone twisted pair. There is also a 16-Mbs version available, which we will discuss later in this chapter.

While companies can run the PC LAN Program on a Token Ring Network, this hardware platform can also run LAN Server, or even Novell's NetWare network operating system. Token Ring Network uses a NETBIOS software program that is loaded into each machine. We will see that the hardware for this network differs from the simple bus architecture (in which there is always some danger of data collision). Token ring topology permits only one network workstation at a time to hold the token required to send messages.

Token Ring Network Hardware

The PC Adapter

The Token Ring Network requires an adapter card in an expansion slot of each node (network workstation). Figure 4.12 illustrates the configuration of this circuit card. There is an exchange of data buffers and control blocks between the network workstation's memory (RAM) and the adapter card. The card's RAM is actually mapped into the workstation's memory, in a section IBM calls *shared RAM*. This technique reduces the overhead required for I/O between adapter card and workstation.

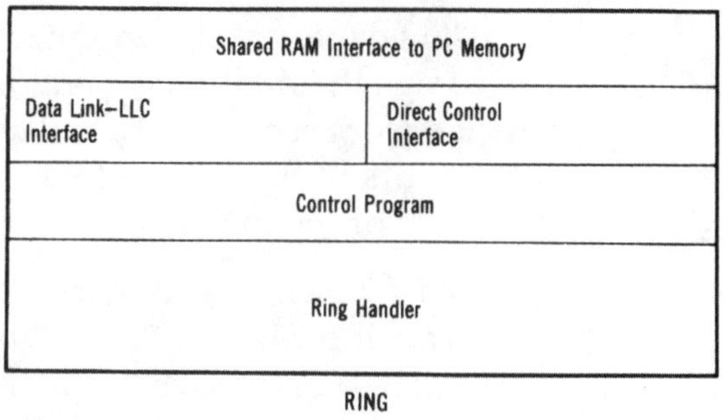

```
+-----------------------------------------------------------+
|            Shared RAM Interface to PC Memory              |
+----------------------------+------------------------------+
| Data Link–LLC              | Direct Control               |
| Interface                  | Interface                    |
+----------------------------+------------------------------+
|                     Control Program                       |
+-----------------------------------------------------------+
|                      Ring Handler                         |
+-----------------------------------------------------------+
                          RING
```

Figure 4.12   Token Ring Adapter Card Structure (Courtesy of IBM Corporation)

The Token Ring Adapter Card contains microcode to provide error checking, token generation, address recognition, and data transmission.

Figure 4.12 also reveals the two interfaces found on the adapter card. The *Data Link LLC Interface* contains some microcode (ROM) that supports these logical link control functions (as defined by the IEEE 802.2 standards). The *Direct Interface* provides a way for a user program to read logs (on such matters as error status information) maintained by the adapter card.

The adapter card in each network workstation handles token recognition and data transmission. Among the adapter's network responsibilities are frame recognition, token generation, address recognition, error checking and logging, time-out controls, and link fault detection.

One adapter on each network ring is designated as the *active token monitor*—in contrast to the other adapters, which function as *passive monitors*. Should normal token activity become disrupted, the station with the active token monitor becomes responsible for error recovery procedures. Note that any one of the remaining adapter cards can assume an active role should something happen to the active token monitor.

The adapter card comes with two different diagnostic programs. The *Adapter Diagnostics Program* is used *before* the adapter card is attached to the ring. It simply checks the adapter and the attaching cable, and ensures that the card can perform self-diagnostics successfully. A second program checks the adapter card *after* it has been connected to the ring, and ensures it can perform the "Open" functions required to connect it to the ring media.

The adapter itself can detect permanent errors (such as loss of receive signal) and then generate a notification signal to initiate automatic network recovery. The adapter detects recoverable errors (such as bit errors in the transmitted message) and reports them to a ring diagnostic program.

IBM's *Token-Ring Network PC Adapter* is available for workstations in a self-contained Token Ring Network. PCs are attached directly to the token ring through this adapter, while the PS/2 family has its own Token Ring adapter cards.

Multistation Access Unit (MAU)

The multistation access unit (MAU) is a wiring concentrator which permits up to eight network workstations to be either inserted or bypassed on the ring.

The *multistation access unit (MAU)* is a wiring concentrator which permits up to eight network workstations to be either inserted or bypassed on the ring. This unit is mounted either on a rack (located in a nearby wiring closet) or in a housing (on a wall or tabletop). The MAU is actually a passive device; it contains bypass circuitry designed to detect the presence or absence of a signal from a network workstation. Should the MAU detect a defective device or damaged cable, it will bypass this particular workstation, to avoid losing data and the token that circulates throughout the ring.

Figure 4.13 illustrates how the workstations are actually attached to the MAU. Although up to eight different workstations can be connected in what looks like a star architecture, notice that the topology within the MAU is really a ring.

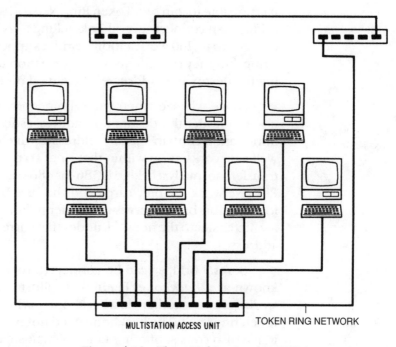

MULTISTATION ACCESS UNIT   TOKEN RING NETWORK

Figure 4.13 Three Multistation Access Units

Each multistation access unit contains 10 connector jacks. Eight of these ports are used to connect network workstations, while the remaining two ports are used to connect other multistation access units.

Token Ring Network Connectivity

One of the major strengths of the IBM Token Ring Network is that IBM provides the hardware and software required to connect this network with other networks, PBX systems, remote PCs, and mainframe computers. We will take a close look at how easy it is to connect this network to the rest of the world.

Network Bridges

A network node serves as a bridge, connecting two or more Token Ring Networks together. The bridge computer contains network adapter cards for each network, and the appropriate bridge software. Several bridges can be joined by a high-speed link known as a backbone.

It is possible to join two Token Ring Networks using a *bridge* PC. In fact, bridges can connect several Token Ring Networks—each of which can contain up to 260 workstations. Bridges appear to be a normal node on a ring, but they route frames of information between rings, by examining the destination addresses contained on the frames.

As we will see when we examine how the token is passed from node to node, the destination addresses found within the frames of information contain specific addresses which identify a specific ring as well as a workstation within that ring. To perform this high-speed data transfer, normally a bridge is 386- or 486-based, containing two Token-Ring Network Adapter cards and the IBM Bridge program. The RAM found in this bridge serves as a buffer to hold several frames while they await transfer to the network nodes that correspond to their destination addresses.

Several bridges can be connected together via a high-speed link known as a *backbone.* Figure 4.14 illustrates three Token Ring Networks joined together via a backbone—which is, in this case, actually a token ring itself. The backbone need not be a higher-speed token ring; it may also consist of other kinds of high-speed channels, including an RF (radio frequency) channel within a broadband CATV system. In this situation, each bridge would consist of a modem that would switch the data onto a broadband channel.

Connecting PC Network and the Token Ring Network

The Token-Ring Network/ PC Network Interconnect Program running on a dedicated PC workstation with adapter cards for both networks can serve as a bridge.

Many companies may find a need to connect a PC Network (perhaps performing a departmental function) with a larger Token Ring Network encompassing the entire company's activities. IBM offers the *Token-Ring Network/PC Network Interconnect Program* to serve this purpose.

It is necessary to dedicate an IBM PC to running the interconnect program and the NETBIOS program. Since adapter cards from each network are installed in two of the PC's expansion slots, it is possible for workstations in one network to share resources of the other network through this "bridge" PC.

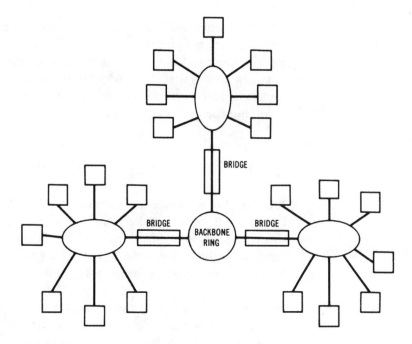

Figure 4.14   Backbone Ring Connecting Three Token Ring Networks

This Interconnect Program can handle up to 16 application names for each network. This means that 16 is the maximum number of attaching devices on one network that can be identified to the other network. It is also true that some applications require the use of multiple names. Since the file server function on the PC Network Program requires the use of three names, a maximum of five file servers on one network can be identified to the other network. Because of this limitation, running multiple Interconnect programs might be necessary in order to identify all the devices that workstations need to address.

The Interconnect program permits a maximum of 32 active sessions. When a name on one network connects with a name on the other network, two sessions are created—one for each network. During the program's configuration phase, it identifies the devices on each network, and stores them in a configuration file. The operational phase of the program concerns itself with actually receiving information from one network and forwarding it to the other network.

While the Interconnect program is running, it monitors several kinds of on-line data. It is possible, for example, to check the status of any adapter on either network. Since PC Network and the Token Ring

Network require different kinds of status reports, there are different screens for each network's adapters. It is also possible to examine interconnect status. This means that the program will display a list of network names that are currently connected. The network administrator can select a connected network pair and examine traffic statistics involving this particular session.

Connecting Token Ring Network with System /370

It is possible to connect Token Ring Network workstations with IBM's System /370 world of Systems Network Architecture (SNA). A 3725 Communication Controller with Token Ring adapters could connect as many as eight Token Ring Networks to an IBM mainframe computer. Workstations on these networks could then communicate with the mainframe computer by using 3270 emulation mode. A *gateway* workstation on these networks could be connected to an IBM System /370 via the network connection with the 3725, or directly (with an SDLC Adapter Card, the PC 3270 Emulation Program, and cabling). The gateway station can function as a normal network workstation, network print server, or file server, depending upon the amount of gateway activity the unit has to handle.

The SNA Advanced Program-to-Program Communication (APPC/PC)

The *Advanced Program-to-Program Communications* program provides a program-to-program protocol (LU 6.2) that permits peer-to-peer conversations. These can take place between applications running on an IBM PC and such logical units as a System 36/38, System 370, Series 1, and another IBM PC. While this program does not provide direct connectivity between sessions on the Token Ring Network and sessions on the SDLC link, it does provide an application programming interface; this allows a program to be written to communicate between these logical units.

Asynchronous Communications for the Token Ring Network and PC Network

IBM offers an *Asynchronous Communications Server Program* which allows workstations on the Token Ring Network or PC Network to access ASCII applications via switched communication lines. Using this program, network administrators can link workstations in their IBM network with a Rolm CBX II, a PBX, or public switched networks. Each Asynchronous Communications Server gateway station provides up to two dial lines, and it is possible to have more than one of these nondedicated gateway stations on a network.

The Asynchronous Communications Server program runs in background mode. It can establish outbound calls to such valuable services as the IBM Information Network, The Source, and Dow Jones News/Retrieval Services. Because modems are shared resources on the network, this program provides very cost-effective service to workstations that need this type of information. If all phone lines are being used, the program provides queuing of these requests.

The program also accepts inbound calls directed toward particular workstations on the network that run communication programs; it provides transparent ASCII data transfer between the caller and the network workstation.

> **Note:** While the Asynchronous Communications Server Program operates on both the PC Network and Token Ring Network, it will only work on the PC Network if the PC running the PC Network Program is configured as a Redirector.

An external ASCII device, in order to communicate to a network workstation, will need to perform a two-step procedure that establishes communications. Remote asynchronous devices cannot have direct access to other resident server functions (such as file servers, print servers, or message servers).

After establishing contact with the asynchronous communications server, the caller must be able to provide the name of the network workstation. Some electronic mail programs that have their own private protocols will not work with this software. Other programs that cannot use the asynchronous communications server (for the same reason) include host security applications, which require the ability to disconnect and then immediately call back.

Connecting a Token Ring Network with a PBX

Just as AT&T has integrated its LANs with its PBX telephone systems, IBM has accomplished much the same thing between its Token Ring Network and Rolm's CBX II telephone equipment. Connection is possible through the Asynchronous Communications Server and a number of digital interfaces, such as these:

 Rolm's DataCom Module (DCM)

 Integrated Personal Computer Interface (IPCI)

 Integrated Personal Computer Interface AT (IPCI/AT)

 Data Terminal Interface (DTI)

Attachment to a Rolm PBX (such as the CBX II) permits network workstations to share the CBX II's resources—including its modem-pooling report capability. An even more significant reason for considering this connection is the CBX II's capability of switching among several different computer systems—including those with different protocols. An office which has several different types of office automation equipment (including PCs and other ASCII terminals) can bridge the communication gap between the IBM world and the rest of the world that uses ASCII—provided it has this PBX and the necessary protocol converters (such as IBM's 3708, 3710, or 7171).

IBM sees this Token Ring Network connection with Rolm's CBX II as a way for PC workstations to access IBM Office Systems—including DisplayWrite/370, PROFS, and Personal Services/370. Because of the CBX II's architecture, it can operate attached ASCII terminals at much higher speeds than in the past. An IBM 3161/3163 and Rolm workstations (such as the Cedar, Cypress, or Juniper) can operate at up to 19.2 Kbs through an IBM protocol converter. Figure 4.15 illustrates the many different devices, including Rolm's CBX II, that can be connected to the Token Ring Network.

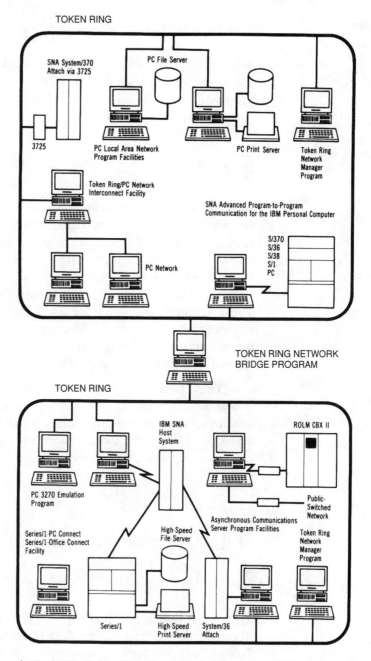

Figure 4.15 IBM's Token Ring Connectivity (Courtesy of IBM Corporation)

Printing in the Token Ring Network

As we pointed out earlier, the PC Network Program offers printer server functions which include a printer queue. IBM offers an additional program, the *IBM LAN Print Manager* to connect the Token Ring Network with its very fast and powerful 3820 laser printer.

IBM's 16-Mbs Token Ring

IBM offers a 16-Mbs version of its Token Ring Network. Unlike the 4-Mbs version (which can run on unshielded twisted-pair wire), this version requires IBM type 1, 2, or 9 shielded cabling. This network also requires its own network adapter cards, which have 64K of onboard RAM (compared to 8K in earlier versions). The new version supports frame sizes up to 18K (compared to the previous limit of 2K in the 4-Mbs ring). These larger frame sizes are ideal for transmission of images in an engineering environment. Because of their greater memory and additional circuitry, these 16-Mbs network interface cards may also be run on 4-Mbs with greater network efficiency.

The 16-Mbs network uses a technique known as *early token release*. A workstation may transmit a token immediately after sending a frame of data, instead of waiting for the return of the original token. The use of more than one token on the same ring at the same time increases network efficiency and speed; tokens are timed to avoid collision.

Data Transmission on the Token Ring Network

The PC Network is a bus topology, utilizing Carrier Sense Multiple Access with Collision Detection (CSMA/CD) to avoid collisions; the Token Ring Network is, by contrast, a *non-contention network*. Because of the nature of a token ring architecture, only one network node can send information at any given time. We will take a close look at how information is actually transmitted and received on this network, and also at how network problems are diagnosed.

Information to be sent across the network is formatted into *frames*. Figure 4.16 illustrates the fields found within these frames. Notice that the frame contains both the destination node address and the address of the source workstation. In very large networks, in which multiple rings are tied together with bridges, an optional *routing information* subfield (RI) follows the address fields, indicating the sequence of bridges that must be traversed to reach the correct ring.

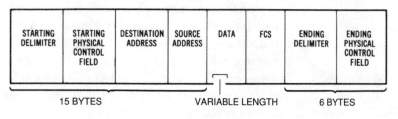

Figure 4.16   Token Ring Information Frame

When a mailbox's flag is up, the postman knows that there is a letter to be picked up. In much the same fashion, the token that circulates around the ring has a bit sequence that tells the various nodes whether it is carrying a message or is free to be used. The first byte of the physical control field, the starting delimiter field, and the ending delimiter field comprise a special token identifier. One of these bits is known as the *token bit;* when it is set to zero, it means the token is identified as a token, and is ready to be used. When a node has information to send, it captures this token and then adds the source and destination addresses, as well as the other fields seen in Figure 4.16. It then changes the zero to a one, meaning that this frame is now an *information frame.*

The information frame moves through the ring until it reaches the destination node— a workstation which recognizes its own address in the destination address field. This workstation copies the information that has been sent and then returns the information frame to the sender as a token.

Upon return receipt, the sender removes the header (first 15 bytes) and issues a new token. This new token is ready to circulate to the next node that needs to send a message. Each network node gets a chance to use the token, because no one node is allowed to transmit continuously.

Errors can occur on a Token Ring Network, and IBM has developed safeguards to prevent network downtime. As we indicated earlier in our discussion of the adapter cards, the circuit cards required in each network node perform such tasks as frame recognition and token generation. A node designated as the active token monitor runs the IBM Token-Ring Manager program. This program monitors the network for transient errors and permanent errors.

A *transient error* is a "soft" error, often intermittent, which usually can be corrected by retransmission. A node detects soft errors by monitoring all frames, verifying the validity of the frame-check sequence which accompanies the message. Each node keeps track of these errors, and reports them if they exceed a threshold amount. An operator can use a function called *Soft Error Conditions* to display the conditions of all stations reporting transient errors. The node detecting these errors sets the "error detected" flag in the physical trailer portion (6 bytes) of the frame.

In contrast to these "soft" errors, there are also *permanent errors* that represent a serious threat to the network's continued operation. When a node sends a message and receives the token back, it examines it to see if the address-recognized flag has been set by the destination node. If the flag has not been set, the location of this defective node is identified. The wire concentrators are able to bypass such faults in the network, and keep the network operating.

A complete disruption of the network signal can be caused by the complete failure of an active node's receiver and/or transmitter, or by a break in the wiring. The next network node downstream from the defective node sends out a special network signal called a *beacon*. This frame contains the address of the node sending this special message, as well as the address of the node immediately upstream from it (presumably the defective node). The normal response to this signal is for the wiring concentrator involved to bypass the defective node.

Breaks in the actual wiring of the network may not be as easy to resolve. The entire ring may have to be reconfigured to bypass a particular break. Since each node has the ability to perform self-diagnostic tests (which can identify errors in its wiring), it is a good idea to run these tests if there is no obvious break apparent in the network wiring.

What Have You Learned?

1. LAN Manager is Microsoft's OS/2-based network operating system that also features Microsoft's Windows graphics user interface.

2. LAN Server is IBM's OS/2-based network operating system that groups file servers by domains.

3. A PC Network workstation can be configured as a Redirector, Receiver, Messenger, or Server.

4. Token Ring Network requires a NETBIOS software program.

5. It is possible to connect Token Ring Network and PC Network with the Token-Ring Network/PC Network Interconnect Program, using a dedicated workstation with adapter cards from both networks.

6. It is possible to connect Token Ring Network with a PBX through an asynchronous communications server and a digital interface.

7. Token Ring Network can be connected directly to IBM mainframes and minicomputers.

8. The Token Ring Manager program monitors the network for both transient and permanent errors.

Quiz for Chapter 4

1. Microsoft's LAN Manager has a graphical user interface called
   a. Presentation Manager.
   b. Windows.
   c. the Finder.
   d. VIEW.

2. LAN Manager runs on a file server, which runs an operating system called
   a. PC DOS.
   b. OS/2.
   c. the Macintosh operating system.
   d. Windows.

3. LAN Server groups file servers into
   a. logical units.
   b. domains.
   c. kingdoms.
   d. fiefdoms.

4. A file server running LAN Server can be linked to an IBM mainframe using
   a. Communications Manager.
   b. AC/DC.
   c. twisted-pair wire.
   d. AppleTalk.

5. On PC Network, the interface between PC DOS applications and the network adapter controller is known as
   a. SNA.
   b. BIOS.
   c. UNIX.
   d. HDLC.

6. The PC Network configuration that is limited to accepting requests for applications directed to servers, and passing these requests along to the servers, is
    a. the Messenger.
    b. the Redirector.
    c. the Receiver.
    d. the Server.

7. Network-request keys on PC Network consist of
    a. Ctrl-[ALT]-Break.
    b. Ctrl-[ALT]-[DELETE].
    c. Ctrl-Esc.
    d. Ctrl-[PRTSCRN].

8. The PC Network command to share resources is
    a. LINK.
    b. SHARE.
    c. NET SHARE.
    d. JOIN.

9. Programs in PC Network normally are set up with the following default:
    a. Read/Write/Create/Delete
    b. Read Only
    c. Read/Write
    d. Write/Create/Delete

10. Tasks a user performs on his own machine are known as
    a. background tasks.
    b. foreground tasks.
    c. remote tasks.
    d. server-initiated tasks.

11. The Token Ring Network's topology follows IEEE standard
    a. IEEE 802.3.
    b. IEEE 802.4.
    c. IEEE 802.5.
    d. IEEE 802.2.

12. Token Ring Network's wiring concentrators are found on its
    a. adapter cards.
    b. network translation cards.
    c. multistation access units.
    d. active network monitors.

13. Two Token Ring Networks can be joined together with a
    a. backbone.
    b. bridge.
    c. spinal tap.
    d. T1 high-speed connection.

14. Several bridges can be joined together with a
    a. backbone.
    b. bridge.
    c. spinal tap.
    d. T1 high-speed connection.

15. To establish peer-to-peer conversations between applications running on an IBM PC and a System 370, IBM provides
    a. modems.
    b. an Asynchronous Communications Server.
    c. the Advanced Program-to-Program Communication Program.
    d. synchronous connections.

16. To establish cost-effective calls between network workstations and services such as The Source and Dow Jones News/Information Network, IBM provides
    a. SDLC protocol.
    b. an Asynchronous Communications Server.
    c. HDLC protocol.
    d. Dow Jones software.

17. When a network workstation wishes to use a token, it must check to see
    a. if the token bit is set to zero.
    b. if the token bit is set to one.
    c. if the token bit has been removed.
    d. if the token beacon signal is on.

18. Transient network errors are
    a. vagrant bits looking for a free transmission.
    b. errors caused by user error.
    c. errors normally corrected by retransmission.
    d. errors that extend across a bridge to a second network.

5 | Novell's NetWare

About This Chapter

In this chapter we'll survey the LAN software that dominates today's market, Novell's NetWare. We will examine its file-server software, sophisticated network security, and accounting options. In addition to viewing some of NetWare's powerful utility programs, we will take a look at Novell's blueprint for the future, and its newest product (NetWare Lite, designed for a small peer-to-peer network).

Novell's Philosophy

Novell's approach to serving the LAN user is unique in that it has chosen to concentrate its efforts on producing software that will run on other vendors' network hardware. NetWare runs on virtually any IBM or compatible, and supports all the major LAN vendor hardware discussed in this book—including the Apple Macintosh and ARCnet products. Novell's philosophy is to make itself a de facto industry standard by dominating the marketplace. Does a major corporation insist on purchasing IBM's Token Ring Network? Novell is happy to supply compatible NetWare to enhance the token ring's performance.

Topology

Novell's network operating system, NetWare, can run on a number of different topologies. Depending upon the hardware you select, NetWare can run on a network configured as a star, a string of stars, a token ring, and even a bus. Running NetWare on 3Com's EtherNet bus hardware, for example, results in a bus topology; when running on ARCnet hardware, NetWare functions efficiently in a token bus environment. Northern Telecom and other PBX manufacturers offer their customers NetWare, utilizing the star topology of a PBX, while Proteon runs NetWare on hardware organized as a string of stars.

NetWare and the Concept of a File Server

NetWare is designed for true network file-server support. To understand this approach, it is helpful to study how a file server functions under Novell's software. Under the OSI model, Novell's file-server software resides in the Application layer, while the disk-operating software (DOS) resides in the Presentation layer. In effect, the file-server software forms a *shell* around DOS, able to intercept commands from application programs before they can reach the DOS command processor. As we will see in a moment, the workstation user is not aware of this phenomenon. The user simply asks for a data file or a program, without worrying about where either is located.

To understand this interaction between the file server and the individual workstations, let's look at what happens when a workstation issues a request for a particular file. As Figure 5.1 illustrates, the network interface to the network file server (the *interface shell*) resides in each workstation. It is responsible for intercepting DOS commands from an application program.

When an application program requests a specific file, the shell must first determine whether the request is for a local file (residing on the workstation's own disk drives) or a network request for information located on a file server. If the information is located on the workstation's own drives, the request is passed back to the DOS command processor, where it is handled as a normal I/O operation. As a particular file is located and loaded into the workstation's CPU for processing, the user notices the red light on the disk drive go on.

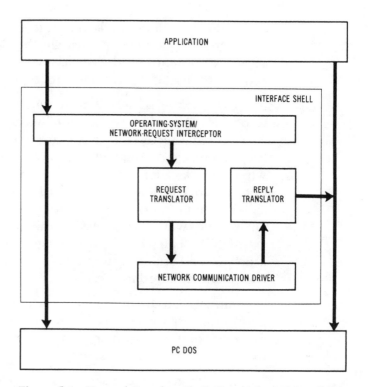

Figure 5.1   Network Interface Shell (Copyright, 1986 Novell, Inc.
All Rights Reserved)

What if the requested file is located on a file server? In this case, the request translator issues a "read" request to the file server—which locates the file and transmits it to the workstation in the form of a *reply packet*. The packet is received by a *reply translator,* which converts this information into a form that DOS on the local workstation can handle. DOS then provides the application program with this data.

The workstation is completely unaware of the internal mechanics of this operation. The network file server is so fast that local and network responses will appear to be equally fast except in cases of unusually heavy network traffic.

Techniques for Speeding Up the File Server

Directory hashing is a method of mapping and indexing directories and their files to

Novell's NetWare uses a number of techniques to speed up the response time of its file servers. One technique is *directory hashing,* which can be likened to an efficient indexing system. The software maps

minimize the number of entries a file server must examine in order to locate a specific file.

Disk caching is a technique for keeping often-requested files in RAM for rapid response to workstation requests.

Elevator seeking is a technique that enables the file server to determine the order in which to execute file requests, based upon the current location of the disk heads.

all the directory files and keeps all this information in RAM. When a workstation requests a particular file, the file server need only examine a few directory entries to locate that file. Since this information is in RAM and not on disk, it is a very fast procedure.

Disk caching is a second technique Novell uses for rapid file-server response. It illustrates just how intelligent a Novell file server can be. In effect, the file server anticipates future workstation file requests and keeps an image of frequently requested portions of its drive in RAM. When a workstation makes a second request for additional material from this area of the server's hard disk drive, it is already located in RAM and does not require a second hard disk access. Since disk access is in milliseconds while RAM access is in microseconds, a "smart" file server's use of disk caching can represent significant time savings for network users. Second and third requests for cached information can be processed one hundred times faster.

Another advantage of disk caching is that the file server can perform all disk writes as a "background" operation—which means it is capable of performing other procedures while sending this information to requesting workstations.

Another technique used to speed up Novell's file-server response time is *elevator seeking.* Imagine a file clerk who is given a series of files to locate. The first three files are Johnson, Anderson, and Jackson. If the clerk actually pulled the files in this order, it would be inefficient, since two of the files are located in the same drawer. Elevator seeking is a technique which allows the file server to execute requests in the most effective manner relative to the current position of the disk heads. The result is a throughput increase (up to 50%) and a decrease in wear and tear on the disk drives.

File Management Under NetWare

NetWare allows the supervisor to define directory access. In a moment, we'll take a look at how a department might establish its users; presently, an even more fundamental issue is the nature of the files themselves.

Certain users may want to run single-user MS-DOS or PC DOS applications in a multiuser environment. The system administrator can designate a program or file as *shareable* (capable of being shared) or *non-shareable* (restricted to one user at a time). NetWare also contains a default file-locking function, which means these single-user programs could be accessed by different users, one at a time.

If a file is non-shareable, different users can view the file in Read Only mode, but they cannot write to it while it is being used in Read/Write mode by a specific user. Programs or files designated as shareable with record-locking capability operate in true multiuser fashion; several users can read and write to them simultaneously, as long as only one user is writing to a specific record at a time.

One feature of NetWare is that an application program can specify all the records it needs before telling the file server to lock these records. This technique ensures that two application programs which need overlapping records cannot create a deadlock in which both wait for unavailable records.

Setting Up Directories Under NetWare

NetWare uses a hierarchical file structure. A diagram of this structure would resemble a mature tree, with main branches having smaller branches (which, in turn, have even smaller branches of their own). As an example, imagine that the Widget Company has just installed a NetWare network with several distributed file servers. Now it is time to set up some directories on the first file server.

Let's assume that Sales and Personnel will be using this file server. Beth and Barbara are the two sales administrators; Phil, Paul, and Peter handle personnel functions. As Figure 5.2 illustrates, Widget has named its first file server "FS1." Under the SALES directory are these two subdirectories: BETH and BARBARA. Each sales administrator has created subdirectories under her own directory. Beth has created the subdirectories EASTERN.RGN, CUSTOMER.LST, and WESTERN.RGN. Notice that under WESTERN.RGN Beth has created two additional subdirectories: SALES.RPTS and PROSPECTS. Barbara has not yet created as many subdirectories, but she certainly has that option in the future.

The Personnel department has created directories for each of its administrators. Since Phil, Paul, and Peter all have distinct functions, each has created two subdirectories to handle his specialized reports.

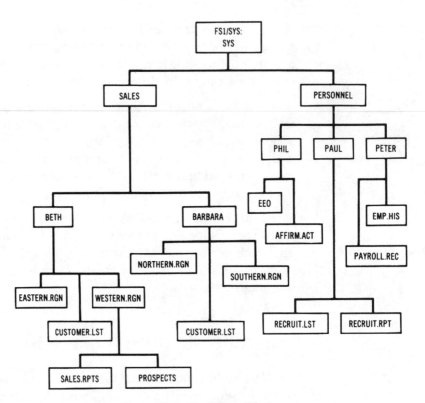

Figure 5.2 NetWare's File Structure

Within the directories and subdirectories of both departments, the system administrator will load appropriate files. Under Beth's CUSTOMER.LST directory, for example, will be found the following files: CURRCUST.E, CURRCUST.W, OLDCUST.E, and OLDCUST.W. To send a letter to former Widget customers living in the western region—to announce a new program designed to entice them to buy widgets again—Beth writes a form letter and performs a mail merge with the OLDCUST.W. and OLDCUST.E files.

When designating subdirectories, Novell follows the convention that a slash (/) or a backslash (\) must be used to separate a directory from its subdirectory. The names of all succeeding subdirectories must also be separated in the same manner. To indicate the pathway for OLDCUST.W, for example, Beth would type

`FS1/SYS:SALES/BETH/CUSTOMER.LST/OLDCUST.W`

Since we have written a pathway for OLDCUST.W, the last directory named is the directory we wished to specify.

Mapping Network Drives: A NetWare Shortcut

Network drives are logical and not physical drives. By assigning directories to specific network drives, a user is able to move quickly from directory to directory, without having to remember the exact pathways.

NetWare requires that network directories be accessed via specific *network drives.* Network drives point to network directories and not to physical disk drives; each workstation may assign 26 logical drive letters (A through Z).

Let's assume we want to assign the WESTERN.RGN directory to network drive F. We would type the following:

```
MAP F:=FS1/SYS:SALES/BETH/WESTERN.RGN
```

Typing the colon following the drive letter assigns this directory to the drive. Now we can type F: from a DOS prompt to go directly to this directory. By assigning frequently used directories to different network drives, it becomes a simple matter to jump back and forth among network directories without having to remember pathways or type in their long names correctly.

Search Drives Save Time

Search drives permit users to locate files, even though they might not know in which directory the files reside. They effectively add NetWare directories to the work-station's DOS path. It is even possible to locate files on other file servers using this technique.

One of the most common network error messages indicates that a file cannot be found. This usually means that the file doesn't exist in the directory in which you are working. Often you cannot remember exactly where it resides. To avoid this situation, use NetWare *search drives;* these enable the operating system to locate program files in directories other than your default directory. The software permits you to define up to 16 search drives (Search1:, Search2:, etc.). By placing universally used programs in a public directory and then mapping a search drive, the file server locates the requested programs, even if they are not in the current directory from which the request is made. This approach has a major advantage: rather than having to copy the same program into several people's individual directories, you can map a single copy to a search directory, which allows everyone to access it from their current directories.

Search drives also can be mapped to directories on different file servers. The result is that a system administrator can make file access painless for naive users; all they need do is specify a particular file or program that has been mapped to a search drive. Even if the file is located on a distant file server, it will appear on the user's screen as if it resided on his or her local disk drive.

System Security

While vendors who market only network security systems may offer more elaborate systems, Novell's NetWare offers by far the most extensive security system available as part of a network package. NetWare provides file-server security in four different ways:

The login procedure

Trustee rights

Directory rights

File attributes

The Login Procedure

NetWare requires a valid username, file-server name, and password at login.

NetWare provides security at the login stage by letting the supervisor require a valid *username* (user identity) and a valid *password*. As a matter of convenience, the network administrator normally allows the user to use his or her initials or name as the username. Fred Firestone's username, then, might be FREDF.

The user must also know which file server he is using. Fred's login to file-server FS1, for example, might look like this (NetWare doesn't care if users use uppercase, lowercase, or a combination):

```
LOGIN FS1/FREDF
```

NetWare now waits for a password to be typed. The software doesn't announce the correctness or incorrectness of the login at this stage, but all three variables must be correct to clear this security level. In the event of an unacceptable login, NetWare will not indicate (for security reasons) whether the username, file server, or password is incorrectly typed. Let's observe Fred's login procedure. We'll begin with Fred's typing the command

```
LOGIN <ENTER>
Enter your login name:

FS1/FREDF <ENTER>
Enter your password:
```

For security reasons, Fred's password will not appear on the screen when he types it. One important point to make here is that the password is associated with the user, and not with the machine. With his username and password, a user can work on any available workstation.

Trustee Rights

Each user has up to eight usage rights assigned by the network supervisor.

The network administrator (Novell's term is *network supervisor*) is responsible for the network's security as well as its operation. The supervisor makes each user a *trustee,* and provides each with specific rights in certain directories. These rights normally extend through all subordinate directories, unless the supervisor specifically limits a user's access. These rights may be extended to the user either as an individual or as part of a user group. The range of possible trustee rights is listed here (these vary from version to version):

Read from open files

Write to open files

Open existing files

Create (and simultaneously open) new files

Delete existing files

Parental (create, rename, and erase subdirectories of the directory)

Set trustee and directory rights in the directory

Set trustee and directory rights in its subdirectories

Search the directory

Modify file attributes

Users can be given any combination of these rights in a directory. A user with Read, Open, and Write rights (for example) can open any file in that directory, read its contents, and write to the file. Without Search rights, however, the user would have to know the name of the file in order to access it; he or she would be unable to search for it with the DOS DIR command. Notice, also, that without the Delete right, a user would be powerless to delete any existing files.

NetWare trustee security has many different levels and potential combinations. A user needs Parental rights as well as Delete rights, for instance, to delete an entire subdirectory. The network supervisor also establishes directory security. Normally, when a directory is established, all trustees enjoy all directory rights, but the supervisor can, if needed, limit these trustee rights within the directory. For example, within a specific directory, all or certain users might be limited to simply reading information.

A *maximum rights mask* for a directory means that users enjoy all eight trustee rights within that directory. Since this is a mask, only those user rights that are also directory rights will match, and represent a particular user's rights within the directory. For security purposes, users must have rights to search a directory in order to "see" a file.

Through security equivalences, a supervisor can set the trustee rights of a particular user as equivalent to the rights of a particular user group or groups, or a number of different individuals.

The network supervisor assigns each user to a *user group,* and then may assign trustee rights directly to the entire group. These rights may also be assigned to user groups indirectly, through *equivalences.* A user or user group may have up to 32 security equivalences.

A supervisor may establish, for example, that one user group may have all the rights already found within another user group; the two groups become equivalents. The supervisor may set up a group called "Everyone" and make all user groups' rights equivalent with this group. Obviously, this is more efficient than setting rights for each user. All members of the word processing pool, for example, are part of the same user group and share the same trustee rights. A NetWare supervisor, setting an assistant's rights as temporarily equivalent to his or her own, would enable the assistant to function as supervisor.

A user's *total rights* comprise those as an individual user, plus those as part of a user group, plus all the trustee rights of any other users or user groups for which this user has a security equivalence.

File Attributes Security

NetWare security permits a user to determine whether an individual file may be modified. Let's assume that Frieda, the NetWare supervisor, has been having trouble with other network users changing the contents of

A user who establishes a file can set the attributes for that flag using the FLAG command. File attributes prevail over individual trustee rights.

a particular file (CSTCONFG). Her rights include Modify privileges for this file's directory. Using the FLAG command, she restricts the file's use to Read Only. Frieda is in her default directory (where the file resides), so to effect the change she types

```
FLAG CSTCONFG SHAREABLE READ ONLY <ENTER>
```

Now the CSTCONFG file can be shared by other users who can read—but not change—the contents. Frieda could have changed all the files in her default directory to the same shareable Read Only status by typing

```
FLAG *.* SHAREABLE READ ONLY <ENTER>
```

There are four combinations of attributes that a user can select for a file (or group of files) with the FLAG command:

Shareable, Read Only

Shareable, Read/Write

Non-Shareable, Read Only

Non-Shareable, Read/Write

By typing FLAG and pressing Enter within a directory, you can see a list of the flags on files within that directory.

File attributes take precedence over trustee rights, because NetWare uses a logical "AND" function to determine rights. Let's assume that Stan has Read/Write rights to a particular directory. The CUST file in that directory has been flagged as Shareable, Read Only. NetWare examines Stan's user rights and the file's attributes, using an AND function that accepts only those terms that appear in both lists. Since the Read function appears in both lists, Stan can only read the CUST file.

Network Utilities

The four levels of network security we have been discussing are all handled by NetWare's powerful series of utility programs. At this point, we'll examine the two utility programs used in conjunction with network security: SYSCON and FILER.

The SYSCON Utility

SYSCON enables users to view information about the file servers they are logged into, their login procedure, the user groups that include them, and their trustee rights and network security equivalences. With proper network security, users can change these variables through this utility.

The *SYSCON* utility is used for system configuration. It handles many of the security functions we have been discussing (such as establishing passwords, user groups, access to file servers, trustee rights, and equivalences).

Because some of its functions can be performed by nonsupervisors, SYSCON is loaded into the SYS:PUBLIC directory. SYSCON is a menu-driven program. From DOS, typing SYSCON and pressing Enter gives the Available Topics menu shown in Figure 5.3.

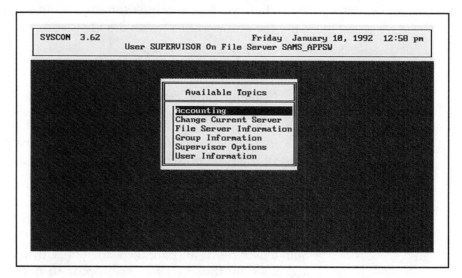

Figure 5.3   SYSCON's Available Topics Menu

Notice that even though you might not be a network supervisor, you can still view information regarding your own status on the network. For example, you can view a list of user names (Figure 5.4). The Available Topics for users (as we saw in Figure 5.3) include Change Current Server, File Server Information, Group Information, Supervisor Options, and User Information.

Figure 5.5 displays the groups to which a particular user belongs. An editorial department, for example, might want to make all staff members part of the WRITERS group, which entitles them to Read Only privileges. Any member of this group would be able to look up a project file for basic information, but only certain members of the department would have individual trustee assignments enabling them to change a file.

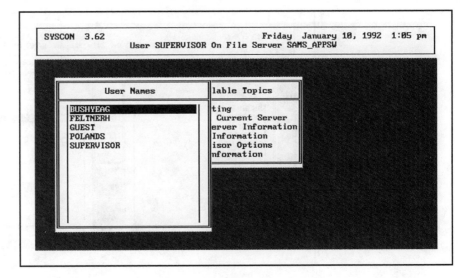

Figure 5.4 Viewing Users on a File Server

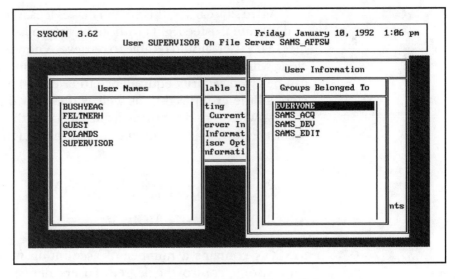

Figure 5.5 Identifying a User's Group

Novell's NetWare allows users to examine their own security equivalences and trustee assignments. In Figure 5.6, the supervisor has chosen to examine his security equivalences—and discovered he has security equivalences with Polands, as well as with the groups EVERYONE, SAMS_ACQ, SAMS_DEV, and SAMS_EDIT.

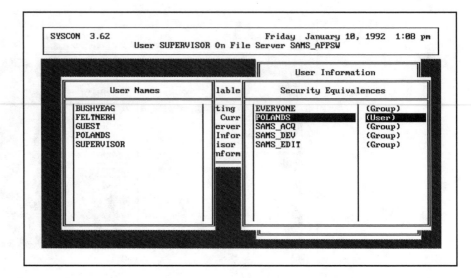

Figure 5.6 Displaying Security Equivalences

As we saw earlier, this system makes it easy to add new users—and to duplicate trustee rights without having to list each of several dozen files that a user should be able to retrieve. A new Personnel Department clerk, who will cover Frieda's assignments during her summer vacation, can be given security equivalence to Frieda—automatically giving the clerk all the group rights, as well as the individual rights Frieda now enjoys. When Frieda returns from vacation, the clerk can be given a security equivalence to another department clerk.

Enhancing Security with SYSCON's Accounting Restrictions

SYSCON contains a number of accounting functions that enable a supervisor to control the degree of users' network access, as well as the cost. We'll look at a couple of examples of how NetWare permits supervisors to perform these tasks. As Figure 5.7 reveals, a supervisor can designate the hours an employee can use the network. In this example, Carol has been restricted to logging into the network between 7:00 a.m. and 7:00 p.m. on weekdays.

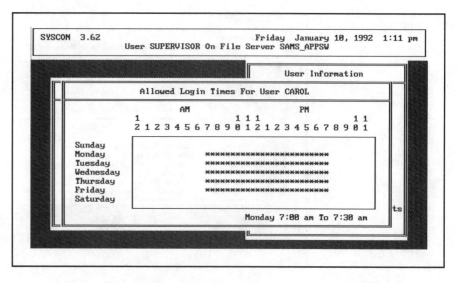

Figure 5.7 Carol May Log In Between 7:00 a.m. and 7:00 p.m. Monday Through Friday

The supervisor can limit incorrect password attempts and lock an account that has exceeded the limit, as shown in Figure 5.8. Other accounting restrictions enable a supervisor to establish an account expiration date for an employee who is temporary. Supervisors can also require users to change passwords at certain intervals and use passwords of certain lengths. Finally, additional options permit a supervisor to charge users for their disk storage and processing time. Users can even be charged higher rates during peak computing time to discourage unnecessary file transfers and report printing.

NetWare's Login Scripts

Login scripts permit network users to have their network search drives automatically mapped, key information displayed upon logging in, and the proper disk operating system software loaded into their network workstation.

At any given time, a user can utilize the NetWare utilities menu to examine his or her login script and make any necessary changes. The *login script* is a shortcut, a way to tell NetWare how to go through a preassigned set of steps to customize the network's environment, and to display certain information when you log in to the network. We'll see in a moment that it is possible to have a different login script for each file server you use and for different days of the week as well.

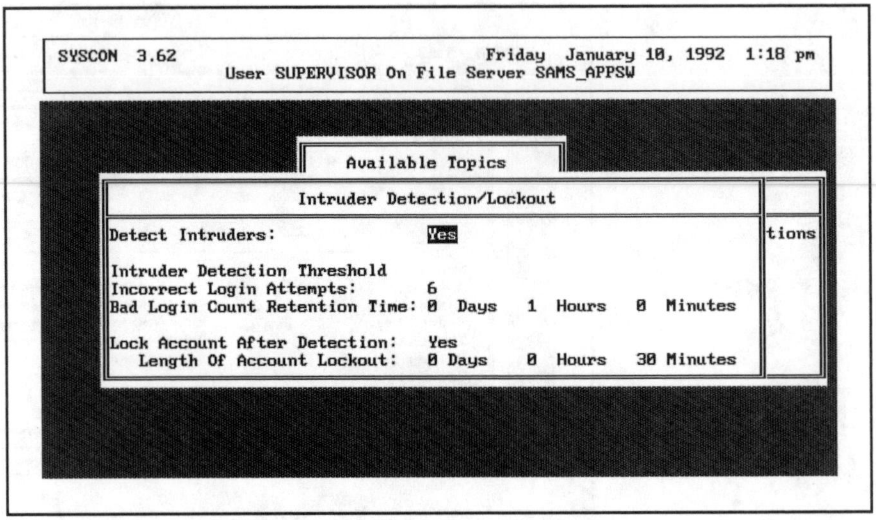

```
SYSCON 3.62                          Friday  January 10, 1992  1:18 pm
                    User SUPERVISOR On File Server SAMS_APPSW


                         Available Topics

                      Intruder Detection/Lockout
Detect Intruders:                    Yes                           tions

Intruder Detection Threshold
Incorrect Login Attempts:        6
Bad Login Count Retention Time:  0  Days    1  Hours    0  Minutes

Lock Account After Detection:    Yes
   Length Of Account Lockout:    0  Days    0  Hours   30 Minutes
```

Figure 5.8 Intruder Detection Locks an Account After a Specified Number of Incorrect Login Attempts

While it is possible for each user to design an individual login script, one of the major advantages of this procedure is that the network supervisor can set up a login script for a new user that will shield the novice from the intricacies of a network environment. The SETLOGIN command defines a login script.

While NetWare permits the mapping of different search network drives, this information is erased each time the user logs off the system. One of the major uses of a login script is to provide NetWare with this information automatically when the login script is executed. A login script for Peter might include the following:

```
map *1=sys:user/Peter
map *2=sys:apps/sprdsht
map *3=sys:public
map *4=sys:apps/wp51
map *5=sys:sales/cust.lst
```

With this login script, Peter is able to access files in different directories, without even knowing where these files exist. By typing cust.lst, for example, Peter will retrieve this information without knowing the full pathname. As a new user, Peter need not even know what a pathname is, as long as his network supervisor has set up this login script for him.

NetWare provides that a number of different variables can be placed in a login script—including the time, day of the week, month, and year. The login script can also identify the specific file server the user is addressing. Scripts use a command language that is clearly explained in Novell's documentation. The commands include an "IF...THEN" combination which permits you to individualize scripts for each day of the week. Frieda, for example, might want to remind herself of a staff meeting that is always held Mondays at 10:00 a.m. She could have the following login script:

```
IF DAY OF WEEK="Monday" THEN
WRITE "Another week. Don't forget the staff meeting at 10 a.m."
```

When Frieda logs in on a Monday morning, her computer screen will display the following:

```
Another week. Don't forget the staff meeting at 10 a.m.
```

You can individualize each day's script, not only with the date and time and standing appointments, but also with the actual set of procedures normally performed that day. A payroll clerk may only go through the actual check-printing routine on the 1st and 15th of a month. The script could specify that if the date were the 1st or the 15th, the network should log the clerk into a different file server where the check-printing program resides, load the program, and make sure the appropriate printer is on-line. The clerk would need only to use the correct login name and password to begin the check-writing procedure.

The INCLUDE command enables you to link a number of text files and place them in a login script.

Another useful login script command is INCLUDE. This command enables you to establish a series of text files that can serve as *subscripts* for your login. It is possible to have as many as 10 levels of INCLUDE commands, accessing different subscripts.

There are a number of very practical uses for these subscripts. Let's say several people are working on a project with a tight deadline. Although some of these individuals are scattered throughout a large four-story building and others are at remote locations, it is essential that they all know the progress of the project on a daily basis. A project manager could establish a file for announcements under the PROJECT directory. Each night before leaving work (or even late at night from home, with the proper remote equipment), the project manager could use the word processing program to write a text file that addressed all members of the team. Each member's login script then would have an INCLUDE command to access this file. As a team member, Frieda might include the following in her login script:

```
IF DAY OF WEEK="Monday" THEN BEGIN
WRITE "Another week. Don't forget the staff meeting at 10 a.m."
INCLUDE SYS:PROJECT/ANNCMENT
END
```

NetWare's interpretive shell permits workstations with different operating systems to share information.

NetWare—particularly its login script procedure—addresses a critical problem for many major companies: the proliferation of types of computers and of operating systems. On a NetWare file server, different operating systems can share files because of the *interpretive shell.* MS-DOS 5.0 files can coexist with PC DOS 2.2 and MS-DOS 3.3 files.

A company can establish an identifier macro command within users' login scripts to ensure that a user whose software is PC DOS 2.2 (for example) loads the proper 2.2 versions of his programs, and not 3.3 programs. Novell suggests the following login script to map search directories for differing machines and operating systems:

```
MAP S2:=SYS:PUBLIC\%MACHINE\%OS VERSION
```

The FILER Utility

FILER permits users to display and change key information about directories and files that they control. For security, a user may specify which directories and files will not appear when the contents are listed.

The *FILER* menu utility program controls volume, directory, file, and subdirectory information. Earlier we discussed a situation in which Frieda wanted to ensure that other users did not change a file within a directory she had established. To accomplish this, Frieda could change the directory's maximum rights mask or change the file's attributes. As the network supervisor, Frieda has *absolute control* of the network.

Let's assume that Frieda wished to make the change at the directory level. Using the FILER utility, she could examine the maximum rights mask for that current directory. The maximum rights consist of the following:

Create New Files

Delete Files

Modify File Names/Flags

Open Existing Files

Parental Rights

Read from Files

Search for Files

Write to Files

Frieda places the *selection bar* (displayed on the screen) on the right she wishes to delete, and then presses the Delete key. NetWare will ask if she wishes to revoke this particular right (Yes or No). When she presses her Select key, the right is revoked and removed from the maximum rights mask.

The FILER utility also permits adding, viewing, or deleting trustee rights for a particular directory, as well as viewing and deleting file attributes. A security feature available under FILER is the ability to specify a *directory exclusion pattern.*

A network supervisor, for example, could establish a network-wide directory exclusion pattern for all directories whose names begin with PROJ. This would mean that the even more secretive information for the Jove, Jupiter, and Saturn projects (PROJJOV, PROJJUP, and PROJSAT) would not be displayed with a directory listing.

It is also possible to specify a file exclusion pattern within directories. Let's say that within the directories of each of the secret projects is a budget file (PROJBUD) only the project manager needs to see or use. A file exclusion pattern for the .BUD pattern ensures that even those users with sufficient security to enter the project directories won't be able to see the budget files listed when they request a listing of all the files in that particular directory.

Printing Utilities

NetWare offers the PRINTDEF utility to define print devices, modes of printing, and types of forms. The CAPTURE/ENDCAP utility is designed to redirect a workstation's LPT ports, while the PRINTCON utility is used to set up print job configurations.

PRINTDEF

PRINTDEF is a printer definition utility program which enables the network supervisor to define the types of network print devices (printers, plotters, etc.), the modes of network printing (draft quality or final printout), and even types of forms (wide, 8.5" x 11", etc.). By typing PRINTDEF and pressing Enter, you will see the PrintDef Options screen;

selecting Print Devices at this point reveals a list of whatever print devices have been defined.

A network supervisor can define the control codes associated with the network's various printers once, and then use other NetWare printing utilities to create customized printing jobs. Using PRINTDEF, a supervisor can define several print modes required for a specific print job. A desktop publishing program's print definition might include emphasized printing and proportional spacing (for example), while budget analysts might want a print job defined for printing very wide spreadsheets in compressed mode.

CAPTURE/ENDCAP

CAPTURE is particularly valuable for a network supervisor who must install software that insists on sending all print data to LPT1.

The *CAPTURE/ENDCAP* utility is designed to allow you to redirect a workstation's LPT ports to network printer devices, queues, and files. CAPTURE is capable of redirecting up to three LPT ports; these ports are logical so that a PC need not have three physical ports. In fact, CAPTURE does not work with serial ports COM1 and COM2.

CAPTURE is particularly valuable for a network supervisor who must install software that insists on sending all print data to LPT1. You can redirect the print data to the network's print queue 2 as follows:

```
CAPTURE LOCAL=1 QUEUE=PRINTQ_2
```

Note that these CAPTURE commands are temporary and are effective only until another CAPTURE command is executed, an ENDCAP command is used, or you log out of the file server.

PRINTCON

The PRINTCON utility can be used to set up print job configurations using the options available under the NPRINT and PCONSOLE utilities.

The *PRINTCON* utility can be used to set up print job configurations using the options available under the NPRINT and PCONSOLE utilities. As a supervisor you may define standard configurations for specific users and their specific documents (since this data is stored in each user's mail directory on the server each one normally logs into). Figure 5.9 illustrates a typical print job for a routine text file using a laser printer.

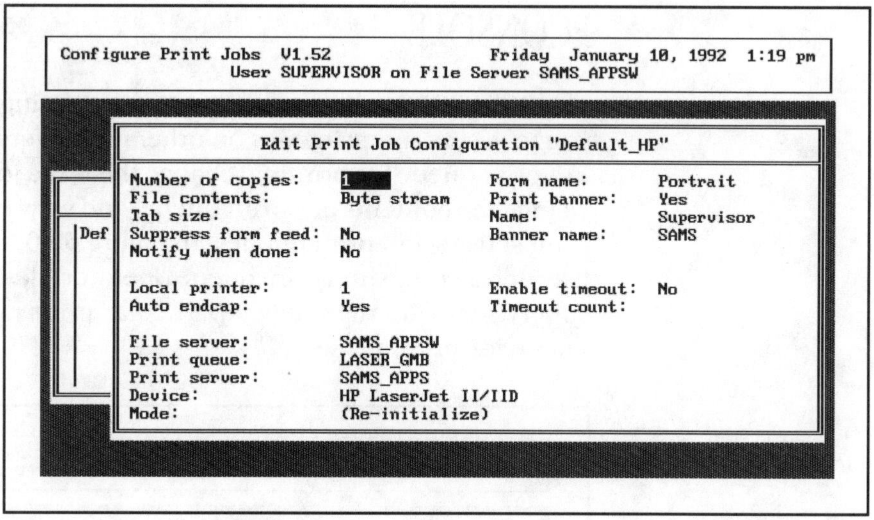

```
Configure Print Jobs  V1.52                 Friday  January 10, 1992  1:19 pm
                       User SUPERVISOR on File Server SAMS_APPSW

               ┌──────────────────────────────────────────────────────┐
               │          Edit Print Job Configuration "Default_HP"     │
               │                                                        │
        ┌──┐   │ Number of copies:   1         Form name:     Portrait  │
        │  │   │ File contents:      Byte stream  Print banner:  Yes    │
        │  │   │ Tab size:                     Name:                    │
      Def│  │   │ Suppress form feed: No        Name:          Supervisor│
        │  │   │ Notify when done:   No         Banner name:   SAMS     │
        │  │   │                                                        │
        │  │   │ Local printer:      1         Enable timeout: No       │
        └──┘   │ Auto endcap:        Yes        Timeout count:          │
               │                                                        │
               │ File server:        SAMS_APPSW                         │
               │ Print queue:        LASER_GMB                          │
               │ Print server:       SAMS_APPS                          │
               │ Device:             HP LaserJet II/IID                 │
               │ Mode:               (Re-initialize)                    │
               └──────────────────────────────────────────────────────┘
```

Figure 5.9 A Typical Print Job Configuration

Once these configurations are defined, a user simply selects one, without having to specify print options. As we'll see shortly, we can specify Carol's LOTUS standard printer configuration (as well as her WORDPERF configuration) once, and she will never have to grapple with answering printer definition questions.

NPRINT

NPRINT is a fast way to print a document on a network using print configurations already established.

Once a job configuration has been set up under PRINTCON, it can be used with the *NPRINT* command. Since PRINTCON contains a detailed description of your form, printer, number of copies, etc., all you need specify with the NPRINT command is which file you want printed:

```
NPRINT file job =BUDMONTH <ENTER>
```

The specific parameters you defined in the BUDMONTH configuration will be used for printing the document. As another example, assume you wanted to print three copies of the file "WESTERN" without a banner. You would issue the following command:

```
NPRINT SYS:MARKETNG\SALES\REGIONS\WESTERN C=3 NB <ENTER>
```

PCONSOLE

The *PCONSOLE* utility controls network printing. This program enables you to access and print files on other file servers, examine jobs waiting in a print queue for printing, change the way a job is printed, physically change the contents of a print queue, and view information about both print servers and print queues. In Figure 5.10, the supervisor is both a user and a designated print queue operator (designated by her network supervisor) who may view a particular print job as it waits in a print queue for printing.

```
NetWare Print Console  V1.51              Friday  January 10, 1992  1:29 pm
              User SUPERVISOR On File Server SAMS_APPSW Connection 2

                         Print Queue Entry Information

Print job:          448            File size:          16660
Client:             SUPERVISOR[2]
Description:        TEMPFILE.TXT
Status:             Ready To Be Serviced, Waiting For Print Server

User Hold:          No             Job Entry Date:     January 10, 1992
Operator Hold:      No             Job Entry Time:     1:29:02 pm
Service Sequence:   1

Number of copies:   1              Form:               Portrait
File contents:      Byte stream    Print banner:       Yes
Tab size:                          Name:               Supervisor
Suppress form feed: No             Banner name:        SAMS
Notify when done:   No
                                   Defer printing:     No
Target server:      (Any Server)   Target date:
                                   Target time:
```

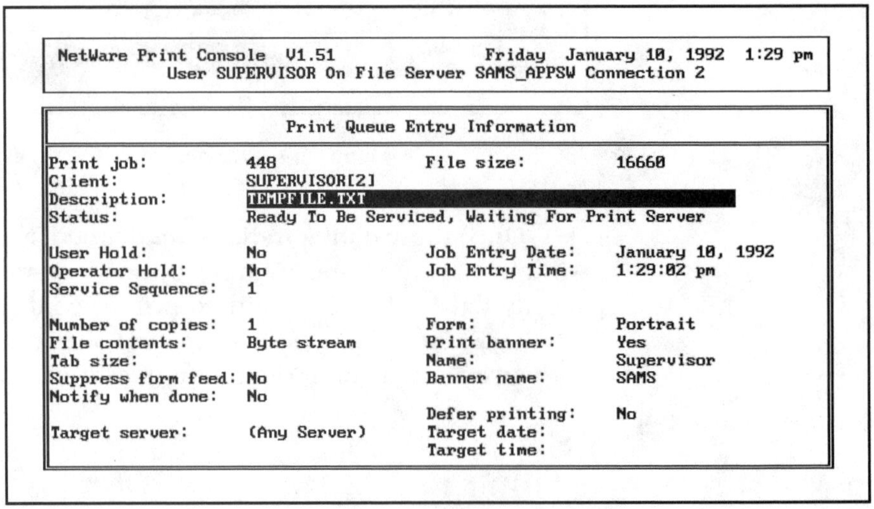

Figure 5.10 NetWare Displays Print Queue Information

NetWare Bridges and Gateways to Other Networks

NetWare not only allows intrasystem operation but supports bridges and gateways that link networks to other networks, as discussed in the following sections.

Bridge Software

Novell's bridge software permits two networks to be linked. A bridge PC must contain the network interface cards for both networks, as well as the bridge software.

NetWare makes it possible for networks to communicate with other networks, as well as with mainframe computers. A bridge connects networks using different hardware. One network, for example, might use ARCnet's interface cards and cabling, while another network uses IBM's Token Ring interface cards and cabling. NetWare provides *bridge software,* which permits these two networks to share information.

The software resides on a *bridge workstation,* usually dedicated to this purpose. This computer must have at least one floppy disk drive, and two available expansion slots to hold the two networks' corresponding interface cards. The cards are cabled to their respective networks, but the bridge is designed to remain invisible to both sets of network users. Alternatively, the file server can contain the bridge circuit card, thus creating an internal bridge.

SNA Gateway for Micro-Mainframe Communications

Novell's SNA gateway hardware and software provide micro-mainframe communications through a gateway PC. This unit provides IBM 3270 terminal emulation for the entire network. The gateway software also has the ability to perform file transfers and disk and printer spooling.

Novell's SNA gateway software provides five different hardware options: Token Ring, Coax, CoaxMux, Remote Synchronous, and Remote High Speed Synchronous. Up to 128 host terminal/printer sessions to as many as 97 workstations are possible under a NetWare gateway from a Token Ring Network. NetWare gateway software permits multiple gateways on the same network, sending mainframe print jobs to LAN printers, viewing the current status of the gateway, and pooling LU sessions.

Since the IBM mainframe world uses synchronous communications, Novell recommends its Synchronous/V.35 Adapter board (which contains an RS-232-to-V.35 interface). This adapter, when used with an Intel 80386-based workstation serving as a gateway, makes possible transmission speeds of up to 64 Kbs. Figure 5.11 illustrates how the gateway workstation connects the network with an IBM mainframe by use of modems.

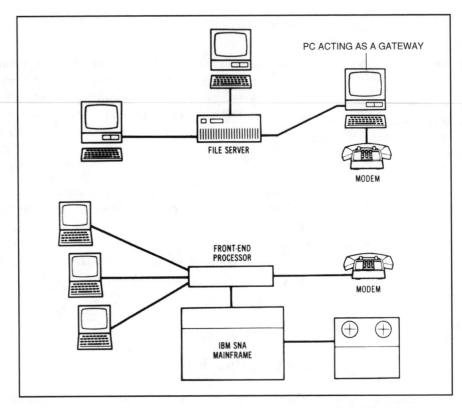

Figure 5.11   Sample NetWare SNA Configuration (Copyright 1986, Novell, Inc. All Rights Reserved)

Asynchronous Communications Server

Novell also offers *asynchronous communications server (ASC)* software. This allows a workstation acting as a server to support simultaneous asynchronous connections for up to 16 asynchronous ports for dial-up service.

System Fault Tolerant Netware

Any company that relies completely upon computers for information processing is fearful of a system failure. Novell has developed *System Fault Tolerant NetWare* to overcome this potential disaster. This

Novell offers three levels of System Fault Tolerant NetWare. Features include the duplication of file allocation tables, disk drives, and even the file server.

special version of NetWare comes in three different levels, each with progressively more protection.

What makes Novell's approach so unusual is that while it has provided the software tools for hardware duplication (to prevent downtime), the user may purchase off-the-shelf hardware in order to realize a significant cost savings.

Level I NetWare protects against partial destruction of the file server by providing redundant directory structures. For each shared network volume, the file server maintains extra copies of file allocation tables and directory entries on different disk cylinders. If a directory sector fails, the file server shifts immediately to the redundant directory. Then the server uses a *hot fix* feature to place the bad sector in a "bad block" sector table, and stores the data in another location. The user, not inconvenienced, is unaware of this automatic procedure (depicted in Figure 5.12).

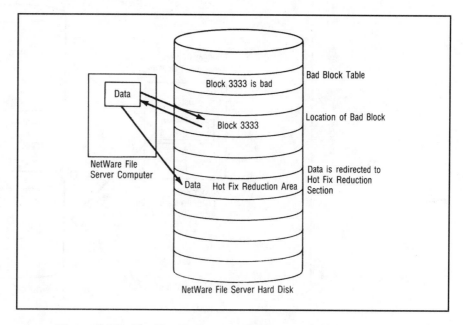

Figure 5.12 The Hot Fix Feature of System Fault Tolerant NetWare

When a Level I system is powered up, it performs a complete self-consistency check on each redundant directory and file allocation table. It performs a read-after-write verification after each network disk write, to ensure that data written to the file server is re-readable.

Level I software's hot fix feature checks a sector before trying to write data to it. If a disk area is bad, the disk drive controller will write its data to a special hot fix area. The hot fix feature then adds the bad blocks to the "bad block" table, so there is no possibility of losing data by writing it to these bad blocks in the future.

Level II software includes the protection offered by Level I, plus a number of additional features. At this level, Novell offers two options to protect the LAN against the total failure of the file server. The first option is *mirrored drives,* which means supporting two duplicate hard disk drives with a single hard disk controller (as illustrated in Figure 5.13). Every time the file server performs a disk write function, it mirrors this image on its duplicate hard disk. It also verifies both hard disk drives to ensure complete accuracy. If there is a system failure, the system switches to the mirrored file server and resumes operations.

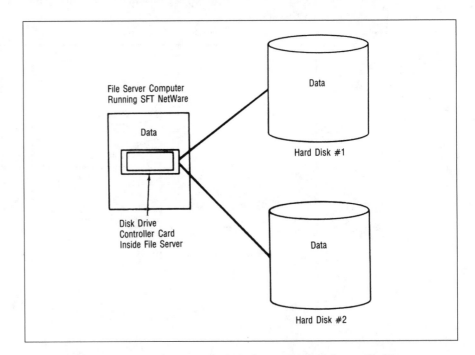

Figure 5.13   Disk Mirroring with System Fault Tolerant NetWare

The second option under Level II is for *duplexed drives:* virtually all the hardware is duplicated, including the disk controller, interface, and power supply (as illustrated in Figure 5.14). If a disk controller or

With duplexed drives, the disk controller, disk drive, and even the cables and interfaces are duplicated. Because both drives perform disk reads, file server performance is virtually doubled.

disk drive fails, the system switches automatically to the duplexed alternative and records this fact in a log. The performance of a duplexed system is far superior to that of a single system because of *split seeks.* If a certain file is requested, the system checks to see which disk system can respond more quickly; if two requests occur simultaneously, each drive handles one of the disk reads. In effect, this technique doubles the file server's performance.

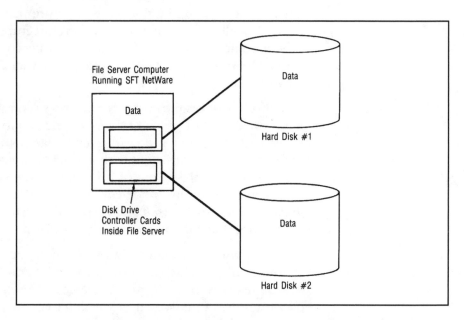

Figure 5.14   Disk Duplexing with System Fault Tolerant NetWare

The Transaction Tracking System ensures that the data integrity of a database is maintained if the network is disrupted in the middle of a database transaction.

Level II also includes a Novell feature known as the *transaction tracking system (TTS),* which is designed to ensure the data integrity of multiuser databases. The system views each change in a database as a transaction that is either complete or incomplete. If a user is in the middle of a database transaction when the system fails, the TTS rolls the database back to the point just before the transaction began. This action is known as *automatic rollback.* A second procedure performed by the TTS is *roll-forward recovery:* the system keeps a complete log of all transactions to ensure that everything can be recovered in the event of a complete system failure.

Level III software incorporates all features from Level II and adds a duplicate file server connected by a high-speed bus. If a file server fails, the second file server immediately assumes control over network operations.

Novell, NetWare, and the Future

In this section, we'll examine Novell's future plans for NetWare. We'll look at Novell's vision of a universal architecture that will be able to accommodate a number of different protocols concurrently. We'll also examine Novell's three major products: NetWare 2.2, NetWare 3.1, and NetWare Lite.

Novell believes the computer industry is now in a second stage of LAN connectivity, in which LANs are connected to mainframe computers by gateways. Over the past several years, Novell has planned an architecture to be consistent with a future characterized by increased connectivity, seamless flow of information between large and small computers, and multivendor compatibility. Novell's plan, known as *Universal Networking Architecture (UNA),* is to move toward a network architecture that will encompass any platform.

In addition to terminal emulation with an increased number of sessions available, gateways now provide file transfer capabilities for a network user. Even so, this second stage of LAN connectivity is still not "user-friendly." A network user wishing to connect with an IBM mainframe must know a lot about that system in order to bridge the gap between microcomputer and mainframe—including how to access the gateway, log on to a mainframe, and use a 3270 terminal.

Ease of use, peer-to-peer connectivity, and transparency for end users will characterize the third stage of LAN connectivity.

The major emphasis today is still on the mainframe or host computer. The LAN user is concerned with accessing mainframe applications, and not with direct peer-to-peer communications between a microcomputer program and a mainframe program. Such concepts as peer-to-peer communication, ease of use, and transparency for end users will characterize the next (or third) stage of LAN connectivity.

Novell sees this third stage as a time in which (for example) an individual database record can be updated with information from various programs running on different-sized computers that use different protocols and operating systems. All these differences will be resolved by NetWare in a manner that is transparent to the end user.

One evidence that Novell is very serious about its UNA is its inclusion of MHS in every package of NetWare. Licensed from Action Technology, MHS provides CCITT X.400 electronic mail standards; these standards are the key to making electronic mail programs that run on different computers able to provide a universal "envelope." The destination LAN's own electronic mail program can open and decode this "envelope."

NetWare versions 2.2 and above reflect Novell's philosophy in yet another way. IBM has been modifying its System Network Architecture to incorporate peer-to-peer communications; the idea is to let programs communicate directly with other programs, without having to go through a mainframe computer. NetWare v2.2 permits Advanced Program-to-Program Communications (APPC) through the addition of *Value-Added Processes (VAPs)*. We'll return to VAPs later in this chapter.

NetWare and the Use of Heterogeneous File Servers

Novell is committed to having a variety of different types of computers serving as file servers.

Novell has been developing file-server software that enables a variety of different types of computers to serve as file servers under NetWare. A DEC VAX computer, for example, can do so with NetWare VMS. The VAX's file-server capabilities are transparent to the end user, who still sees DOS files in their familiar format.

NetWare for the Macintosh now permits an IBM DOS-based machine to serve as a file server for an AppleTalk network. NetWare translates the native AppleTalk commands from Macintosh workstations into its own Network Core Protocol, processes the commands, and then translates its own commands back into the AppleTalk protocol the Apple workstations understand. This entire process is transparent to Apple users and PC users alike.

In December 1988, Novell announced its NetWare server strategy would include support for Network File Systems (NFS) and IBM's Server Message Block (SMB) protocols. Novell also indicated it would support LAN Manager clients with the NetBEUI/DLC protocol. Novell's long-range NetWare server strategy, however, is to provide a broad platform capable of supporting several different kinds of file servers—including those running under UNIX, VMS, and OS/2.

Novell also committed itself to developing a powerful version of NetWare capable of utilizing platforms based on Intel's 80386 and 80486 chips. Later in this chapter we'll examine the current NetWare 3.11 version, and what Novell promises in future versions. Support of OS/2 will include support for Microsoft's Named Pipes and IBM's APPC. Figure 5.15 represents what Novell calls its "Novell Vision" of a heterogeneous file-server environment.

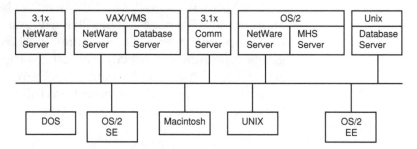

Figure 5.15 The Novell Vision (Courtesy of Novell)

Native-mode file servers perform with much greater efficiency than host-mode file servers.

Novell differentiates between *native-mode* and *host-mode* file servers. Native-mode file servers are designed for a specific hardware platform (a dedicated NetWare Intel 80386-based file server, for example) and so are inherently more efficient. Host-mode servers, on the other hand, run on top of an operating system such as UNIX or OS/2 (which also supports such services as file and print functions).

There is a movement in the computer industry toward server-based database applications that use such host-based server platforms as OS/2 and UNIX. Novell has indicated it will support both its own native-mode server and those host-mode servers which support database applications.

Novell showed its commitment in this area by signing Fox Software as its firm OEM (original equipment manufacturer) for *NetWare SQL (Structured Query Language)*. The two companies have agreed to jointly develop a database server; it will be based on NetWare SQL, using features found in Fox Software's FoxPro database program.

The FoxServer will process requests to see if they are in SQL format or dBASE format (since FoxPro uses a dBASE-like language). This approach will enable developers to create applications in either dBASE or DQL to work on the SQL server. Eventually the software will support DOS, OS/2, and Macintosh operating systems all using NetWare on the same network.

Portable NetWare

Portable NetWare, written in the C language, provides a scaled-down version of 80386-based NetWare. It will be licensed for recompilation to computer manufacturers, who will offer it on their own minicomputers and mainframes.

Novell has developed a version of NetWare that will run on platforms from mainframe and minicomputer vendors. *Portable NetWare* represents a scaled-down version of Novell's Intel 80386-based software. It will be licensed to computer companies that will recompile it to run on their own systems. Portable NetWare runs as a host-mode operating system application; minicomputers can serve as both hosts and NetWare servers. Vendors such as Prime, Data General, Hewlett-Packard, NCR, and Unisys have agreed to port NetWare to their minicomputers, allowing them to function as file servers.

Network users' computers will be able to communicate with these larger machines as terminals and as network workstations. As terminals, they will be able to run minicomputer and mainframe software (NetWare VMS users can have their workstations emulate a DEC terminal and run DEC programs in much the same way). As workstations, network users' machines will also be able to run PC-based SQL database programs, then save their files on the larger machines in NetWare file format.

Novell has written its portable NetWare in the C programming language to make it easier to port from machine to machine. The software is compliant with the U.S. government's Posix standard for operating system interoperability.

NetWare's Movement Toward Protocol Transparency

A virtually universal NetWare platform would provide support for multiple protocols—and Novell has been moving toward this vision. It would enable a user to have transparent access to a number of computing resources; these might include multiple server/client protocols and various subnet protocols.

Novell views the future as a time when the microcomputer will be at the center of computing, and not a mere appendage to mainframe computers. Apple Computer's John Sculley has expressed much the same viewpoint. To make this dream come true, however, the artificial barriers separating computing resources must be eliminated.

The various protocol differences create incompatibilities for UNIX-based minicomputers, DEC computers running VMS, SNA-based IBM mainframe computers, and other computing resources (such as Sun workstations running NFS protocol). Novell envisions a time when its software will help break down the barriers that make communication difficult among these different platforms.

Novell's Open Link Interface

Open Link Interface (OLI) software provides an interface between up to 16 different LAN adapter cards and up to 32 different protocol stacks.

Open Link Interface (OLI) software offers an interface between LAN adapter cards and different protocols. The Open Link Interface serves as a Novell response to LAN Manager's Network Device Interface and Protocol Manager features. OLI can handle as many as 32 transport protocols—and 16 different adapters—simultaneously. A single network will be able, accordingly, to support multiple protocols and different types of adapter cards.

Instead of leaving the network manager to grapple with the multiprotocol issue, OLI will make the entire matter transparent to users. In effect, OLI acts as a standard network interface, so that vendors need only develop network software with one generic driver. OLI will provide the necessary translations required, as well as the appropriate network drivers.

Open Link Interface is composed of a Link Support layer which contains two programming interfaces: *Multiple Link Interface (MLI)* for LAN-adapter device drivers, and *Multiple Protocol Interface (MPI)* for LAN protocols. The Link Support layer coordinates the sending and receiving of packets by sorting the packets it receives into the correct protocol stack—which could consist of as many as 32 queues for such disparate protocols as IPX/SPX, TCP/IP, OSI, and AppleTalk.

Among the many vendors who welcomed Novell's OLI announcement in early 1989 were Apple, Compaq, and Western Digital Corporation. Sytek Corporation also indicated support for OLI by incorporating it into its Multiple Protocol Architecture and LocalNet Integrated Network Connectivity products. Sytek will develop drivers for baseband and broadband network adapter cards that use Novell's Multiple Link Interface. Novell indicated it would provide OLI-compliant drivers for its own LAN adapters, as well as for those offered by IBM and 3Com

Corporation. Open Link Interface is consistent with Novell's philosophy of offering a universal platform for different network operating systems.

NetWare 2.2

At one time, Novell had several different versions of NetWare—including one that offered system fault tolerant features. NetWare 2.2 consolidated features found in different versions of NetWare into a single package. Offered in 5-, 10-, and 100-user licenses, NetWare 2.2 is designed for medium-sized networks with file servers based on the Intel 80286 microprocessing chip.

In addition to offering hot fix, disk mirroring, and disk duplexing (features associated with system fault tolerance), NetWare 2.2 offers Macintosh support. While previously the various NetWare packages could not be bridged, companies can bridge their NetWare 2.2 LANs, regardless of whether they have 5-, 10-, or 100-user licenses.

NetWare 2.2 offers print server software that permits up to 16 printers to be located anywhere on the network. Up to 1,000 concurrent open files are permitted per server. This version of NetWare's network operating system permits up to 32 volumes per server, with each volume having a maximum size of 255 megabytes.

Value-Added Processes (VAPs)

Value-Added Processes (VAPs) are software interfaces that permit third-party developers to write programs to these interfaces so that their applications will run a NetWare 2.2 server through the VAP interface.

A *Value-Added Process (VAP)* is a special program which runs on a dedicated server, permitting the server to host additional applications that users can access without requiring additional servers. A VAP is actually a software interface that permits third-party developers to write programs to it; their applications will run on the NetWare server through the VAP interface.

To the NetWare 2.2 operating system, a VAP appears to be a logical workstation, capable of making all kinds of requests for operating system functions. It can request that a particular process be scheduled and run, order that a report be generated, or request that a printer queue be emptied. In effect, the VAP is the process that permits the application program to run and perform its functions.

The computer industry's movement toward SQL (structured query language) database servers is an example where NetWare's concept of a VAP becomes very useful. A database management system can run as a VAP on a server, without requiring a second (dedicated) system server for database management.

Dozens of VAPS can communicate with each other using *Internetwork Packet Exchange (IPX)* protocol—facilitating the application programs they support—without the user being aware of this process. The user is aware of only the application program currently running.

NetWare for the Macintosh is actually a VAP application—known as DTALK when it communicates with Apple's LocalTalk hardware, and as ETALK when it communicates with EtherNet hardware. Additional VAPS are required to manage Macintosh printing functions; another manages the NetWare printing queue.

NetWare 3.11

NetWare 3.11 supports up to 250 nodes per server, up to 32-Gb volumes (with 32 physical drives per volume) for a total of 1,024 physical drives per server. It allows 100,000 concurrent open files and 25,000 concurrent transactions.

In May 1989, Novell announced the products it described as its "server platform for the '90s"—NetWare 386 v3.0 and v3.1. This network operating system (now called NetWare 3.11) is not a replacement for NetWare 2.2; it is a separate product. NetWare 3.11 supports up to 250 nodes per server, and volumes of up to 32 Gb, with 32 physical drives per volume—for a total of 1,024 physical drives per server. It allows 100,000 concurrent open files and 25,000 concurrent transactions. It also can handle more than 2 million directory entries per volume, with a maximum file size of 4 Gb, and a maximum volume size of 32 Gb. A feature providing Level III system fault tolerance—not yet available— eventually will permit redundant file servers and third-party applications.

Novell's NetWare 3.11 approach is modular. Users can add functions to their server platform by using server-based applications called *NetWare Loadable Modules (NLMs)*. Printing functions, LAN drivers, and various NetWare utilities are among the features available as NLMs. In the near future, Novell expects database, electronic mail, and office automation servers to be written as NLMs; that way they can be loaded or unloaded while the server is running. Figure 5.16 illustrates this feature of NetWare 3.11 architecture.

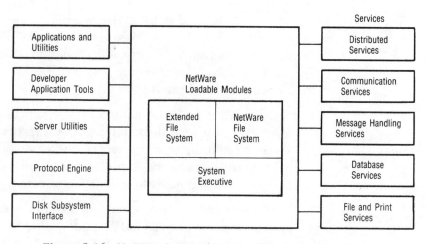

Figure 5.16   NetWare 3.1x Architecture (Courtesy of Novell, Inc.)

There is only one negative associated with NLMs: existing Value-Added Processes (VAPs) that work on NetWare 2.2 servers have to be completely rewritten to work in this NLM environment.

NetWare 3.11 supports XNS, TCP/IP, OSI, and SNA.

NetWare 3.11 supports multiple transport protocols concurrently—including Xerox Networking System (XNS), Transport Control Protocol/Internet Protocol (TCP/IP), Open Systems Interconnect (OSI), and Systems Network Architecture (SNA)—as illustrated in Figure 5.17.

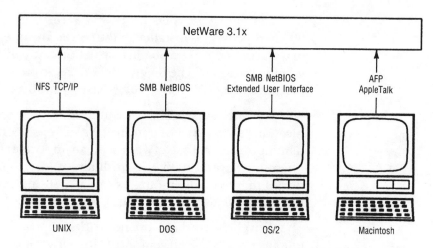

Figure 5.17   NetWare 3.1x Supports Multiple Protocols

As of the end of 1990, NetWare 3.11 also supported Microsoft's Named Pipes and Server Message Block, IBM's NETBIOS Extended User Interface, Advanced Program-to-Program Communications, Apple's AppleTalk and Apple Filing Protocol (AFP), and Sun Microsystems' Network Filing System (NFS).

NetWare 3.11 adds a number of significant network management features. These include better network statistical reporting, better print services (including print servers), and password encryption. NetWare 3.11 provides network status—even monitors and alerts—as well as access to management functions from remote consoles.

This version of NetWare also offers extended (installable) file system support for CD-ROMs and WORM drives. NetWare 3.11 can configure its server memory automatically, which reduces installation time substantially. Its Extended File Salvage facility enables NetWare 3.11 to retain all user-deleted files until the server runs out of disk space, unless the user has flagged those files for purging. When there is no longer any disk space available, the files are purged in order of deletion.

NetWare 3.11 incorporates other evidence of artificial intelligence. It is capable of fine-tuning its own operation by observing the number of users accessing an application, and when this number drops it can adjust the amount of memory needed at each stage of optimum caching.

NetWare 3.11 is also "80486-aware." This means that if an Intel 80486 processor is installed in the server, the operating system is aware of it and uses the extra 80486 instructions available to it to perform with greater efficiency. The 80386 version has approximately three times the performance of Novell's 80286-based products.

Network supervisors considering NetWare 3.11 will find communications a vital area of concern. Novell has been working on a global naming directory for NetWare 3.11, an important feature for companies operating several networks at different locations. NetWare 3.11 supports EtherNet, Token-Ring, LocalTalk, ARCnet, and Synchronous Data Link Control, as well as T-1 and asynchronous media.

Novell is working on network management features as future enhancements to NetWare 3.11. Its network reporting system will be based on the categories and packet formats of the OSI Common Management Information Protocol. This format will enable NetWare networks to report information to other CMIP-based systems, as well as to NetView (IBM's mainframe network management system). IBM and Novell currently are working together so that NetView will understand over 100 of NetWare's alerts.

Novell offers a NetWare Programmers' Workbench, which provides developers with everything necessary to write distributed applications in the NetWare 3.11 environment. These essentials include two "C" programming language compilers, supplied to Novell by Watcom Systems.

NetWare Lite and Peer-to-Peer Networking

NetWare's centralized file-server approach to networking provides high performance, but small networks might find it too expensive, and it might provide far more capacity than a small network requires. To fill this niche, Novell offers the *NetWare Lite* network, which uses a peer-to-peer approach to linking workstations.

On a *peer-to-peer network,* each workstation can share some, all, or none of its resources with the other workstations. The core communications software occupies approximately 13K of a workstation's RAM. The client software (which enables a workstation to run other workstations' resources) also requires about 13K of RAM. A workstation that wants to run as a server and share its resources with the network runs server software (occupying approximately 50K of RAM).

The program uses menus in much the way that NetWare 2.2 and NetWare 3.11 do. A workstation user can establish, via a menu, the rights different network users have in various directories on that workstation.

What makes NetWare Lite interesting to companies that already have large NetWare networks is that NetWare Lite and regular NetWare can coexist on the same cable. A workstation can be part of both networks; it can access NetWare file servers and also access the resources of other workstations on the NetWare Lite network.

NetWare Lite packets will not cross a NetWare bridge, so the network's growth potential is limited. However, Novell does provide a *migration path* for users who want to upgrade to a NetWare network, because the two networks use the same protocol (IPX) to generate packets.

What Have You Learned?

1. System fault tolerance enables NetWare to provide redundancy of key hardware and software elements to prevent network failure.

2. Three techniques NetWare uses to speed up its file-server response time are directory hashing, disk caching, and elevator seeking.

3. By mapping network drives and utilizing the principle of search drives, a user can retrieve a file without knowing where it is located.

4. NetWare's many levels of network security include the login procedure, trustee rights, directory rights, and file attributes.

5. New network users can immediately enjoy all the rights of another network user if they have the same network equivalences.

6. NetWare users can learn information about their login scripts by using the SYSCON utility.

7. Using the FILER utility, network users can establish directory and file exclusion patterns.

8. Novell's NetWare bridge software and hardware permit two networks to be linked.

9. Novell's SNA gateway software permits up to 128 concurrent SNA sessions with an IBM mainframe.

10. NetWare can search for potential bad disk sectors—and then avoid them—using the hot fix feature of system fault tolerant software.

11. The integrity of a database is maintained, even in the event of network failure, by the Transaction Tracking System (TTS).

Quiz for Chapter 5

1. ARCnet uses a series of active and passive hubs tied together with
   a. fiber optics.
   b. twisted-pair wire.
   c. coaxial cable.
   d. lasers.

2. NetWare file servers keep often-requested files in RAM for rapid response to requests. This is known as
   a. directory hashing.
   b. disk caching.
   c. elevator seeking.
   d. rapid response retrieval.

3. NetWare minimizes wear and tear on disk drives by retrieving files that are closest to the present location of the heads, instead of simply processing retrieval requests in the order in which they are received. This technique is known as
   a. directory hashing.
   b. disk caching.
   c. rapid file retrieval.
   d. elevator seeking.

4. NetWare workstations need not contain floppy disk drives as long as they have
   a. a remote system reset PROM.
   b. NetWare v2.2 and above.
   c. EGA graphics.
   d. at least 256K of RAM.

5. Workstations using different versions of DOS can coexist on a NetWare network because
   a. each workstation does not use the file server.
   b. NetWare provides an interpretive shell.
   c. the differences in DOS versions are not significant.
   d. different machines need different versions of DOS.

6. The PCONSOLE menu utility is designed to handle
    a. printing requests.
    b. photocopying requests.
    c. filing requests.
    d. micro-mainframe communications.

7. Novell's System Fault Tolerant NetWare automatically places bad sectors in a "bad block" table by using
    a. a hot fix feature.
    b. elevator seeking.
    c. mirrored disk drives.
    d. the Transaction Tracking System.

8. The automatic rollback feature of the Transaction Tracking System ensures the integrity of a database by
    a. duplicating each data entry.
    b. rolling back to before the data entry if the entry was disrupted before it was complete.
    c. keeping a log of all data entries.
    d. completing an entry if it is disrupted.

9. The concept of mirrored drives means that
    a. all drives are the mirror opposites of each other.
    b. a second drive keeps an exact copy of the file server's information.
    c. all hardware and software are duplicated, including disk controllers and interfaces.
    d. if one disk drive becomes cracked, the other drive also is cracked.

10. Duplexed drives increase the speed of a file server by about
    a. 3 times.
    b. 4 times.
    c. 2 times.
    d. 6 times.

11. Novell's peer-to-peer network operating system is
    a. NetWare Lite.
    b. NetWare PEER.
    c. NetWare Shrink.
    d. NetWare 2.2.

12. Portable NetWare is written in
    a. COBOL.
    b. FORTRAN.
    c. C.
    d. 4GL.

13. NetWare enables the file server to locate a file quickly, without searching through every directory, by use of
    a. disk caching.
    b. directory hashing.
    c. elevator seeking.
    d. remote system reset PROMS.

14. Network disk drives are really
    a. hard disk drives.
    b. floppy disk drives.
    c. network file servers.
    d. logical disk drives.

15. Different networks can be linked using
    a. a remote PC.
    b. a bridge PC.
    c. a disk server.
    d. spooled disk files.

16. NetWare LANs can communicate with IBM mainframe computers by using
    a. a bridge PC.
    b. an SNA gateway PC.
    c. an asynchronous communications server.
    d. both b and c.

17. A program running on a NetWare 2.2 server that permits the server to host additional applications is known as a

    a. vaporware product.

    b. vampire link.

    c. VAMP.

    d. VAP.

18. Users can shorten the login procedure by

    a. using the NetWare manuals.

    b. using electronic mail.

    c. using elevator seeking.

    d. using login scripts.

CHAPTER

6 | Macintosh Local Area Networks

About This Chapter

In this chapter, we'll examine some of the major Macintosh local area networks. In addition to Apple's LocalTalk hardware and AppleShare software (which comprise an AppleTalk network), we will also look at Novell's NetWare and Sitka's TOPS for the Macintosh.

Apple's Macintosh Hardware and Software

LocalTalk

LocalTalk is the hardware, or the physical equipment, comprising an AppleTalk network.

LocalTalk is Apple's built-in network interface, found in its Macintosh computers and LaserWriters. It handles the physical requirements of network transmission, as well as media access. It can transmit data at 230.4 kilobits per second (Kbs), using a CSMA/CD method of media access control. The LocalTalk cabling system consists of shielded twisted-pair wiring—configured, according to Apple, into a *multidrop bus*. A *drop cable* (a cable coming off the bus) connects a Macintosh to a connection box, which in turn is connected to the network.

While LocalTalk is Apple's network hardware, *AppleTalk* is Apple's family of network software protocols; these control everything from routing to file access. Before examining specific network products, we'll spend some time looking at these important protocols.

AppleTalk Protocols and the OSI Model

Apple has long desired to become a major provider of Fortune 500 local area networks based on its Macintosh, but only recently has it developed a strategy that seems to be working. By developing a set of protocols that are consistent with the OSI model (discussed in Chapter 2), Apple has provided major corporations with some assurance that its Macintosh-based networks will be able to communicate with any IBM PC-based LANs (since IBM has also moved toward OSI-model compatibility). If both computer giants provide OSI-compliant networks, then it is reasonable to assume these networks will be compatible, since they will use the same international standards.

Apple designed its AppleTalk network to be consistent with the OSI model. Apple's network architecture follows the layered approach developed by the OSI to facilitate communications among heterogeneous networks. It is worth taking some time to examine this architecture, since it is so critical to Apple's desire to make Macintosh-based LANs an integral part of corporate America.

The Physical Layer

Figure 6.1 illustrates the structure of the protocols found in an AppleTalk network within the context of the OSI model. At the level of the *Physical layer,* Apple provides an interface for its own LocalTalk hardware. The LocalTalk circuitry is included with every Macintosh, so that only a LocalTalk cable is needed to connect Macintosh computers together. As mentioned earlier, the problem with LocalTalk for larger networks is its limited transmission speed (approximately 230 Kbs).

For users requiring greater speed than the 230 Kbs of Apple's LocalTalk hardware, Apple File Protocol also supports EtherNet and Token Ring Network.

For companies requiring faster network transmission, an AppleTalk network is also capable of implementing EtherNet (10 megabits per second, or Mbs) and IBM's Token Ring Network (4 Mbs). Both of these approaches would require network interface cards (as well as appropriate network software) in each network workstation. Apple and several other vendors offer this equipment.

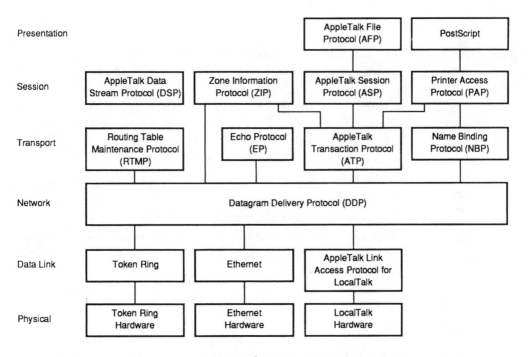

Figure 6.1   The AppleTalk Suite of Protocols

The Data Link Layer

At the *Data Link layer,* an AppleTalk network provides a link access protocol for Apple's own AppleTalk, as well as one for EtherNet and IBM's Token Ring hardware. In the not-too-distant future, there also will be a protocol for Standard Microsystems' popular ARCnet.

These link access protocols provide the Data Link layer with directions for formatting a packet into frames; the frames are given specifically defined fields, as well as a header and a trailer (which include important control information). These protocols also provide specific directions for handling data collisions. As indicated earlier, Apple provides a traditional CSMA/CD approach for both detecting and avoiding data collisions.

The Network Layer

The Network layer can access routing tables to establish a network path. It also can use the Name Binding Protocol to translate the network server's name into an acceptable internet address.

The *Network layer* takes responsibility for the physical details of ensuring that a packet will be routed correctly from one network to another. Apple includes a *Datagram Delivery Protocol (DDP)* that provides a means of addressing specific logical ports or sockets on different networks. This protocol is responsible for establishing the route a datagram will take from its source workstation address to its destination workstation address.

This Datagram Delivery Protocol is absolutely critical for Apple's interconnectivity with other networks, because it can access key information from routing tables to establish a network path for the datagram. It can also use a Name Binding Protocol (found in the Transport layer above it) to translate the network server's name into an acceptable internet address.

The Transport Layer

The Routing Table Maintenance (RTM) protocol can provide alternative routes if a particular bridge is disabled.

An AppleTalk network's *Transport layer* consists of four distinct protocols, all designed to facilitate the arrangements necessary to route a datagram from one network to another network. While the Network layer handles the "nitty gritty" details of the routing, the Transport layer is responsible for deciding exactly what transport services (including acknowledgement of delivery, error checking, etc.) are required.

The *Routing Table Maintenance (RTM)* protocol provides the key information necessary for bridges to connect similar networks, and for routers to connect different networks together. This protocol provides detailed information on which bridges must be addressed (and how many "hops" it will take) to transmit a datagram from network 1 to network 4. The RTM protocol can provide not only the preferred route for transport, but also alternative routes if a particular bridge is disabled.

We have already mentioned a second Transport layer protocol—*Name Binding Protocol (NBP)*—in conjunction with the activities of the Network layer. The NBP is responsible for matching workstation/server names with internet addresses. We might think of NBP as a service similar to one provided by many post offices. While post offices would like to receive full address information, often a letter addressed simply to "The Gas Company" will be routed (with the proper address added) to the city's lone gas company. The actual addressing, then, is transparent to the network user.

Transaction Protocol (TP) and Echo Protocol (EP)

The *Transaction Protocol (TP)* provides a guaranteed class of service for transport of datagrams. It makes it possible to have an acknowledgement that a datagram was delivered error-free. This protocol is a critical component of OSI-compatible Transport layers, since a specific class of service may be required by certain network application programs.

The *Echo Protocol (EP)* is the final standard found in an AppleTalk network's Transport layer. It provides an "echo" function by enabling the destination workstation to echo the contents of a datagram to the source network workstation. This echoing technique enables the network to know that a particular workstation is responding and active; it also enables the network to measure the round-trip delays encountered.

The Session Layer

The *Session layer* on OSI-compatible networks is concerned with the establishment of a communications session. In an AppleTalk network, there are four protocols found in this layer: the *Data Stream Protocol (DSP), Zone Information Protocol (ZIP), Session Protocol (SP),* and *Printer Access Protocol (PAP)*.

Data Stream Protocol (DSP)

The *Data Stream Protocol (DSP)* is concerned with the major task of the Session Layer: establishing a communications session between nodes. The DSP can establish full duplex communications, detect and eliminate duplicate datagrams, and request retransmission to ensure error-free service.

Zone Information Protocol (ZIP)

The *Zone Information Protocol (ZIP)* is involved in mapping networks into a series of *zone names.* These zone names become instrumental in helping the NBP determine which networks are found in which specific zones. This information is also critical for establishing a delivery path for both routers and bridges.

Session Protocol (SP)

The *Session Protocol (SP)* found at the Session layer in an AppleTalk network is concerned with the correct sequencing of datagrams when they arrive out of order. The Session Protocol is also concerned with packaging data into correctly sized datagrams, and with establishing break points during conversation sessions to ensure efficient communication.

Printer Access Protocol (PAP)

The *Printer Access Protocol (PAP)* found in an AppleTalk network is concerned primarily with stream-like service for devices such as printers (or streaming tape systems) when a network wishes to communicate with such a device.

The Presentation Layer

The *Presentation layer* in an OSI-compatible network is concerned with the way data is presented, and with the type of syntax that will be used. In an AppleTalk network, two major protocols are located in the Presentation layer: the AppleTalk Filing Protocol (AFP) and Postscript Protocol (PP). They coexist and provide different functions.

AppleTalk Filing Protocol (AFP)

The *AppleTalk Filing Protocol (AFP)* provides a critical interface for file server software—in particular, Apple's AppleShare and Novell's NetWare. Since other computers with Macintosh-like interfaces can now function as file servers on a Macintosh AppleTalk network, the AFP also provides the interface for them.

The AFP is concerned primarily with file structure. It provides the foundation for a network's hierarchical structure of volumes, directories, and files—as well as appropriate login techniques. It also enables AppleTalk workstations to access a local (or even a remote) file server. A special Translator program within AFP translates native AppleTalk file system calls into whatever equivalent is required by the file server being accessed.

PostScript Protocol (PP)

The Presentation layer's *PostScript Protocol (PP)* provides the appropriate interface to ensure effective communications between network workstations and PostScript devices (such as Apple's own LaserWriter).

The first versions of AppleTalk software limited users to 32 workstations per *zone* (a workgroup unit assigned arbitrarily by a network administrator). There was also a 254-node limit per network. Under Phase 2 AppleTalk, however, it is possible to have up to 256 zones per network—with support for up to 16 million AppleTalk devices, and routing support for up to 1,024 interconnected AppleTalk networks. While these numbers are theoretical, this routing support for a large number of workstations does make interconnectivity easier for companies that have several small networks.

AppleShare

AppleShare is Apple's file server software for an AppleTalk network. Hard disks attached to the file server are known as *volumes*. Within each volume, files are stored in *folders* (which correspond to "directories" under MS-DOS). Interestingly enough, AppleShare provides security and access at the folder level, and not the file level. AppleShare's administrative software, *Admin*, is used for such supervisory chores as setting up network users and workgroups, and providing reports for network users. These reports can provide valuable information, such as the size and accessibility of individual folders on a volume.

Security includes logins, the access to a folder discussed previously, and even the ability to make files in a folder invisible to anyone but the person placing the files there.

AppleShare makes full use of the Macintosh graphic interface. (Figure 6.2 illustrates how a user would connect to a file server.) Apple IIe and Apple IIGS computers can function as AppleShare workstations, and can share their files with other network users of an AppleShare file server. Apple IIe computers require an Apple II Workstation Card, while the Apple IIGS has LocalTalk hardware built-in. PC users can also connect to an AppleTalk network by installing a LocalTalk PC card. They then can access AppleShare files and printers. AppleShare PC software includes the MS-DOS Redirector, which converts all DOS file system requests to *Server Message Blocks (SMBs)*. A special program then converts SMBs to AppleTalk Filing Protocol calls that can be understood on an AppleTalk network. The PC user will still see a conventional MS-DOS screen, since Apple's software follows all MS-DOS conventions.

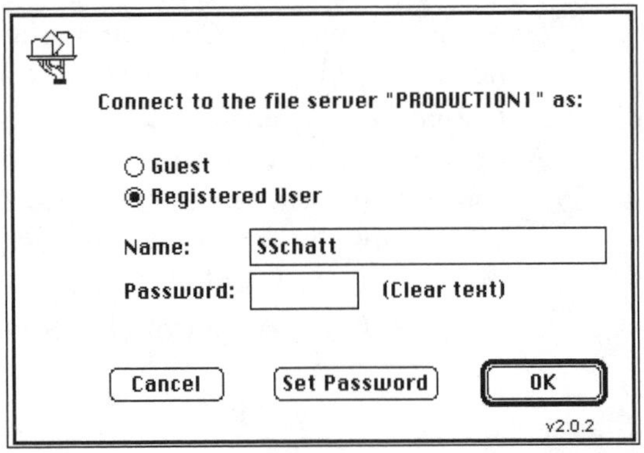

Connect to the file server "PRODUCTION1" as:

○ Guest
◉ Registered User

Name: SSchatt

Password: [   ] (Clear text)

[Cancel] [Set Password] [OK]

v2.0.2

Figure 6.2 Connecting to an AppleShare File Server

AppleShare Server 3.0 added a number of significant features, in part because it takes advantage of Apple's System 7 operating system. Because System 7 is a true multitasking operating system, other servers and application programs can run at the same time as AppleShare runs on one Macintosh computer.

AppleShare 3.0 supports up to 120 simultaneous users. It provides on-line CD-ROM exchange, as well as the ability for users to share folders or entire disks. Users can protect their data by choosing one of these options that will apply to other network users:

Can't see enclosed folders

Can't see enclosed files

Can't write to folder

Can't write to or see folders

Can't write to or see files

AppleShare 3.0's print server function can run as a background task on the AppleShare server. A print spooling feature supports up to five AppleTalk printers, with a log that can accommodate up to 1,100 jobs.

Another very useful feature of AppleShare 3.0 is that newly created folders are available to all users by default, and folders inherit the access privileges of the folder or volume in which they are placed. This server software now also permits multiple "superusers," so that a network manager can delegate responsibilities to workgroup managers.

NetWare on the Macintosh

How NetWare 2.2 Translates AppleTalk Network Commands

NetWare 2.2 uses a Service Protocol Gateway (SPG) VAP to translate Macintosh workstations' AppleTalk system calls into NetWare commands.

NetWare 2.2 uses a *Service Protocol Gateway (SPG),* illustrated in Figure 6.3, to translate workstations' native commands (in this case, AppleTalk system calls) into NetWare commands. It interprets these commands and then responds with commands that are translated back into commands acceptable to the network's hardware configuration.

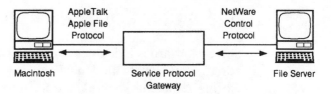

Figure 6.3 The Service Protocol Gateway Translates Protocols

NetWare's Service Protocol Gateway is a Value Added Process (VAP) that translates AppleTalk commands into its own *Network Core Protocol (NCP)*. SPG is an application that runs on top of a network operating system; it allows NetWare and third-party processes to be linked into the network operating system running on a file server or bridge. For a NetWare file server to provide file services to Macintosh workstations, the SPG VAP and a special LAN-driver VAP must be installed, as well as additional VAPs for print services.

The NetWare for the Macintosh Network Loadable Module

As discussed in Chapter 5, NetWare 3.11 utilizes network loadable modules (NLMs) to add network functions. The NetWare for the Macintosh NLM enables Macintosh users to take full advantage of NetWare services, and allows them to access information on an Intel 80386-based file server. Enhanced printing support enables Macintosh users to manage their own print jobs within a queue. Macintosh, DOS, and OS/2 users can send print jobs to an Apple LaserWriter and compatible printers. The printers themselves can be connected to the serial or parallel port of a NetWare 3.11 file server, a NetWare Print Server, or a DOS workstation serving as a remote printer.

The Macintosh NetWare NLM includes an *AppleTalk router* that can determine its own network and zone configuration by analyzing data it receives from AppleTalk. This feature frees network managers from having to provide configuration information. AppleTalk data packets can be routed across ARCnet, EtherNet, LocalTalk, and Token Ring cabling.

Bridging the Gap Between the Macintosh and IBM PC

Since NetWare is a distinct and hardware-independent network operating system, it provides an effective bridge between the IBM and Apple worlds. A Macintosh workstation utilizing NetWare v2.15 (and above) is able to see and access both the Macintosh and the PC files displayed on its NetWare file server. DOS files are stored in standard HFS format; in addition, no conversion is needed for files produced by application programs available for both machines (such as Microsoft Word, Page-Maker, and WordPerfect).

Under NetWare, a Macintosh network can utilize an IBM Intel 80286-, 80386-, or 80486-based computer as a file server.

One major advantage of Novell's approach is that a Macintosh network can utilize Intel 80286-, 80386-, and 80486-based computers as file servers; these units provide high performance at lower prices than comparable Macintosh units. Also, since NetWare is capable of handling up to 2 gigabytes of disk storage on a single file server, large-capacity hard disks are still less expensive for IBM machines than their Macintosh counterparts.

DOS-based workstations on a Macintosh network under NetWare can utilize Apple printers.

Equally important, NetWare supports Macintosh print spooling, because it is compatible with the AppleTalk Printer Access Protocol. IBM PC workstations under DOS or OS/2 can access ImageWriters and LaserWriters that are part of an AppleTalk network. These printers can be configured on IBM software (as C Itoh Prowriters and Diablo 630 printers, respectively). The network also has PostScript printer drivers built into its AppleTalk protocol suite.

Because NetWare is able to distinguish its own IPX packet format from Apple's format for its own file server, AppleShare file servers can also be accessed on a NetWare network. Similarly, Macintosh computers using EtherPort network interface cards and running NetWare can access IBM PC workstations that use standard EtherNet network interface cards and also run NetWare.

NetWare for the Macintosh contains a utility program that converts Apple file names to DOS file names, since the two operating systems have different rules for naming files. DOS limits file names to eight characters, without spaces between the letters; Apple files can contain up to 31 characters. DOS interprets a period in a file name as the *separator* between file name and extension, and lists the first three letters after a period as the extension. The Apple file name My Proposal is translated into the DOS file name MY; the Apple Mr. and Mrs. Smith file becomes MR.AND in DOS.

One problem with this automatic conversion process is that since the program truncates Apple names, it is possible that two files could appear to have the same DOS name. The solution is to convert the two Apple file names in such a way that the last character in the second file name in the DOS display appears as a number. This way, the Macintosh files MY.FILE 1 and MY.FILE would appear on a DOS workstation's screen as MY.FIL and M1.FIL. DOS files are displayed in Apple folders with the word DOS appearing in the document icon, and all letters appearing in uppercase. Figure 6.4 shows what a Macintosh user would see.

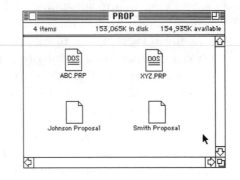

Figure 6.4 DOS and Apple Files Displayed

How NetWare Volumes Are Depicted on the Macintosh

NetWare will display a list of available volumes in a *volume dialog box*. You may select as many volumes as you wish to work with. One very nice feature of this login process is that you can specify that your name and password be saved along with the list of volumes you have selected. From that point on, each subsequent time you log in to the network, you'll be logged into these volumes automatically.

NetWare volumes on the Macintosh are depicted using the Macintosh icons (pictures). A SYS volume, for example, could be selected and clicked to reveal several file folders (including LOGIN, MAIL, PUBLIC, and SYSTEM).

A volume can contain several different types of folders: *gray, dropbox, plain, black-tab gray,* and *black-tab plain.*

You may drop files into drop-box folders, but may not see what is inside.

- A gray folder is unavailable for use; this means you cannot open it, copy files into it, or make any modifications.

- The arrow above dropbox folders symbolizes that you can drop files into these folders, but you cannot see what's inside.

- Plain folders permit you to open them and see the files contained therein. Your rights, a subject we will discuss shortly, determine what else you can do with these files.

- Finally, black-tab folders enable you to modify the folder's security. You can change your own rights inside the folder, which may result in a change of the folder's color from gray to plain. (You cannot read the files in black-tab gray folders.)

Several of these folder types are shown in Figure 6.5. To create a new folder, you simply select the New Folders command from the File menu. When an unlabeled new file folder appears on your screen, you can type a name for it. NetWare will convert a Macintosh file folder name (by eliminating spaces and truncating it) into a form DOS will accept.

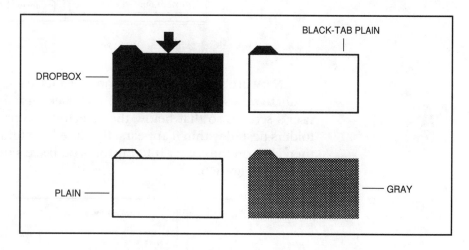

Figure 6.5   Different Types of Folders Available

Files can be named and saved directly into a specific folder which exists on a specific volume, as shown in Figure 6.6. Files can be flagged to give them any of the following special attributes: Read-Only, Shareable, Hidden, Indexed, Modified Since Last Backup, System, and Transaction Tracking.

Security on a Macintosh NetWare Network

The equivalent to NetWare's Parental rights does not exist on an AppleTalk network.

Users on Macintosh networks which contain both AppleShare and NetWare file servers will find that files on the AppleShare server will have AppleShare privileges, while files on a NetWare server will have NetWare rights. There is no AppleShare equivalent to NetWare's Parental rights. In this section, we'll examine how the Macintosh version of

NetWare displays such information as effective rights and trustee rights, as well as a number of other security issues.

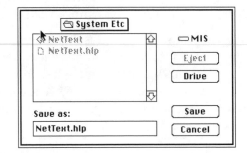

Figure 6.6   Files Can Be Saved Directly into a Specific Folder

NetWare's Macintosh version permits users to select a parent folder to view security options; double-clicking at this point changes the user's screen, so that below the selected parent folder, a list of the folders nested within it appears. If you select a folder at this point, and then click on the Folder Info button, you'll see a display similar to that shown in Figure 6.7.

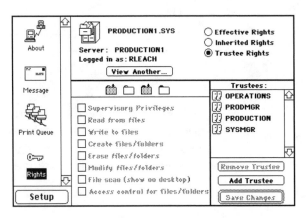

Figure 6.7   Options for Files

The folder's (or volume's) effective rights displayed in Figure 6.7 are the assigned trustee rights; these are included in the maximum rights mask. The Macintosh version of NetWare uses pen, paper, and folder icons, which are already familiar to Macintosh AppleShare users. While NetWare on the Macintosh offers essentially the same type of rights found on a PC-based network, the icon-oriented appearance is striking. Figure 6.8 illustrates how you can view groups and add trustees you want to assign to a folder.

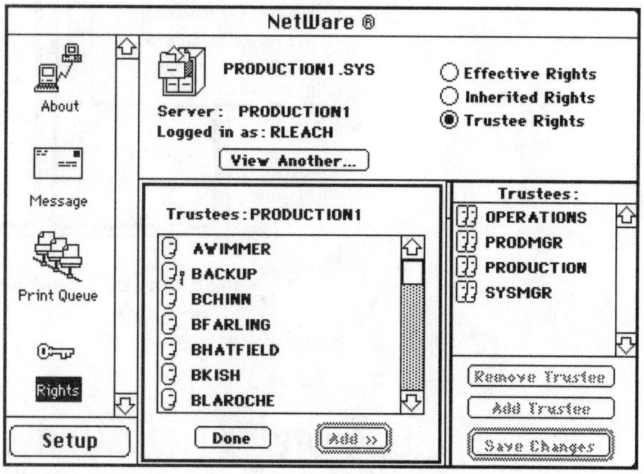

Figure 6.8 Viewing Groups and Trustees

The NetWare Control Center

The NetWare Control Center contains key information on users, groups, servers, volumes, folders, and files.

The heart of NetWare for the Macintosh user is the *NetWare Control Center.* Here network information concerning users, groups, servers, volumes, folders, and files may be viewed and modified.

The Network Control Center probably will appear as an icon on a file server. When you double-click on this icon, it begins to search for NetWare file servers. If you are not logged on to some of these file servers, you may do so by double-clicking on the file server icons as they appear.

The NetWare Control Center menus include the following: Server, Volumes, Folders/Files, User, and Groups. A sample screen appears in Figure 6.9.

Note that the Server window is divided into left and right panels. The left panel contains icons for each file server on the network, while the right panel contains icons that enable you to access appropriate information on users, groups, and volumes linked to that file server. You may access information on only one file server at a time.

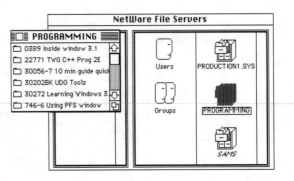

Figure 6.9   The NetWare Control Center

Printing Under NetWare for the Macintosh

On a mixed NetWare network—containing both IBM and Apple computers and printers—DOS machines can utilize both the Apple printers and their own non-Apple network printers. The Macintosh workstations, on the other hand, can print only to the Apple printers. One major limitation of AppleShare software is that it does not use a print spooler; instead, it sends files directly to its printers.

Novell developed its Macintosh version of NetWare so that Macintosh workstations can spool to an AppleTalk queue server that emulates an Apple printer. This queue server will then forward the files to a NetWare print queue for spooling and eventual printing.

The Chooser menu permits Macintosh users to see NetWare queues and the Apple printers attached to the network. Novell suggests that the supervisor create a separate print queue for each AppleTalk printer on the network.

There is one other major consideration when printing under NetWare. NetWare print services do not emulate printer control codes or page description languages. This means that application programs running under NetWare must supply these printer drivers.

TOPS on the Macintosh

Sitka's *TOPS* is one of the pioneers in Macintosh networking. Its TOPS/ Macintosh makes it possible to link Macintosh computers with PCs and Sun workstations. Unlike other networks described in this chapter, TOPS uses a peer-to-peer distributed approach; workstations share resources, in contrast to a centralized file server approach. TOPS runs on LocalTalk and EtherNet cabling systems.

When using LocalTalk cabling, TOPS generally runs on workstations daisy-chained together (with a maximum of 32 stations per daisy chain). A *TOPS FlashBox,* using FlashTalk, enables the network to transmit data three times faster than AppleTalk's 230 Kbs. A *TOPS Spool* program permits spooling to an Apple LaserWriter, while *TOPS NetPrint* enables a DOS workstation running a DOS application to print to an Apple ImageWriter II or LaserWriter. A *TOPS Translators* program serves as a data file format translator, translating PC file formats (such as WordStar, WordPerfect, and dBASE IV) into common Macintosh formats—and vice versa.

Publishing Resources

It is possible to share your files with others on the TOPS network by *publishing* a drive or folder containing your files. When you publish a drive or folder, it is called a *volume,* and its icon becomes black to denote its published status.

It is impossible to publish an individual file; to make a file available, place it in an otherwise-empty folder (or on a floppy disk) which is then published. Users who wish to make use of a published resource select the folder or disk by clicking on its icon and then clicking on the Mount button.

Some Considerations When Sharing Resources Under TOPS

When you share your Macintosh's resources with other workstations on a TOPS network, there are some important facts to keep in mind. It is far more efficient to organize your files into folders according to access. In other words, documents you do not wish to publish can be grouped together, while documents you wish to share (but only with password restrictions) can also be grouped together.

Another consideration when planning to share resources is the different nature of file names on different machines. While a Macintosh file, directory, or folder name can have up to 31 characters (including blank spaces), a DOS file is restricted to 8 characters with no blank spaces and a 3-character extension. UNIX file names can be up to 256 characters in length. Since names will be truncated when moving to another machine, it is important to select names carefully.

Printing Under TOPS

As mentioned earlier, TOPS offers a background print spooler called TOPS Spool. This utility generates a PostScript file as the file sent to the LaserWriter is redirected to a temporary disk file. Figure 6.10 illustrates a TOPS Spool screen.

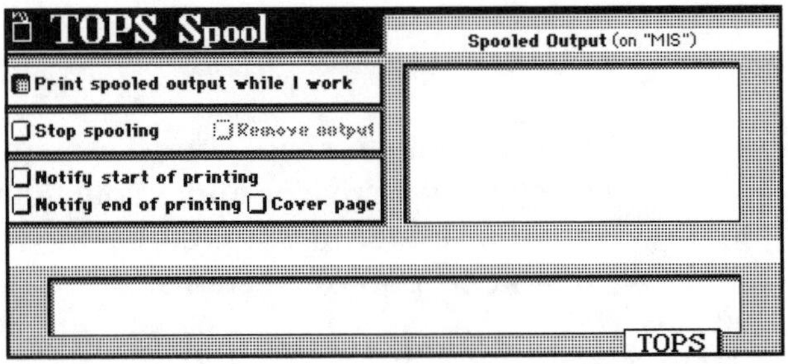

Figure 6.10 A TOPS Spool Screen

Translating Files with TOPS Translators

Earlier in this chapter, we indicated that TOPS has a utility program that makes it relatively easy to translate from one file format to another. Figure 6.11 displays the TOPS Translators screen.

Notice that you also set the direction of the file transfer. Another screen available with this utility indicates your preferences. You specify whether you want to be notified if there are file name conflicts, and whether you want to assign all file names or let the program assign them.

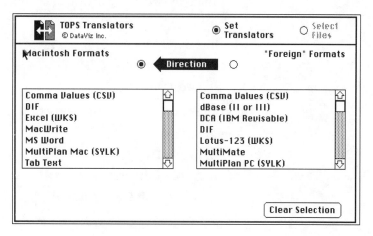

Figure 6.11   TOPS Translators Understand Both the Macintosh and the PC Worlds

What Have You Learned?

1. LocalTalk describes the physical network hardware Apple offers for its network.

2. AppleTalk describes the family of networking suites offered by Apple.

3. AppleShare is Apple's centralized file-server software.

4. NetWare uses a Service Protocol Gateway to translate AppleTalk commands into NetWare commands, and vice versa.

5. Apple's System 7 is a true multitasking operating system that enhances Apple network operation.

6. TOPS is a distributed network environment in which workstations share resources by "publishing" them.

7. TOPS makes it easy for Macintosh computers to communicate with Sun workstations, as well as with IBM PCs.

Quiz for Chapter 6

Apple's network hardware is known as

    a. CheapTalk.

    b. TinkerTalk.

    c. AppleTalk.

    d. LocalTalk.

2. Apple's major network protocol is called

    a. SpeakEasy.

    b. Apple Filing Protocol.

    c. Apple Universal Protocol.

    d. Macintosh OSI Protocol.

3. AppleTalk networks transmit at speeds of

    a. 1 Mbs.

    b. 4 Mbs.

    c. 230.4 Kbs.

    d. 188 feet/second.

4. AppleTalk provides link access protocol for all but one of the following:

    a. LocalTalk

    b. EtherNet

    c. Token Ring

    d. Xnet

5. AppleTalk networks are mapped into a series of

    a. zones.

    b. area codes.

    c. regional centers.

    d. AppleAreas.

6. Apple's LaserWriter requires the _____ protocol.
    a. Applesoft
    b. PostScript
    c. RS-232-C
    d. V.35

7. Security under AppleShare is at the _____ level.
    a. bit
    b. file
    c. folder
    d. document

8. Under Phase 2 of AppleTalk, it is possible to have up to _____ zones per network.
    a. 32
    b. 64
    c. 128
    d. 256

9. To translate AppleTalk system calls into NetWare commands, NetWare uses
    a. SBM.
    b. SPG.
    c. NETBIOS.
    d. SPM.

10. Under NetWare on the Macintosh, a 31-character Macintosh file name would be converted into a DOS file name of _____ characters with an extension.
    a. 5
    b. 8
    c. 15
    d. 31

11. Under NetWare, a gray folder is
    a. read-only.
    b. create-only.
    c. delete-only.
    d. unavailable for use.

12. Under NetWare, information concerning users, groups, servers, volumes, and folders is found in the
    a. Help file.
    b. NetWare Control Center.
    c. group file.
    d. information folder.

13. AppleShare 3.0 takes advantage of Apple's latest operating system, known as
    a. OS/2.
    b. System 7.
    c. AppleTalk.
    d. NetWare.

14. NetWare for the Macintosh running on NetWare 3.11 is actually a(n)
    a. VAP.
    b. VAD.
    c. NMN.
    d. NLM.

15. AppleShare Server software permits
    a. only one supervisor.
    b. multiple users with supervisory rights.
    c. no supervisor.
    d. remote supervision.

16. TOPS represents a
    a. distributed network.
    b. centralized network.
    c. centralized file server.
    d. centralized workstation.

17. To share a resource with another workstation, a TOPS workstation must first _____ it.

    a. publish

    b. mount

    c. copy

    d. delete

18. To increase LocalTalk speed under TOPS, use

    a. TOPSBURN.

    b. FLASHBURN.

    c. FlashTalk.

    d. Flasher.

19. To translate from file format to another under TOPS, use

    a. TOPS Translators.

    b. TOPS Convert.

    c. TOPS File.

    d. MAC-to-PC TOPS.

20. To spool a file for printing under TOPS, use

    a. Spool It.

    b. PrintSpooler.

    c. StorePrint.

    d. TOPS Spool.

7 | AT&T's Local Area Networks

About This Chapter

AT&T's STARLAN is a low-cost bus network that illustrates the company's *open architecture* philosophy. In this chapter we will take a close look at STARLAN's hardware and software, and explore why it might be an ideal solution for a small department—or a large company that is considering departmental networks. Because AT&T is committed to linking its DOS-based STARLAN with its UNIX-based minicomputers, we will look at what this connection can mean for a company. We will also examine how STARLAN links to AT&T's powerful Information Systems Network (ISN), and how ISN offers true office voice and data integration. Finally, we will look at how ISN supports the new Integrated Services Digital Network (ISDN) standards that will become more and more important in the near future.

STARLAN and STARLAN 10 Hardware

AT&T designed the STARLAN network to be as simple as possible. Up to 10 PC workstations can be linked together by installing a Network

Access Unit (NAU) in each workstation's expansion bus, and then using unshielded twisted-pair telephone wire to daisy-chain these units together. Each NAU has three telephone jacks. One unit's IN jack is connected to the OUT jack of another unit. The third jack is used for connecting an analog phone to a workstation. One workstation with a hard disk is designated as the file server; each workstation installs a copy of the STARLAN software. AT&T refers to workstations that utilize a file server as *clients*. Figure 7.1 shows how a small daisy-chained STARLAN network would look with an AT&T 6300 Plus used as a file server. The maximum distance permitted for a daisy-chained STARLAN network is 400 feet.

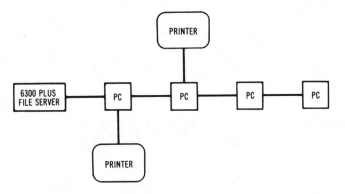

Figure 7.1   A Small STARLAN Network

The Network Access Unit (NAU)

Each network workstation requires a Network Access Unit (NAU) circuit card. STARLAN NAUs may transmit at 1 megabit per second (Mbs), while STARLAN 10 NAUs transmit at 10 Mbs. Both networks use CSMA/CD to avoid data collisions.

As we just pointed out, a *Network Access Unit (NAU)* is required in each workstation on the network. There are actually three different kinds of NAUs. STARLANs with PCs (or PC compatibles) as file servers require the PC NAU. IBM PS/2 microcomputers require an MC 100 NAU designed for this computer's microchannel bus. AT&T's own 3B2 minicomputers utilize a 3B2 NI card which is EtherNet-compatible. STARLAN NAUs transmit at 1 Mbs, while STARLAN 10 units can transmit at 10 Mbs. Each NAU comes with a 10-foot, twisted-pair, modular cable. Longer cables can be ordered from AT&T. The limitation on cord distance between any two network devices is 328 feet (100 meters).

In addition to the three telephone jacks we have already mentioned, each NAU also contains 8K or 32K of RAM, a network address

ROM, and a CSMA/CD controller. STARLAN is a baseband-technique *contention network* (workstations compete to use the bus to transmit their data), using a CSMA/CD approach to transmit data at 1 Mbs. The NAU uses a *shared memory system* which makes it appear that the memory resides in the host's main memory, even though it is physically found on the NAU itself. The CSMA/CD coprocessor accesses this memory, as do the computer's read/write operations.

Network Hub Units (NHUs)

A Network Hub Unit (NHU) can link 11 workstations directly together in a star topology, or can be used as a master unit (with 11 secondary NHUs) to create a two-tier network with up to 1,210 units.

A *Network Hub Unit (NHU)* is used to expand a STARLAN network beyond 10 workstations; it enables a network supervisor to link up to 11 directly connected workstations, up to 800 feet from the NHU, in a star topology. It also makes it possible to use one NHU as a master unit, and link up to 11 secondary NHUs (each with a star topology) — creating what is known as a *two-tier star.* This arrangement can support up to 100 active workstations and as many as 1,210 physical connections.

The NHU also contains one port to connect existing coax-based EtherNet networks. 3B2 NIs installed in 3B computers can also be attached to the NHU via the AUI.

An NHU can be mounted in a telephone wiring closet, or in the same room as the workstations. The NHU has one port labeled OUT, used to connect it to another NHU or to a *network repeater unit (NRU).* A connector on the NHU connects to a wall-mounted transformer that provides low-voltage AC.

The NHU is also responsible for amplifying and retiming network signals before transmitting them, detecting and isolating problems caused by a faulty device or connection, and detecting the presence of network traffic and collisions (indicating these with its LEDs). Each NHU must be within 10 feet of a commercial power outlet that is not switch-controlled. Figure 7.2 shows how an NHU creates a star topology.

An important network design consideration is that NAUs and NHUs are not interchangeable between STARLAN and STARLAN 10. It is possible, though, to bridge the two networks (a subject that will be discussed later in this chapter).

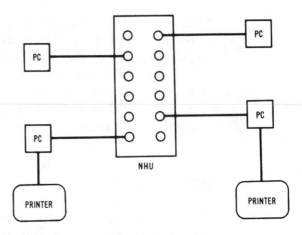

Figure 7.2   NHU Linking PCs Together

Media

It is possible to use the new IEEE 10BaseT standard—two pairs of unshielded twisted-pair wire—for STARLAN. STARLAN 10 wiring is also consistent with AT&T's Premises Distribution System 62.5125-micron optical fiber cabling. An AUI Adapter is available that provides connections to EtherNet boards. As mentioned previously, the AUI port on the NHU supports a variety of connections, including standard thick coax, thin coax, fiber optic, and broadband coax cable.

File Servers

Workstations can access applications and share resources from either a DOS-based server or a UNIX System V-based server. A small group of DOS workstations can be daisy-chained together, sharing resources without the need for a dedicated server. AT&T's PC6386 WGS is a PC workstation that can run UNIX and file-server software, but AT&T also recommends its 3B2 family of minicomputers for this function. These larger computers, when configured with SCSI Host Adapters, permit up to 15.9 gigabytes of disk storage.

AT&T offers file-server software; a 1-Mbs STARLAN network can use the company's own proprietary software, which includes a 3B2

DOS Server Program and a PC6300 Network Program. AT&T also offers a 386 Server Program, a DOS Server Program, and a 3B2 Server Program; these run under OSI protocols. The STARLAN 10 network must use a special version (3.1) of these programs.

With regard to the number of simultaneous clients possible on a network, AT&T supplies recommended maximum numbers—as well as the absolute maximum number. Since AT&T's recommendations are designed to keep the network running optimally, we'll use these values.

While a 6386 WGS has a recommended simultaneous client maximum of 32 under DOS, this number increases to 64 under UNIX—illustrating the advantages of a true multiuser, multitasking operating system. The 3B2 minicomputer can support 50 simultaneous users. While the smaller workstations can only support 3 printers (2 parallel and one serial) attached to the file server, the 3B2 minicomputers can support up to 11 parallel printers and 45 to 88 serial printers.

STARLAN Software

STARLAN's network software is consistent with the OSI specifications discussed in Chapter 2. Figure 7.3 indicates the network's different protocol layers.

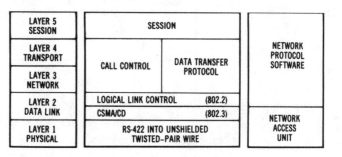

Figure 7.3   STARLAN Protocol Layers (Courtesy of AT&T)

- The *Physical layer* is concerned primarily with providing transmission on a baseband network. The medium used is 24-gauge building telephone wiring (consisting of two un-shielded twisted pairs), dedicated to STARLAN.

- The *Data Link layer* regulates this contention network, using CSMA/CD techniques consistent with IEEE 802.3 standards. Notice that the logical link control is consistent with IEEE 802.2 standards, and uses the *LLC Type-1 connectionless protocol* (which governs the rules under which logical connections are made).

- The *Network* and *Transport layers* create point-to-point connections between two network endpoints, and include flow control, call administration, and error handling.

- Finally, the *Session layer* uses MS-DOS protocols to establish sessions with application programs. It has a set of additional commands to enable it to establish sessions with UNIX-based computers running under STARLAN.

STARLAN Packet Structure

As pointed out in our earlier discussion of the OSI standards, the *packet* for one network layer becomes part of the *information field* of the next lower layer. The *MAC sublayer* of STARLAN follows the IEEE 802.3 standards, and is shown in Figure 7.4.

PREAMBLE	SFD	ADDRESS	LENGTH	LLC DATA	PAD	FCS

Figure 7.4   The MAC Frame

The MAC frame begins with a *Preamble* used to synchronize receiver and transmitter. The *Start of Frame Delimiter (SFD)* is responsible for letting the hardware know when the synchronization is over and the message begins. The *Address* part consists of both a destination address and a source address. The *Length* field indicates the number of octets in the LLC data portion of the packet. *User data* is found in the next field, the LLC Data area. The final two packet portions are the *Packet Address Destination (PAD)* and *Frame Check Sequence (FCS)*. The PAD is used to pad any packets that fall below the acceptable minimum of 64 octets of information. Finally, the FCS detects errors so that the MAC layer can discard defective packets.

Using STARLAN

STARLAN's network software is very similar to IBM's PC Network Program, in that both programs are designed to be as easy as possible for beginners to use. Both DOS-based programs offer experienced network users the opportunity to use DOS commands to access the network, and even let users create DOS batch files to customize operations. Both programs also offer beginners the opportunity to perform virtually all major network functions through the use of menus.

All STARLAN commands can be classified under three categories: Administration Services, File Sharing Services, and Printer Sharing Services. These commands can be entered four different ways: typing a command string, using command prompts, responding to network prompts, and using menus.

All STARLAN commands are classified under *Administration Services, File Sharing Services,* or *Printer Sharing Services.* The Login and Logout commands are found under Administration (AD)—along with commands to modify passwords, view statistics, and add/delete users. To log on under STARLAN, a user simply types a *command string,* providing the type of command (AD), the actual command, a DOS path, and a password:

```
LOGIN AD servername \username /pass=password
```

To give several consecutive commands for the same command service, the user can use *command prompts* to avoid typing the command service repeatedly. Typing the command service and pressing Enter yields the prompt (AD, FS, or PS) from which the user can enter the commands. For instance, if the user wants to log in and then get help on how to use the ADDUSER command, he or she would type the following:

```
AD>login servername \user/pass=password help adduser
```

Rather than using command prompts, the user can choose to respond to STARLAN's prompts by merely typing a command prefix and the command name and then pressing Enter. The user will then be prompted by STARLAN to supply the file server name, the username, and a password if needed. By using these *network prompts,* a new user can enjoy the faster network operation (rather than going through several menus), without needing to memorize all the network command structure.

The fourth way to enter commands is to use the *STARLAN menus.* These menus can be accessed by typing the command MENUS. Figure 7.5 shows what the STARLAN Main menu displays.

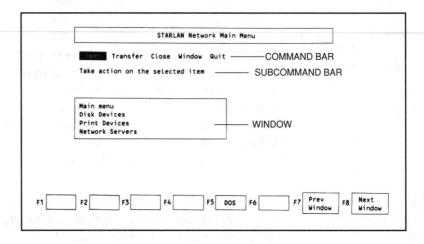

Figure 7.5 The STARLAN Main Menu

Notice that there is a *Command Bar* displaying the commands available from this menu (Open, Transfer, Close, Window, Quit). The line below this is known as the *Subcommand Bar.* It contains subcommands or command descriptions. A *window* indicates the items to be selected. The last line contains the *screen label keys,* which indicate which function key to press for a particular command. Notice that only three function keys (F5, F7, and F8) are active on this Main menu. The commands on the Command Bar (and the items in the window) can be accessed by using the arrow keys. Commands can also be entered by typing the first letter of the command (as seen in the Command Bar), followed by pressing Enter. To open a highlighted file, for example, a user need only type o and then press Enter.

File Sharing

Each user has his own personal home directory, which may be protected with a password.

Each user has his own personal *home directory* (located on the file server), which may be protected with a password. Upon logging on to STARLAN, a user needs to establish a link between his workstation and his home directory. Note that a user can only log on to one file server at a time. STARLAN's FS LINK command establishes this connection.

STARLAN offers the ability to share files among multiple users.

Since one of the major advantages of a network is the ability to share files, STARLAN offers a number of options in this area. It is possible to copy files from your home directory to another user's directory. It is also possible to place a copy of a file you wish to share in another subdirectory. To share files, the subdirectory must be shared with other users; this is done by using the FS SHARE command. In most cases you will eliminate a password, or use a password different from your own personal password.

The final option for sharing information is to share your home directory. The major disadvantage of sharing files in your own personal home directory is that other users will have to know your password in order to link their directories with yours, thus you will lose your security.

It is possible to establish various levels of access to files on a file server. The four levels of shared file access under STARLAN are *read, write, create,* and *exclusive.* The *exclusive* option prevents two users from trying simultaneously to update a file (which would wipe out valuable information). The network administrator normally establishes the access level. These options are outlined in Table 7.1.

Table 7.1. Levels of STARLAN Shared Access

Key	Access	Meaning
R	Read	Files in a shared directory can be read.
W	Write	Files in a shared directory can be written to.
C	Create	Files can be created in a shared directory.
E	Exclusive	Only one user at a time can access a shared file.

After placing material in a directory or subdirectory so it can be shared, the user must provide a *sharename* and *pathway.* Let's assume that Georgia has created a subdirectory called REGMTG in her home directory. This material contains the budget she is developing for a regional meeting. While Georgia wants to share this information with others in her group, she wants to keep her working copy from being changed. The solution is to use the DOS command MKDIR (make directory) to create a subdirectory called REGPROJT:

```
MKDIR E: \REGPROJT
```

The next step is to copy the contents of the subdirectory REGMTG over to this new subdirectory, using the DOS COPY command:

```
COPY C: REGMTG D: \REGPROJT
FS SHARE \REGPROJT
```

STARLAN will want to know a sharename—a name by which users will access this shared subdirectory. Georgia decides on BUDGET.

```
Sharename? BUDGET
SERVER1\GEORGIA\REGMTG shared as GEORGIA\BUDGET
```

At the moment, anyone on the STARLAN network can share this file. If Georgia wants to limit access, she could use the FS MOD command and create a password:

```
FS MOD BUDGET/pass=password
SERVER1\GEORGIA\BUDGET modified
```

It is always possible to see a list of shared directories on a network by using the FS DIR command:

```
FS DIR
Object list for \SERVER1\*...
GEORGIA C:\USER/HOME 0 links
TAX C: \TAX/RWC 0 links
```

Bridging STARLAN and STARLAN 10 Networks

AT&T offers a standalone desk bridge unit in two different configurations. The 1:10 bridge connects a STARLAN network to a STARLAN 10 network, while the 10:10 bridge can link two STARLAN 10 networks (or link a STARLAN 10 and an EtherNet network).

A bridge unit contains a motherboard and two LAN circuit boards.

A *bridge unit* contains a motherboard and two LAN circuit boards. The 10:10 bridge contains two AUI ports, while the 1:10 bridge contains one AUI port (for connection to a STARLAN 10 network) and one modular jack (for connection to an NHU). The bridge is IEEE 802.3- and EtherNet-compatible. It can link a range of media—including twisted-pair, 10BASE5 (thick coax), and 10 BASE2 (thin coax). It also supports fiber-optic MAU connections.

There are some restrictions to AT&T's bridges. Only two networks can be bridged, and they cannot be bridged to a third network. The maximum cable length between hub unit and bridge is approximately 750 feet.

STARLAN Network Management

The *STARLAN Network Manager (SNM)* is AT&T's management software designed to handle networks with more than 100 nodes. The program can be run from a host computer, from an RS-232-C terminal, or from a PC with terminal emulation. Release 1.0 runs on the 3B2 minicomputer or the 6386 WGS, and manages the 1-Mbs STARLAN network. Release 2.0 runs on a 6386 WGS, and can manage both the 1-Mbs and 10-Mbs versions of STARLAN.

SNM uses an INFORMIX-based, on-line database called the *Network Configuration Database (NCD)*. This database can be configured to include such information as the building location of each node, as well as moves and changes.

The SNM polls nodes to determine their status and provides a network map. The program provides on-line, real-time reporting of any network errors, as well as traffic data (in bytes per second, or as a percentage of media capacity utilized). The SNM also can monitor network traffic in terms of packets per second, and provide error statistics (including the number of collisions and retransmissions).

Electronic Mail on an AT&T LAN

PMX/STARMail is the LAN equivalent of AT&T's Mail Private Message Exchange software. In addition to being able to link STARLAN and STARLAN 10 networks, the mail system can link to public AT&T mail service (where messages can be delivered by the U.S. Postal Service, Airborne Express, and Telex, as well as electronically).

The mail service is X.400-compatible, a critical consideration for companies considering future OSI compatibility. AT&T's Mail Service also contains gateways to IBM's DISOSS and PROFS—as well as HP, Wang, and DEC Office Systems (through AT&T's Mail Exchange).

PMX/STARMail is a graphics-oriented program that contains a DESK where messages are prepared, an IN BOX that holds incoming mail, an OUT BOX used for outgoing messages, and a WASTEBASKET for messages to be deleted. The program contains a message editor, as well as the ability to attach word processing documents or spreadsheets to mail. What makes this particular mail program so unusual is that it reflects AT&T's ability to make communications between UNIX and DOS transparent to the end user.

STARLAN and Information Systems Network (ISN)

At first glance, STARLAN appears to be an effective network for a department or small business, but of limited value to a larger company. AT&T provides a growth path for companies that need more sophisticated network functions. *Information Systems Network (ISN)* is a high-speed network capable of providing integrated voice and data transmission—as well as providing interfaces to PBXs, IBM mainframes, EtherNet LANs, and its own STARLAN networks. Figure 7.6 shows the ways that ISN can integrate communications for a large company.

The STARLAN Interface Module (SIM) connects STARLAN networks, increasing the effective distance available.

AT&T offers a *STARLAN Interface Module (SIM)* to connect STARLAN networks via its ISN. This option increases the effective distance for a STARLAN to several thousand feet. Each SIM has two jacks that can be used to connect workstations on a STARLAN network, or to an NEU located on an ISN concentrator or packet controller.

The SIMs come in two versions. The B version provides a bridge between multiple STARLAN networks through ISN; the C version provides a connection between STARLAN nodes and RS-232 devices that are not on the STARLAN network but are on ISN. So an AT&T DOS workstation on a STARLAN network (for example) could access a 3B2 computer on ISN.

The heart of ISN is a *packet controller* that acts as switch and management center. Concentrators collect data from host computers, STARLANs, and other devices; they pass this data to the packet controller through multiplexed channels, each composed of a pair of optical fibers. ISN breaks down messages to very short packets (18 envelopes of 10 bits of data each), and interleaves the packets into a sequence of time slots on the transmission bus.

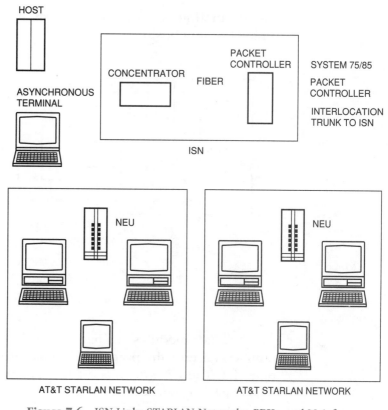

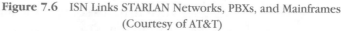

Figure 7.6 ISN Links STARLAN Networks, PBXs, and Mainframes
(Courtesy of AT&T)

The transmission across this short bus is so fast that ISN maintains (in effect) virtual circuits or direct links between communicating devices with virtual circuits—more than enough for most large businesses.

The ISN packet controller contains three buses: the *transmit bus,* which carries packets from sending modules to the switch; the *receiving bus,* which carries packets away from the switch to device interface modules; and the *contention bus,* which determines the order of access to the transmit bus. (See Figure 7.7.)

As Figure 7.7 illustrates, under ISN all modules having data packets ready to send compete with each other for access to a time slot on the transmit bus. Each module transmits its own *contention code* to the contention bus, one bit at a time. If the module recognizes that another module has a higher contention code, it ceases transmitting. The winning module accesses the next time slot available for data packets on the transmit bus.

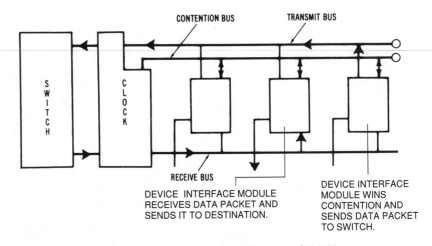

Figure 7.7   ISN Bus Design (Courtesy of AT&T)

The data modules that have lost this round have their contention numbers raised at this point, and begin competing for the next available time slot. The ISN switch is capable of a maximum switching rate of 48,000 packets per second.

Figure 7.8 illustrates some of the interfaces available through ISN. In addition to linking STARLAN networks, ISN users can (with the proper protocol) interface directly with asynchronous hosts or IBM 3270 terminals—eliminating the need for costly cluster controllers.

Users can establish two sessions per terminal, and switch between applications. Each protocol converter on the network contains seven asynchronous ports and one synchronous port. ISN supports Type A coaxial cable at 2.358 Mbs, as well as IBM 3278/9 and 3178/9 terminals.

A company with several departments might find it cost-effective to tie together several departmental STARLAN networks, and use ISN to enable all networks to communicate with the company's distant IBM mainframes. ISN supports both a BSC and an SNA/SDLC interface. The synchronous traffic can share T1 facilities with an AT&T PBX, thus eliminating expensive long-distance modems.

ISN also offers an EtherNet bridge consistent with IEEE 802.3 baseband network standards. Companies with EtherNet networks that

Companies with EtherNet networks that are too far apart to communicate though direct cabling can communicate through ISN.

are too far apart to communicate though direct cabling can communicate through ISN. The ISN EtherNet bridge is a 10-Mbs CSMA/CD module that terminates the Physical and Data Link layers of the OSI model. It supports *Transmission Control Protocol/Internet Protocol (TCP/IP)*, as well as *Xerox Network System (XNS)* devices.

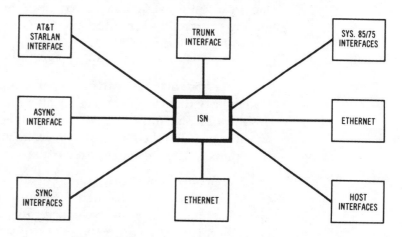

Figure 7.8   ISN Interfaces (Courtesy of AT&T)

ISN and Network Management

The star topology provides excellent diagnostic reports and management tools.

ISN is a star topology just like STARLAN. As we saw earlier, star-architecture networks usually provide excellent diagnostic reports and management tools. Because of ISN's star topology, it is able to provide detailed traffic and performance statistics. It also makes adding new users easy; the network supervisor simply assigns a new device to an unused port and gives it an address.

The negative side of star topology networks has always been the danger that the entire network will collapse with the collapse of the central processor. ISN provides a measure of protection by utilizing nonvolatile memory for its storage of configuration and fault data. In the event of a power failure, it utilizes automatic system recovery when power is restored. It also monitors the functioning of various modules, including the control processor, and reports faulty modules (with an indication of the type of module, a description of the faults, and the time they occurred).

AT&T's StarGroup

AT&T's *StarGroup* is its UNIX-based network operating system based on Microsoft's LAN Manager. It supports file service for DOS, OS/2, Macintosh, and UNIX client workstations, and also supports Microsoft Windows' graphic user interface. StarGroup supports a number of protocols—including OSI, AppleTalk, TCP/IP, and IBM's NetBEUI. Eventually it should also support NetWare's IPX protocol.

A network manager can create, on a StarGroup file server, a UNIX subdirectory that can be shared by all supported client workstations. This means a Macintosh user (for example) can access this data-shared data area by using the NET USE command and indicating a drive letter that points to the particular directory structure.

StarGroup handles the different file naming conventions used with different operating systems. Because DOS users are limited to eight characters and a three-character extension for file names, they must first run the *uren utility program* to translate Macintosh and UNIX file names (which can be much longer and, in the Macintosh case, can include spaces).

Sharing Printers with StarGroup

StarGroup supports LocalTalk-attached Apple LaserWriters, serial or parallel printers attached to DOS workstations, and remote UNIX printers. All print queues created under StarGroup are, in reality, UNIX print queues. Even though these print queues are created from a Macintosh workstation, they can be controlled from the UNIX console, as well as from DOS and OS/2 workstations.

StarGroup's File Server

The *StarServer S* file server is based on an Intel 33-MHz 80486 microprocessor; it features 128K of external RAM cache, plus the microprocessor's 8K of internal RAM cache. The StarServer S comes with 4M of RAM, expandable to 64M. Its EISA motherboard can support 10 EISA or ISA circuit cards.

A StarGroup file server can process DOS tasks by using the UNIX Simul-Task program in conjunction with the StarGroup Simul-Task Client Interface Program. A network manager can create a program running on a DOS virtual machine that will, on a scheduled basis, execute a DOS batch file to perform tasks on the file server — or on any other workstation.

ISDN and AT&T's Voice/Data Integration

ISDN standards define a digital interface that is divided into B and D channels.

In Chapter 3 we examined *Integrated Services Digital Network (ISDN)* architecture and discussed how these standards eventually would result in an office-automation revolution. ISDN standards define a digital interface that is divided into B and D channels. *B channels* are capable of carrying voice, data, and video signals, while *D channels* carry signaling and control information to manage the network. Furthermore, ISDN postulated two types of interface: the *Basic-Rate Interface (BRI)* and the *Primary-Rate Interface (PRI)*. Although BRI is designed for small-capacity devices (such as terminals) and PRI is designed for large-capacity devices (such as PBXs), both interfaces carry one D channel and several B channels. The B channels transmit at 64 Kbs each, for both BRI and PRI; the D channels transmit at 16 Kbs for BRI, and 64 Kbs for PRI.

Imagine an office with a STARLAN network and an AT&T System 75 PBX phone system, using AT&T's ISN. Let's assume that a network user needs to send a voice message—accompanied by a video display and several data files—to another user. Using ISDN standards on AT&T's ISN, the user's *premises equipment* (equipment that is at that site—in this case, the PBX and data terminal) transmits signals to establish communications with the network. Once the link is established, the video, voice, and data are sent in digital form into the network, using its B channels. The network, in turn, sends this information to the addressee.

Figure 7.9 illustrates AT&T's approach to integrating its services while following ISDN guidelines. In this *premises-switched* ISDN architecture, the switch takes place at the user's location and not at the telephone company's central office.

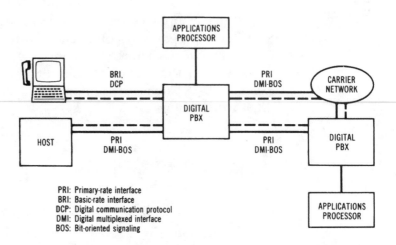

Figure 7.9 AT&T Premises-Switched ISDN Architecture (Courtesy of AT&T)

An example of ISDN in action—which AT&T likes to cite as an illustration of what we can expect in the future—is its E911 service. When a customer calls the emergency 911 number, the call is routed to an operator who sees the caller's telephone number and address appear automatically on the console screen. A computer has searched a very large database, recovered the key customer information, and transmitted it to the operator's screen—while simultaneously routing the voice signal there. In the future, offices will be able to link their networks with several other kinds of networks, in a manner transparent to the network user. Figure 7.10 summarizes how ISDN integrates these networks into a coherent system.

Another example of how AT&T is integrating voice and data applications in the modern office is its use of *Unified Messaging Systems (UMS)*. A company with UMS probably also has a PBX system (such as AT&T's System 75), and probably has AT&T's AUDIX voice-mail service as well. Managers in this company might use *Office Telesystem (OTS)* to link with the UMS.

Employees in this office can choose whether to read their messages on their terminals or hear them spoken. They can reply by voice, or by typing the replies at the keyboard. Let's assume an employee calls in to retrieve his or her phone messages. Using such AT&T supplementary products as Mailtalk or Speak-To-Me, the employee can hear the messages spoken by a computer.

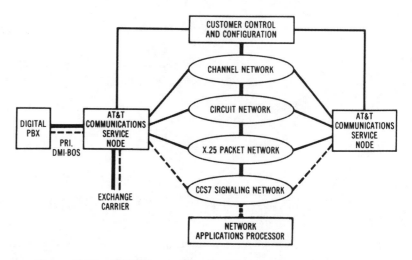

Figure 7.10   AT&T Communications Interexchange Carrier ISDN
Architecture (Courtesy of AT&T)

The Office Telesystem (OTS) uses the same structure as UMS (so that it can receive UMS messages), but it adds a number of handy management functions. OTS is available for up to a hundred users. It can provide an AT&T DOS-based workstation user (or a 3B2 UNIX-based minicomputer user) with an electronic calendar (which includes resource scheduling). It can also handle telephone management by providing multiple directories, speed dialing, and the option of writing telephone memos. OTS also offers a text processor and access to external databases. AT&T hopes to expand services such as these to provide a truly integrated office, where voice and data messages are exchanged effortlessly.

AT&T Connectivity and Other International Standards

AT&T provides LAN interfaces for several international standards.

While ISDN is a standard waiting to be implemented, AT&T has chosen to support several other international standards by providing LAN interfaces.

- A *TCP/IP UNIX System Interface* consists of hardware and software that permits an AT&T 6386 WGS to access TCP/IP networks.

- The *TCP/IP WIN/3B* software provides TCP/IP links for a 3B minicomputer.
- The *AT&T UNIX System V NFS* software enables AT&T users to access computers using this protocol—especially Sun Engineering workstations.
- Finally, AT&T offers an *X.25 Packet Assembler/Disassembler (PAD)* with software for its 6386 WGS and 3B2 computers.

What Have You Learned?

1. A STARLAN network can daisy-chain up to 10 workstations together, with one node serving as the file server.
2. STARLAN is a network following the CSMA/CD protocol. It transmits data at 1 Mbs, while STARLAN 10 transmits at 10 Mbs.
3. STARLAN software contains three types of commands: Administration Services, File Sharing Services, and Printer Sharing Services.
4. STARLAN network security consists of a LOGIN password, password requirements for using a directory or subdirectory, and data encryption.
5. Several STARLAN networks can be connected together using Information Systems Network (ISN) and the STARLAN Interface Module (SIM).
6. The ISN packet controller utilizes a Transmit Bus, a Receiving Bus, and a Contention Bus.
7. Under ISDN guidelines, a company can transmit voice, data, and video signals simultaneously.

Quiz for Chapter 7

1. STARLAN permits up to 10 workstations to be daisy-chained together in what kind of network architecture?

   a. Star

   b. Bus

   c. Ring

   d. Token Ring

2. The expansion bus of each STARLAN workstation must contain

   a. at least 640K.

   b. a Network Hub Unit (NHU).

   c. a Network Access Unit (NAU).

   d. a Network Interface Unit (NIU).

3. STARLAN follows the IEEE 802.3 guidelines for avoiding data collisions using

   a. CSMA/CD.

   b. packets.

   c. tokens.

   d. one-way communications.

4. To connect different offices within the same building, a STARLAN would use

   a. coaxial cable.

   b. a wiring closet.

   c. Network Interface Units (NIUs).

   d. an analog phone signal.

5. A 1:10 bridge links

   a. a STARLAN and a STARLAN 10 network.

   b. 2 STARLAN networks.

   c. 2 STARLAN 10 networks.

   d. 2 EtherNet networks.

6. Under STARLAN, which of the following can be used as file servers?

    a. AT&T 6386 WGS

    b. AT&T 6300, 6300 Plus, and IBM compatibles

    c. AT&T 3B2

    d. all of the above

7. STARLAN will only work with which version of DOS?

    a. DOS 2.1

    b. DOS 3.0

    c. DOS 3.1 and above

    d. DOS 2.2

8. To connect more than 10 workstations in a STARLAN network, it is necessary to use a

    a. Network Cable Connection (NCC).

    b. Network Interface Unit (NIU).

    c. Network Repeater Unit (NRU).

    d. Network Hub Unit (NHU).

9. More than 100 workstations can be connected in a STARLAN network by using a Network Hub Unit connected to

    a. other Network Hub Units (NHUs).

    b. 10 daisy-chained workstations.

    c. Network Repeater Units (NRUs).

    d. Network Interface Units (NIUs).

10. The practical limit when daisy-chaining workstations together under STARLAN is

    a. 200 feet.

    b. 400 feet.

    c. 600 feet.

    d. 800 feet.

11. Using a Network Hub Unit, a STARLAN network can extend a maximum of

    a. 400 feet.

    b. 800 feet.

    c. 1,000 feet.

    d. 1,200 feet.

12. STARLAN workstations are connected using

    a. two pairs of unshielded, twisted-pair, 24-gauge telephone wire.

    b. coaxial cable.

    c. fiber optic.

    d. data-grade cable.

13. Under STARLAN, a user may log in to

    a. only one file server at a time.

    b. only two file servers at a time.

    c. only three file servers at a time.

    d. an unlimited number of file servers.

14. To protect files from being destroyed by two people trying simultaneously to write to them, STARLAN lets shared files be

    a. write-only.

    b. read-only.

    c. create.

    d. exclusive.

15. The electronic mail program that works on STARLAN is known as

    a. Mail.

    b. Electronic Messenger.

    c. PMX/STARMail.

    d. Postman.

16. Two STARLAN networks can be connected together through ISN by using

    a. coaxial cable.

    b. STARLAN Interface Module (SIM).

    c. ISN Interface.

    d. broadband cabling.

17. Under ISDN, control signals are transmitted using
    a. the one D channel.
    b. any one of the several B channels.
    c. a special C channel for control.
    d. a token-passing protocol.

18. For limited devices, ISDN has established
    a. BRI.
    b. PRI.
    c. DRIP.
    d. SIP.

19. For large devices such as PBXs, ISDN has established
    a. BRI.
    b. PRI.
    c. DRIP.
    d. SIP.

20. The heart of ISN is a(n)
    a. microprocessor.
    b. packet controller.
    c. analog switch.
    d. cardiac coil.

8 | Other Major LANs: ARCnet, 10Net, Vines, and LANtastic

About This Chapter

In this chapter, we will examine four LANs that have captured significant amounts of market share because of the valuable features they offer.

- *ARCnet* is a proven technology that illustrates how a token bus works. It provides a hardware platform for virtually all the major local area network operating systems. While it is one of the oldest LAN products still on the market, a new 20-Mbs version illustrates that ARCnet may be a major player in the LAN market for the foreseeable future.

- *10Net* offers several security features that make it a major government contractor.

- *Vines* may offer a preview of the next stage of network connectivity. Its transparent bridges and global directory (StreetTalk) make it the leader in internetwork connectivity.

- Finally, *LANtastic* has captured a major share of the peer-to-peer network market with a product that proves that a small network does not have to sacrifice functionality.

ARCnet

Reliable and inexpensive, ARCnet uses a media access approach that is non-IEEE standard. It serves as an effective hardware platform for a wide range of network operating systems including NetWare and PC LAN Program.

Attached Resource Computer Network (ARCnet) was developed in 1977 by Datapoint. Today it is available from a number of vendors, including Standard Microsystems, Acer Technologies, Earth Computers, and Thomas-Conrad. ARCnet provides inexpensive, very reliable network hardware that supports a wide range of network operating systems (including NetWare). In fact, the ARCnet Trade Association (ATA) has standardized on Performance Technology's NetBIOS, so that ARCnet users can run virtually any NetBIOS-compatible network operating system on ARCnet, including the IBM PC LAN Program. Standard Microsystems even offers Microsoft's OS/2 LAN Manager software for ARCnet.

What makes ARCnet particularly interesting is that while it has existed outside the IEEE 802 body of standards, its vendors have made a major effort to make it a de facto industry standard; for the most part—because of its low cost, flexibility, and reliability—they have succeeded. While standard ARCnet transmits at 2.5 megabits per second (Mbs), a new version can transmit at 20 Mbs.

Topology

ARCnet offers bus, star, and distributed star topologies, utilizing thin coaxial cable, twisted-pair wire, or optic-fiber cable. This very flexible network permits the intermixing of all these topologies and media.

The star is the most common ARCnet topology. Up to eight workstations can be connected to a central hub, with a 2,000-foot maximum cable length between workstations. A passive hub can be used if distances do not exceed 100 feet. Active hubs can be joined together via an interface on the back of the hub, or through one of the eight ports. In total, the network can stretch up to four miles.

Because of the number of ARCnet vendors, the user will find a wide range of product configurations available. Active hubs, for example, can be purchased with anywhere from four to 32 ports.

A bus configuration that utilizes coaxial cabling can contain up to eight workstations. If a company's computing needs grow, this bus can be linked to a star-configured ARCnet network. A repeater called an

Active Link can expand a coax bus network (by linking two bus cables) or a star network (by increasing point-to-point distances). Active Links can be purchased with various combinations of connectors; twisted-pair, coax, and optic-fiber segments can all be linked into one ARCnet network. Figure 8.1 illustrates a star configuration linked to a coax bus network under ARCnet.

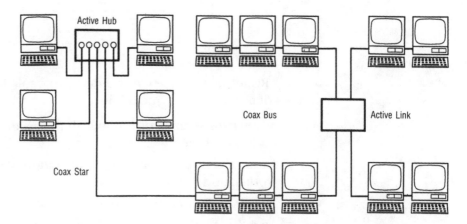

Figure 8.1   Star Configuration Linked to Coax Bus Under ARCnet

At one time limited to RG-62 A/U thin coaxial cabling, today's ARCnet is popular in part because it is also able to use existing unshielded twisted-pair wire, as well as IBM types 6, 8, and 9. Its star configuration makes it easy for a network supervisor to diagnose cabling problems, since a cabling problem is localized to a particular hub-to-node link, and reflected on most ARCnet cards by an LED.

ARCnet's Access Method

ARCnet uses a token bus protocol that is a logical ring but a physical star.

ARCnet uses a *token bus* protocol that considers the network to be a logical ring. The permission to transmit a token is passed in a logical ring, according to the workstation's network interface card address (which must be set between 1 and 255, using an eight-position DIP switch). Each network interface card knows its own address, as well as the address of the workstation to which it will pass the token. The highest-addressed node closes the "ring" by passing the token to the lowest-addressed node. Figure 8.2 illustrates how this process works.

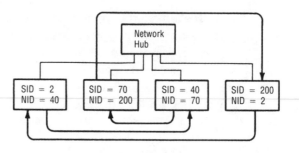

Figure 8.2 ARCnet's Access Method

ARCnet is a *character-oriented* protocol that has five different types of frame formats, including:

- An *Invitation to Transmit,* which passes the token from one node to another.
- A *Free Buffer Enquiry (FBE),* which inquires whether the next workstation can accept a data packet.
- The *Data Packet* itself (up to 507 bytes).
- An *Acknowledgement (ACK),* indicating a packet has been received correctly.
- A *Negative Acknowledgement (NAK),* used to decline an FBE.

An *Alert Burst* of six ones identifies the ARCnet data packet; the other parts follow sequentially. Figure 8.3 illustrates the ARCnet packet format.

ALERT BURST	SOH	SID	DID	DID	COUNT	DATA	CRC	CRC

Figure 8.3 ARCnet's Packet Format

Following the Alert Burst is the *Start of Header (SOH),* which comprises one byte. The *Source Node ID (SID)*—which identifies the node sending the packet—is also one byte, though the packet's recipient is specified by a two-byte *Destination Node ID (DID).* A one- or two-byte *Count* indicates the size of the data field, and it is followed by the *Error Check Characters (CRC);* these last two bytes play a role in where the token goes next.

When node 100 receives the token, for example, it might need to send a packet to node 222. It would first send an FBE to node 222, to confirm its ability to receive a message. When it received an ACK as a response, it would transmit its packet. Upon receipt of the packet, node 222 would respond by verifying the error-checking information (CRC) and replying with an ACK.

If node 222 is silent, node 100 knows there must have been an error in transmission. When node 100 does receive an ACK, it can issue an FBE to the next node to use the token, node 101.

20-Mbs ARCnet

The new 20-Mbs ARCnet adheres to IEEE standards for packet addressing and logical link control.

Datapoint Corporation has developed a 20-Mbs product known as *ARCnetplus,* which remains backward-compatible with existing cable, and with 2.5-Mbs ARCnet. It permits data packet sizes up to 4,224 bytes (versus the traditional limitation of 508 bytes). It is capable of addressing up to 2,047 nodes (versus the historical limitation of 255 nodes).

Perhaps even more important, this new version supports IEEE 802 packet addressing, logical link control, and internet protocol addressing. Chip sets are being built by Standard Microsystems Corporation and NCR's microelectronic products division.

DCA's 10Net and 10Net Plus LANs

10Net products have become a major alternative for companies looking for inexpensive LAN hardware and software that still offers a number of communication and security features.

The 10Net family of LANs has developed over the past few years, until today it offers a wide variety of hardware and software options. Flexible, inexpensive hardware runs software which has features not found on far more expensive network operating systems. For companies that need effective LAN communication links and security, 10Net is assuming an increasingly important role as an inexpensive alternative to NetWare and PC LAN Program.

10Net Configurations and Topologies

A number of different configurations are possible with 10Net. Its network interface cards and software can be combined to form a 1-Mbs bus network topology, or (using the STARLAN approach) a star architecture.

The bus can be up to 10,000 feet in length, while the STARLAN topology supports an 800-foot distance between PC and hub, and a total 8,000-foot network. If 10Net is configured with an EtherNet topology, the network supports a distance of 500 meters/segment, with a 2.5-Km maximum distance (using thick EtherNet coaxial cable); thin EtherNet coax allows 180 meters/segment, with a 900-meter maximum. A fiber-optic 10Net LAN permits a PC-to-hub (or hub-to-hub) maximum distance of 1 Km (the 1-Mbs version) or 3 Km (the 10-Mbs version), with a total network distance of 6 Km. The hardware and software supports up to 3 hub levels, and a maximum of 392 nodes. Figure 8.4 illustrates how repeaters can link different 10Net topologies.

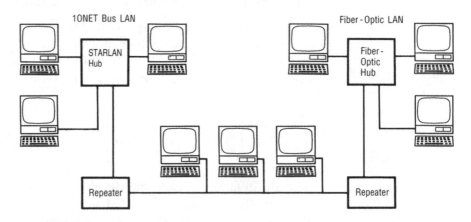

Figure 8.4   Different 10Net Topologies Linked with Repeaters

10Net Plus Software

10Net Plus software is NetBIOS-compatible, and uses the SMB protocol suites. Because the software requires only 110K (with 20K additional RAM for NetBIOS), it has become a popular substitute for the PC LAN

Program on IBM Token Ring Networks, where it can support 4-Mbs transmission over unshielded twisted-pair cabling.

The program also runs with 10Net's own interface cards and a variety of cabling and protocol schemes—including IEEE 802.3 1BASE5 STARLAN over twisted-pair, thick or thin EtherNet coaxial cable (10 Mbs), and fiber-optic cabling (1 Mbs or 10 Mbs).

In Chapter 5, we discussed some special techniques NetWare file servers use to enhance performance. 10Net acts very much in the same way, using such techniques as *prefetch, write buffering,* and *disk caching.*

Among the methods used by 10Net file servers to achieve greater efficiency are prefetch, write buffering, and disk caching.

- *Prefetch* anticipates your next request, and thus speeds up network performance. Rather than merely fetching a 200-byte record that has been requested, 10Net's server fetches 1,000 bytes, under the assumption it will not have to perform another disk access when you request the next record.

- *Write buffering* is a technique in which the file server writes to a buffer, rather than directly to disk—and then transmits a larger block, less frequently.

- Finally, *disk caching* brings an entire track of information into an area of memory known as the *cache,* where it is available upon request.

Some Features That Distinguish 10Net Software

Other features that make 10Net Plus a good value include its pop-up version of the CHAT program, its bundling of the Network Courier electronic mail program, and its menu-driven installation. The Network Courier will be discussed in some detail in Chapter 9's survey of leading electronic mail programs.

- *CHAT* is 10Net's program for brief communications between users.

- A *Bulletin Board* program enables users to leave messages for everyone on the network.

- *CB* permits users to have multipoint public discussions.

- A *group calendaring* program makes it easy to schedule meetings by coordinating a number of individual schedules of network users.

- A *TALLYS* program lets a network manager examine dozens of network statistics—including the number of packets sent and received over the network, the number of collisions, and the number of bad packets sent.

Sharing Network Resources

A superstation is a 10Net network node that shares its resources with the network.

A node that shares its resources under 10Net software is considered a *superstation* (as opposed to a workstation that simply utilizes its own and other nodes' resources). As in the case of many DOS-based network programs, 10Net uses the NET SHARE command to share a resource, and the NET USE command to use a particular resource. Users provide a short name (or *alias*), along with the network name of the device they wish to share. Figure 8.5 illustrates how the NET SHARE command provides information on resources (and their aliases) that have been shared.

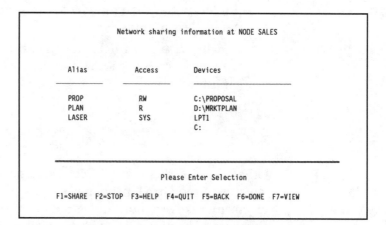

Figure 8.5   The NET SHARE Command

10Net's Levels of Security

10Net provides four different levels of security:

File Security

Directory Security

User Security

Superstation Default Security

At the file and directory levels, attributes can be defined for files, groups of files, or an entire directory. Similarly, files and directories can be limited to a specific user, or to specific groups. A user's *security level* (0 is the lowest and 255 the highest) must be greater than or equal to the *read or write security* of the file or directory he or she is trying to access.

As an example, imagine a file with a read security level of 60 and a write security level of 80; a user would need a security level of at least 80 to have full access to the file. A user with a security level of 70 would be able to read the file but could not update it.

10Net Secure LANs

One area where 10Net LANs have proven to be popular is in government installations that require security. The 10Net Secure LAN incorporates 10Net hardware (a 10Net circuit board and encryption board) and 10Net Plus software. The 10Net encryption board provides *single-keyed encryption* of all data written to the PC's hard disk, and of all data transmitted over the network in conformity with ANSI x9.17 standards.

The hardware and software can function on a single PC, or on the entire network. The 10Net Plus software provides multilevel file access, as well as a full audit trail of user activity, with date transfer security. Users are required to provide a valid ID and password before the DOS boot. Users can also be restricted from use of selected peripherals.

Providing 10Net secure systems for the government has become a major revenue source for Digital Communications, which has installed more than 10,000 nodes. In addition to its 10Net Secure LAN, it also offers a Tempest configuration (featuring government-defined security standards)—and, very shortly, a C2 secure system that conforms to National Security Agency requirements.

Today, government networks utilize the Transmission Control Protocol/Internet Protocol (TCP/IP), developed a decade ago under a Defense Department contract. 10Net offers 10Net TCP, a collection of programs that implement a standard TCP/IP protocol family for PCs running under DOS. It functions as a *terminate-and-stay-resident (TSR)* program that can be run whenever needed for terminal emulation.

Since the U.S. government has already expressed its intention to move from TCP/IP to *Government OSI Profile (GOSIP)*, there is a need to bridge the two protocols. Because the government represents such a major market for 10Net, the company has been working under a joint agreement with Northern Telecom to implement the CMIP protocol—which would permit TCP/IP networks to comply with the network management specifications of the Open Systems Interconnection standard.

Token Ring Bridge

The *10Net Token Ring Bridge* integrates a 10Net LAN with an IBM Token Ring Network. Using a dedicated node as a bridge PC, the program monitors network traffic, and can handle the 1-Mbs and 10-Mbs 10Net transmission speeds as well as the 4-Mbs transmission speed on the IBM network. This software-only product performs bridging at the NetBIOS level.

Vines

Banyan Systems' *VIrtual NEtworking System* (*Vines*, previously an acronym and now a trademark) is a network operating system based on UNIX System V. Vines places a premium on internetwork connectivity, security, and transparent operations. The company offers a number of add-on products, including electronic mail and network management software, which we will discuss later in this section.

Vines supports a wide variety of hardware platforms—including IBM's Token Ring, SMC ARCnet, Interlan EtherNet, 3Com's EtherLink and EtherLink Plus, and Proteon's ProNET-10. It requires a dedicated file server. This can be one of its own models—equipped with an Intel 80286 (Vines/286) or Intel 80386 (Vines/386) CPU—or a comparable IBM AT, PS/2, or compatible unit.

All Vines services—including naming, file, printer, and mail—execute as UNIX processes. These services can be stopped and started from the server without disrupting other services. While computer industry experts have long extolled the multitasking and multiuser capabilities of UNIX, they have pointed out that its wide acceptance by the general public would be hindered by its lack of a user-friendly interface. Although the Vines user interface is menu-driven (as illustrated in Figure 8.6), and Vines is UNIX System V-based, a user must exit this network environment before being able to use UNIX.

```
VINES:  VIRTUAL NETWORKING SYSTEM



         1 - Mail
         2 - Catalog of StreetTalk Names
         3 - Printer Functions
         4 - File Sharing
         5 - Password Update
         6 - Communications with Other Computers



   Use arrow keys to highlight a choice and press ENTER.
   Press F1 for HELP.     Press ESC to exit this screen.
```

Figure 8.6   The Vines Menu

StreetTalk

The key to Vines' internetwork connectivity is its distributed database, StreetTalk, which provides a global directory for network communications.

StreetTalk is Vines' distributed database, which serves as its *resource-naming service. Resources* can represent users, services (such as printers, file volumes, or gateways), and even lists. The StreetTalk name structure is threefold, with each part separated by the @ symbol:

object@group@organization

As an example, Frank Jones, an account executive in PolyTex General's Western regional office, might have a StreetTalk name such as the following:

FRANK JONES@SALES@WESTERN

With StreetTalk and Vines, a user does not need to know pathways, or the location of users (or other resources). If Frank needed to send a message to Bill Taylor working in the Southwestern regional office, Frank would need only know Bill Taylor's name; StreetTalk would take care of the mechanics of finding Taylor's node address and routing the material to him accurately.

To make matters even easier, StreetTalk permits the designation of aliases, or *nicknames,* for users. Figure 8.7 illustrates a menu a network manager would use for adding a user's nickname.

```
Use arrow keys to highlight a choice, then press ENTER


SELECT from list below      SEARCH for other nicknames
ADD a nickname              FIND nicknames for a full name
EXIT this screen (ESC)      HELP (F1)

------------------------------------------------------------

(There are 5 nicknames in group "Sales@Poly".)

1 - cct
2 - ddw
3 - hp
4 - kak
5 - ss
```

Figure 8.7   Adding a User's Nickname Under Vines

If Frank only knew Taylor by the nickname "BT," he could consult the StreetTalk catalog (using a screen similar to the one pictured in Figure 8.8) and find the name corresponding to BT.

```
What would you like to look at?


        Users                   Nicknames
        File Volumes            Groups
        Printers                Organizations
        Lists                   Servers
        EXIT this screen (ESC)  HELP (F1)


Use arrow keys to highlight a choice and press Enter.

------------------------------------------------------------

You are Frank K. Olsen@Sls@Polytex
```

Figure 8.8   A StreetTalk Catalog

Similarly, if Frank had proper access, he could request a file without having to care about the directory—or even the physical location of the file server that contains it. Frank could request BUDPROJ89, and let StreetTalk find and retrieve it, since each file server on a Vines network maintains a StreetTalk directory of all resources known to the network.

Because of StreetTalk's global naming capability, the process would be the same, whether Frank needed to access an IBM mainframe in Arizona, or an EtherNet network running Vines in New Jersey. The network operating system would handle network addressing and communications with the mainframe (which runs SNA) or the EtherNet network (which uses an addressing scheme different from that used by Frank's Token Ring Network). All this work is transparent to Frank, the end user; in each case, he simply selects (from a Vines menu) the name of the resource with which he wants to communicate.

Behind the scenes, the various Vines file servers communicate and exchange StreetTalk information with each other, using what are called *outbound blasts.* These communications occur whenever a new server joins the network, when the administrator adds or deletes group or service information, and every 12 hours from the time the last server came on line.

Security Under Vines

Vines provides several levels of security through its VANGuard program.

Vines provides several different layers of security. A network administrator can require a password for login to the network. He or she can also specify the hours and days permitted for a particular user to log in to the network. Vines version 3.0 and above contains security software known as *VANGuard.* The VANGuard menu is shown in Figure 8.9.

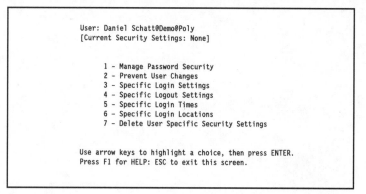

```
User: Daniel Schatt@Demo@Poly
[Current Security Settings: None]


        1 - Manage Password Security
        2 - Prevent User Changes
        3 - Specific Login Settings
        4 - Specific Logout Settings
        5 - Specific Login Times
        6 - Specific Login Locations
        7 - Delete User Specific Security Settings


    Use arrow keys to highlight a choice, then press ENTER.
    Press F1 for HELP: ESC to exit this screen.
```

Figure 8.9   VANGuard Provides Security for Vines

VANGuard lets the administrator limit the number of simultaneous logins, set specific locations from which users must log in, and require users to change their logins at specified intervals. In addition, users' access can be restricted to a specific file server.

Under Vines, each user, service, and communications link has an *access rights list (ARL),* which specifies the users who are authorized to use it. The network administrator can establish the access rights to a file volume, but individual files cannot be restricted.

Printing Under Vines

Under Vines, printers linked to network PCs can be shared in the same way as printers attached directly to file servers. This eliminates the printer-to-server distance limitation, and makes printer location a much more flexible operation. The network administrator determines which printers will be available for which users by assigning a *virtual connection* for each print queue listed in a user profile. The SETPRINT program permits a user to look at jobs in any print queue, use a different print queue, or change printer settings. The Show Print Queue menu in Figure 8.10 illustrates how a user could hold or cancel a print job in a queue.

```
                          Show Print Queue


          CANCEL job          HOLD job          REPRINT job

   -------------------------------------------------------------

   There are 4 print jobs in print queue LaserPrinter@MKT@Poly


   Job    State   Creator              Size   Title   Form Type

   01     Done    Suzie S Marshall@Sa  12033  input   Standard
   02     Ready   Stan Schatt@Mk        3237  input   Standard
   03     Hold    Bill Bones@Sales    434445  input   Standard


   Use arrow keys to highlight a command and press ENTER.
   Press ESC to exit this screen; F1 for HELP.
```

Figure 8.10   The Vines Show Print Queue Menu

Communicating with Other Vines Users

Vines includes two standard intranet communications packages and an optional E-mail program.

For intranet communications, Vines includes two standard network packages—SEND and CHAT—and offers an optional electronic mail program. SEND is a command that enables a user to send a one-line message that will appear at the bottom of another user's screen. To use this command, a user would type SEND and press Enter. Prompts will request the message (enclosed in quotation marks), as well as the name of the recipient. By indicating ALL, a user can send a one-line message to all other users with LANs connected to the sender's server.

The CHAT program creates a window enabling a user to chat with up to four others at one time. The program opens conversation windows for each user. If you are chatting in a private conversation with another user, and a second user expresses a desire to chat, you can either add that user to the discussion or place the first user on hold. Since CHAT works on all Vines networks, five users at different locations can have a sustained "conversation" on a particular project—very much like a conference call.

While Vines does come with an electronic mail package, Banyan's *Mail* program is available as an add-on. A major advantage of this program over others is that it uses the StreetTalk naming convention, so that names and nicknames are consistent. It also features a *store-and-forward* approach that enables it to utilize high-speed links between servers. The Vines Mail program menu displayed in Figure 8.11 shows that it provides most basic mail services, including the ability to organize documents into appropriate folders and a text editor for composing.

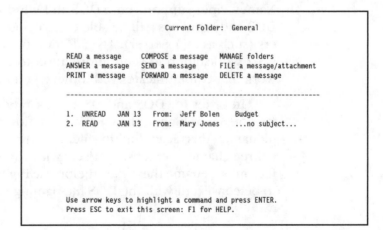

```
                      Current Folder:  General


    READ a message      COMPOSE a message    MANAGE folders
    ANSWER a message     SEND a message       FILE a message/attachment
    PRINT a message      FORWARD a message    DELETE a message

    ----------------------------------------------------------------

    1.  UNREAD    JAN 13   From:  Jeff Bolen    Budget
    2.  READ      JAN 13   From:  Mary Jones    ...no subject...





    Use arrow keys to highlight a command and press ENTER.
    Press ESC to exit this screen: F1 for HELP.
```

Figure 8.11   The Vines Mail Menu

MacVines Mail Gateway allows communication between IBM and Macintosh users.

Banyan offers a *MacVines Mail Gateway* software option that provides communication between Macintosh and IBM microcomputers. Vines Network Mail, in conjunction with CE Software's QuickMail, provides the necessary DOS and Macintosh file conversions. Vines Network Mail includes the Listener and Bridge. The Listener runs as a service under Vines, and talks to the Bridge using AppleTalk protocols. Figure 8.12 illustrates how Macintosh computers and PCs can exchange mail on a Vines EtherNet backbone network.

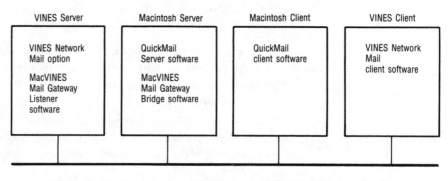

Figure 8.12   Macintosh and IBM-Compatible PCs Exchange Mail on a Vines Network

Vines and OS/2

Vines (version 4.10 and later) supports OS/2 *application programming interfaces (APIs)*, including APIs to named pipes and mail slots. Because Named Pipes supports both DOS and Windows, workstations running DOS and Windows will be able to access OS/2-based application servers (such as SQL Server). The addition of mail slots enables a DOS or OS/2 workstation to send information to any application on the network that communicates with others with mail slots.

In order for DOS and OS/2 workstations to share files on Vines version 3.x or higher, the OS/2 workstation must use DOS-compatible filenames; this means limiting filenames to an eight-character name and a three-character extension. Users with High Performance File System files must rename these files (before saving them to a Vines file server) to be consistent with the DOS file-naming scheme.

Vines and the Macintosh

The Vines option for the Macintosh supports an unlimited number of Macintosh clients across a Banyan network. A Macintosh workstation anywhere on a Vines network can access resources residing anywhere else on the network. The Vines Macintosh software is AppleTalk File Protocol (AFP)-compatible.

Macintosh users access Vines network services as though they were on an AppleShare server; they select Vines servers through the Chooser and access files on the server by double-clicking on the server icon with a mouse. If Vines Mail for the Macintosh is added, Macintosh users can send E-mail across the network without the need for a separate Macintosh mailbox.

Macintosh users can send files to PostScript-compatible printers anywhere on a Vines network, even those connected directly to PCs. Vines for the Macintosh also includes built-in *wide-area packet routing.* (A *wide area network,* or *WAN,* links workstations located at sites covering a large geographic area.) This means that if a Macintosh user wants to send a packet to another user on a network running the TCP/ IP protocol, the user's AppleTalk packets are encapsulated in Internet Protocol (IP) packets and sent over the links connecting the various Vines servers on the WAN.

Banyan's Intelligent Communications Adaptor

Banyan's *Intelligent Communications Adaptor (ICA)* manages six high-speed serial communication ports. Two ports are configured for 64-Kbs synchronous communications. An ICA can support several different protocols, including HDLC, SDLC, and X.25. Because the ICA has its own processor (as well as 512K of dual-ported, zero-wait-state RAM), it reduces overhead on a Vines server. The number of ICAs supported varies according to the Vines file server selected. Banyan's own top-of-the-line *Corporate Network Server (CNS)* can support—in addition to up to 100 simultaneous network users—a maximum of five ICAs or 30 communication ports.

Vines Gateways to Other Networks

Banyan's TCP/IP routing software gives a PC user access to TCP/IP resources.

The major strength of Vines is in its ability to provide transparent access to network resources, regardless of where they are, or what protocol they happen to be using. Banyan's TCP/IP routing software enables a PC user to access TCP/IP resources—whether they reside on a local network or a wide area network—without worrying about these physical details.

As an example, Vines mail can be sent to SMTP mail users using the SMTP Mail Gateway option. Vines mail addresses are automatically converted into the standard SMTP format (user@host@domain) or UUCP-style address (host!host!host!user). The Vines' TCP/IP program encapsulates TCP/IP packets within Vines packets for travel across a Vines network. A server equipped with the TCP/IP routing option strips the Vines headers, and sends the packets to an attached TCP/IP host or gateway.

Emulating an IBM 3274/6 cluster controller, the Vines 3270/SNA option supports up to 96 concurrent sessions per server—with up to 32 sessions supported by a single communications link. The software permits up to four concurrent host sessions and one DOS session per PC. In addition to providing 3278/79 terminal emulation, the software permits host print jobs to be performed on local PC printers, file transfer, and APIs so that users can build DOS-based applications to communicate with SNA host applications.

Banyan also offers a Vines SNA Communications Server. This software includes 3270 terminal emulation features, NetView support, and up to 254 concurrent sessions. This server offers access to IBM Advanced Program-to-Program Communications (APPC) at both the desktop and server. This allows client/server applications to interact at the desktop, server, and host.

Vines and Symmetric Processing

A number of "super" file servers have been developed that utilize multiple processors. Multiple processors use either *symmetric multiprocessor processing (SMP)* or *asymmetric multiprocessor processing (AMP)*. Under SMP, work is divided among processors on the basis of volume of work, with each processor receiving an equal share. Under AMP, work is divided on the basis of job type. Vines (4.0 and above) offers support for SMP on servers such as Compaq's dual-processor SystemPro and AT&T's four-processor StarServer E.

The Vines Applications Toolkit

The Banyan *Vines Applications Toolkit* is an advanced UNIX System V development environment for Vines, providing C language APIs for X.25, TCP/IP, and serial interfaces to support network communications. Several other features are noteworthy:

- The Toolkit provides access to *Vines Socket Communications* protocols, enabling developers to write media-transparent applications.

- A *UNIX/DOS Bridge File Service* enables DOS-based programs to share and interchange source code with the UNIX environment.

- A *Network Compiler* implements *Remote Procedure Calls,* which generate the code required for application-to-application communications.

Vines Network Management

Banyan offers *network management software* which provides LAN and LAN-interface statistics, as well as detailed information on servers, disk activity, and overall network performance. Designed as a network diagnostic tool, this software provides network administrators with information on file server cache size, percentage of cache hits, the number of times the file system was unavailable, and such "vital signs" of overall network performance as total messages sent and received, number of messages dropped, and the average amount of swapping. In addition, network administrators can view activities across multiple servers simultaneously.

Banyan offers the *Vines Assistant* for enhanced network management functions. This software enables a network manager to modify global network configurations, automate maintenance tasks, and monitor server capacity.

Vines now supports IBM's NetView, enabling an IBM host running NetView to monitor a Vines network. Vines also supports the *Simple Network Management Protocol (SNMP)*, which provides the "hooks" necessary to link with SNMP-based network management systems.

LANtastic

LANtastic utilizes a peer-to-peer configuration.

Artisoft's *LANtastic* is a network operating system that uses a peer-to-peer approach—which enables each network workstation to share its resources (such as its hard disk's contents or printer) with other network workstations. For companies that do not need the security and additional features available with a centralized file server, the peer-to-peer approach is relatively inexpensive and efficient.

LANCache

Disk caching can make a peer-to-peer server more efficient by using RAM to speed up disk operations. Artisoft provides a disk-caching program called *LANCache.* This program intercepts any higher-level attempts to access *BIOS interrupt 13 services* (such as DOS calls to load or save a file), and buffers the data exchanged with the hard disk. Thus LANCache works like a NetWare shell program to permit equal access to shared resources.

LANtastic Z

The LANtastic Z program is an ideal tool for transferring files between a laptop computer and a workstation on a LANtastic network.

The *LANtastic Z* program makes it possible to use any uncommitted printer and serial ports to hook up additional PCs to the network—without requiring a dedicated network adapter card. While this approach does slow transmission speed, it proves ideal for transferring files to and from a computer without a network adapter card (such as a laptop).

Because LANtastic Z supports modems, users can access a LANtastic network remotely from a laptop—and share files and network printers—simply by dialing in.

Security on LANtastic

LANtastic's *Username with Password* feature makes it possible to limit a user's access to certain hours, and to certain days of the week. Users can be granted any or all of the following privileges:

Read files

Write files

Modify files

Create files

Delete files

Rename files

Make directories

Delete directories

Look up directories

Execute programs

Change file attributes

If an uninterruptible power supply is connected to a LANtastic network, the network operating system will alert all network users when power is lost that they need to log off. Then it will close all network files, so no data is lost. When power is restored, LANtastic will inform users that their data has been saved.

User Communications with LANtastic

LANtastic has a *Chat* feature that enables users to transmit text messages to each other. A LANtastic menu makes it possible for users to save these messages and read them at a later time. A terminate-and-stay-resident (TSR) program called *LANPUP* alerts users immediately when a message is received. If the Artisoft Sounding Board adapter is installed in network workstations, users can use the *Voice Chat* feature to converse with each other—or even send a voice message that can be saved in digital format and replayed later, in just the same way a user might display electronic mail.

LANtastic for Windows

The *LANtastic for Windows* utility program enables the LANtastic network operating system to be run from a Windows graphical user interface. Network resources can be accessed in different windows. One window might contain E-mail, while a second window monitors network printer queues. Still another window might display a Chat session taking place with another network user.

Because the LANtastic for Windows utility program supports the *dynamic data exchange (DDE)* standard, users can mail data from a spreadsheet or database window (via LANtastic's E-mail) without leaving the application.

LANtastic's Network Management Features

Artisoft's *The Network Eye* is a program that enables one user on a LANtastic network to sit at one network workstation and view the screens and keyboards of all other network workstations. A user can view up to 32 screens simultaneously. It is possible to copy, cut, and then paste text or data from one PC to another PC.

One valuable use of this program, from a managerial perspective, is to give network users access to a modem or fax board installed on a networked workstation.

The *Net Mgr* utility program makes it possible to set up individual accounts. Users can be required to change their passwords, and their network access can be limited to certain times and days. A network manager can use this utility to define groups of users, so that network resources can be shared by all individuals within a group. Users can log into the network and use this utility program's menu to see which servers and network resources are available; they can also access E-mail or view a printer queue.

Hardware for a LANtastic Network

On EtherNet networks, LANtastic supports thick and thin coaxial cabling as well as twisted-pair wire. The *AE-3 EtherNet Adapter* supports all three types of cabling. It contains a 16K RAM buffer (upgradable to

64K), which can be used in either 8-bit or 16-bit slots; the buffer can sense the 16-bit slot and enhance its performance.

Adding an optional *PROM chip (Programmable Read-Only Memory)* from Artisoft makes it possible to boot up a *diskless workstation* from a network server. Network programs can be run on a diskless workstation, but because it has no disk drives, files cannot be downloaded; this approach provides greater security than does a standard PC.

The maximum network cable lengths per segment on a LANtastic EtherNet network are 607 feet with thin coaxial cable, 1,640 feet with thick coaxial cable, and 328 feet with 10BaseT twisted-pair cable.

Artisoft offers a *10BaseT hub/concentrator.* Residing within a host PC, this device has five external 10BaseT ports; these use modular RJ45 telephone-style jacks. Network management software makes it possible to view the status of all ports, and to enable or disable each port individually.

What Have You Learned?

1. ARCnet is a reliable, low-cost LAN that provides a physical star and a logical ring.
2. ARCnet was a character-oriented protocol.
3. Standard ARCnet is capable of transmitting data at a speed of 2.5 Mbs, while a new version provides 20 Mbs.
4. 10Net provides a high-security, low-cost LAN.
5. 10Net's file servers use prefetch, write buffering, and disk caching.
6. A superstation is a 10Net node that shares its resources.
7. Vines is a UNIX-based LAN operating system that runs on a wide range of hardware platforms.
8. StreetTalk is Vines' distributed database, which serves as its resource-naming service.
9. Vines provides effective gateways to TCP/IP networks and IBM mainframes.
10. LANtastic is a peer-to-peer network that permits users to share their computer resources with other network users.

Quiz for Chapter 8

1. ARCnet was developed by
   a. Datapoint.
   b. Standard Microsystems.
   c. Acer Technologies.
   d. Earth Computers.

2. Under ARCnet, a passive hub can be used if distances do not exceed
   a. 50 feet.
   b. 100 feet.
   c. 200 feet.
   d. 500 feet.

3. ARCnet's access method is
   a. polled star.
   b. CSMA bus.
   c. token ring.
   d. token bus.

4. The newest ARCnet version provides speeds of
   a. 4 Mbs.
   b. 16 Mbs.
   c. 20 Mbs.
   d. 50 Mbs.

5. Using a STARLAN approach, 10Net can achieve speeds of
   a. 1 Mbs.
   b. 5 Mbs.
   c. 10 Mbs.
   d. 20 Mbs.

6. 10Net Plus software requires only _____ of RAM.
   a. 50K
   b. 110K
   c. 500K
   d. 640K

7. 10Net's file server will fetch more than the required number of records, a technique known as
    a. profetch.
    b. prefetch.
    c. postfetch.
    d. fetch.

8. 10Net provides network statistics using
    a. Netstat.
    b. Record.
    c. TALLYS.
    d. STAT.

9. A network node under 10Net that shares resources is known as a
    a. workstation.
    b. sharer.
    c. superstation.
    d. altruist station.

10. 10Net provides _____ levels of security.
    a. 1
    b. 4
    c. 6
    d. 10

11. A 10Net encryption board provides
    a. single-keyed encryption.
    b. double-keyed encryption.
    c. double-handed encryption.
    d. sleight-of-hand encryption.

12. A UNIX-based LAN operating system is
    a. ARCnet.
    b. 10Net.
    c. Vines.
    d. NetWare.

13. The distributed database serving as Vines' resource-naming service is called

    a. ORACLE.

    b. SQL Server.

    c. TownTalk.

    d. StreetTalk.

14. A Vines user can communicate with four other users simultaneously with

    a. Mail.

    b. Bulletin.

    c. CHAT.

    d. SEND.

15. Vines/3270 SNA software emulates a

    a. cluster controller.

    b. host printer.

    c. mainframe.

    d. multiplexer.

9 | Electronic Messaging on Local Area Networks

About This Chapter

Electronic messaging is more than electronic mail transmission; it also includes the use of network-based facsimile (fax) machines, many of which work in conjunction with network E-mail systems. In this chapter, we'll take a close look at several different electronic messaging systems that are available for the leading LANs, including some network fax applications.

Since there is an industry movement toward incorporating CCITT standards in electronic mail packages (in order to facilitate internetwork connectivity), we'll examine the CCITT's X.400 set of recommendations. We also will look at Novell's Message Handling System (MHS), a product that network software companies and electronic messaging companies are licensing to provide E-mail services comparable to many offered by the CCITT X.400 set of recommendations. We'll also examine the effects on electronic messaging of the new CCITT X.500 set of recommendations—which provide for the creation of a global mail directory of users.

What Is Electronic Messaging?

Electronic messaging includes more than just electronic mail or "E-mail." It includes gateways to other networks and fax machines, as well as numerous scheduling and organizing features.

Today, *electronic messaging* means much more than simply one network user sending a note to one or more other users. Many electronic messaging programs also include the ability to send mail from one network to another, or even around the world. Often these programs also have the ability to maintain calendars for everyone on the network, schedule meetings, and (in some cases) even send phone messages automatically. More than simply a paperless office mail system, today's electronic messaging programs are designed to handle virtually all intraoffice and interoffice communications, and to link network users with each other and with the rest of the world.

CCITT X.400 and What It Means for Electronic Messaging

In Chapter 2, we mentioned the *International Standards Organization (ISO)* and their *Open Systems Interconnect (OSI)* model, designed to promote a set of standards for internetwork communications. The OSI model designates the Application layer (layer 7) as the location for a *Message Handling System (MHS)*. The purpose of this MHS is to provide a standard for electronic messaging, so that different computer networks will be able to communicate regardless of differences in their operating system environments.

In developing its model, the ISO used a set of standards from the *Consultative Committee for Telephony and Telegraphy (CCITT)*. These evolving standards are usually referred to as the CCITT X.400 set of recommendations; Table 9.1 reflects their scope.

Table 9.1. The CCITT X.400 Recommendations

Standard	Recommendation
X.400	System model and service elements
X.401	Basic service elements and optional user interfaces
X.408	Encoded information and conversion rules

Standard	Recommendation
X.409	Presentation transfer syntax and notation
X.410	Remote operations and reliable transfer system
X.411	Message transfer layer
X.420	Interpersonal messaging user-agent layer
X.430	Access protocol for teletex terminals

While much of this material is too complex to cover in this book, it is important that we look at the basic building blocks of an X.400-compliant system, since virtually all LAN manufacturers have announced support for these international standards.

Basic Elements of an X.400 Message Handling System

An X.400 message handling system includes user agents, message transfer agents, and a message transfer system.

An X.400-compliant MHS includes various elements, each with specific functions. These are the basic three elements:

- The *user agent (UA)* is the software part of the MHS that provides the interface or connection between network user and MHS, enabling the user to retrieve and send messages.

- The UA interacts with a *message transfer system (MTS)*— software which operates in support of the network users, providing the screen display they will see.

- The *message transfer agents (MTAs)* consist of the messages sent by users, plus the commands that provide a number of store-and-forward services; you might want to think of them as a "post office." Sometimes they store messages until a requested delivery time and date. Other times they may have to convert the message into a form that a destination user can understand.

Figure 9.1 illustrates how these elements are related within the structure of the MHS.

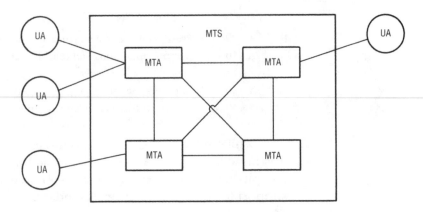

Figure 9.1 A Message Handling System

The MHS provides, on request, a variety of network and internetwork services that enhance electronic communications. These include notice of verified delivery or nondelivery (with an explanation), time and date stamps for submission as well as delivery, multidestination deliveries, alternate recipients, and even different grades of delivery service (including nonurgent, normal, and urgent).

The P1, P2, and P3 Protocols

The P1 protocol provides rules for routing information between two MTAs. The P2 protocol defines the types of services requested. The P3 protocol provides rules for changing existing parameters for electronic mail routing and delivery.

As part of its X.400 recommendations, CCITT has developed three key protocols, or sets of standards. These set rules for routing information, specify services the user can request, and change the parameters of MTAs as needed.

Protocol P1 (defined in the X.411 recommendation) provides rules for routing information between two MTAs. These rules take the form of formatting specifications to be followed in packaging information. The "envelope" for the information consists of the data to be sent, plus several fields that provide such important control elements as the following:

- A *message identifier,* which provides unique identification for where this message originated, as well as the name of the user sending this message.
- A description of how this information should be displayed.

- Information describing the destination user and this user's address.
- Delivery instructions, and instructions for any return receipt information required.

Notice that the type of information defined in Protocol P1 is very similar to the information that the post office requires when you request any kind of special service.

Protocol P2 (defined in the X.420 recommendation) enables users to request particular services, such as the following:

- Restricting the sending of certain messages to authorized users.
- Specifying the types of notification required of the request's recipient (for example, an immediate reply to a message).
- Providing subject information (and even cross-filing data), making it easier for companies that receive large volumes of messages.

Protocol P3 has been defined in the X.410 recommendation. Perhaps the easiest way to understand this set of standards is to think of it as a set of rules for a user or user agent to follow when talking to the "post office" (the MTA) after a message has been transmitted. Under Protocol P3, for example, a user can change existing parameters and conditions to respond to needs such as these:

- The need for a password.
- A need to alter the maximum size permitted in a message.
- The need for a test (before the actual delivery takes place) to see if a message can be delivered.

CCITT X.500 and What It Will Mean for Network Users

The CCITT X.500 set of recommendations will facilitate worldwide electronic mail by providing the basis for a common directory.

One major limitation of CCITT's X.400 set of recommendations is that they do not solve the problem of incompatible post-office-box addresses in the electronic mail services of different networks. The *X.500* recommendations will respond to this problem by providing a standard for a global directory of electronic mail users.

Still in the development stage, the X.500 set of recommendations will have a major impact on worldwide electronic messaging. Sometime in the not-too-distant future, a user on a NetWare network in St. Louis will be able to send a message to a user on an IBM mainframe computer in Paris, as routinely as we now drop a letter into our mailbox and raise the flag to indicate that we want the letter picked up and delivered.

The X.500 uses a hierarchical directory structure. Users access the X.500 directory through a *directory user agent.* This special UA communicates with the directory by using the *directory access protocol.*

Message Handling Service (MHS)

> **Note:** As used in this section only, MHS will refer to a specific messaging program from Action Technologies, and *not* to the CCITT's term "MHS" (as used in the X.400 set of recommendations). This is the only section of the book that will discuss the MHS program.

Message Handling Service (MHS) provides X.400-like control information and a way to connect different electronic mail systems together.

In October 1986, Action Technologies began offering its *Message Handling Service (MHS) program* to developers; beginning in early 1988 with v2.1, Novell began bundling MHS with NetWare without charge. Today, Novell owns Action Technologies' MHS, and is actively soliciting other vendors to write to this interface.

When a user requests that a message be sent, MHS takes this message and places it in an "envelope" that contains X.400-like control information. A *message control block (MCB)* accompanies the message; it is an 18-line ASCII file that provides such information as the desired destination, a date/time stamp, the priority requested, and return notification requirements. Since a three-part MHS message consists of a *header,* the *text* or message itself, and an *associated parcel* (which can consist of any binary encoded data), messages can be sent along with lengthy reports or data files.

Other X.400-like services include the following:

Management of access to user agents

Nondelivery alert

Content type

Delivery notification

Multi-destinations

Relay and forward message

Workgroup addressing

Dead-letter notification

MHS provides store-and-forward service, which means messages can be sent from one network to another with scheduled delivery dates and times.

Just as important, MHS provides gateways to other networks, and even converts messages to the format appropriate for these networks. Since MHS is fully compatible with X.400 recommendations, its "store-and-forward" method of operation means that messages can be sent with delivery dates and times. Companies can schedule noncritical reports for night delivery and even schedule *electronic document interchange*—a process in which information can be transmitted electronically, and then placed in a form running on another computer.

MHS is a utility program that virtually no network users will ever see or use directly. It is a program that enables programmers to develop the application programs (and electronic mail/scheduling programs) that will work in conjunction with it. Since different application programs will share this common interface, it is reasonable to foresee a time—not too far in the future—when programs will use MHS to communicate directly with other programs on different networks.

As an example, a network supervisor at Widget Company's branch in Phoenix might schedule an accounting program to produce a management report that reflects sales and profits for that day. This report could be scheduled to be run each evening and then transmitted at a certain time to the company's New York headquarters so that it could be an agenda item for an 8 a.m. executive meeting. Similarly, this very same report could be scheduled to be produced at night, and then sent immediately to a long list of company managers worldwide. Since MHS keeps workgroup addresses on file, mailing reports to distribution lists is very easy.

Finally, since MHS messages can start executable programs, it also is possible in our example to have one hundred sales branches of our fictitious company compile sales reports at night and then submit them at scheduled intervals to the corporate New York headquarters. At headquarters, the information is received automatically and then transmitted to a database program. The database is scheduled to compile all this data at a certain time and then produce a report with accompanying graphics. Assuming a printer does not suffer a paper jam, this entire scenario can take place without human intervention.

Simple Mail Transfer Protocol (SMTP)

The Simple Mail Transfer Protocol (SMTP) was designed for the Department of Defense as a simple, easy-to-use mail system that could be used to transmit mail from one network using the TCP/IP suite of protocols to another network using the same suite of protocols.

Simple Mail Transfer Protocol (SMTP) was developed for the U.S. Department of Defense as a simple, easy-to-use mail system for the *Internet* (a system of networks connecting major research universities and defense installations). SMTP is part of the suite of protocols known as **Transmission Control Protocol/Internet Protocol (TCP/IP)**, which now runs on a wide range of networks—including those using UNIX or NetWare as their network operating systems.

SMTP often is used to transfer mail between two network workstations connecting remotely. What makes SMTP so easy is that there are only a few commands to type. A list follows:

HELO
A command to identify the sender to the receiver. This is the first command issued during a SMTP session.

MAIL
This command initiates the mail transaction so that data is delivered to a specific network mailbox.

RECPT
The Recipient command indicates the recipient of the mail message.

DATA
This command indicates that the lines of text to come are data.

SEND
This causes mail to be sent immediately, and is often used when someone wants to send a page of data at a time.

SOML
This command can be translated as "send and mail." If a user is logged in, a message is sent to the user's screen. If the user is not logged in, the message is sent as mail to the user's mailbox.

RSET   The Reset command aborts a mail transaction.

VRFY   The Verify command checks to ensure that the user has a mailbox on the receiving system.

EXPN   The Expand command indicates that a message is to be sent to a mailing list, and not to an individual user.

HELP   This command results in a message being displayed.

NOOP   The No Operation command does not really do anything, except cause the mail server to send an "OK" in reply. This is useful for verifying the connection.

QUIT   The Quit command tells the mail server to issue an "OK" reply and close the channel.

TURN   The Turn Around command "turns around" communications so that sender becomes the receiver, and vice versa.

The Coordinator

Developed originally by Action Technologies, *The Coordinator* at one time was sold by Novell as the NetWare Electronic Mail System. Today, it remains one of the leading electronic mail/scheduling programs. Its features include receiving, creating, and sending electronic mail; organizing what the program labels "conversations"; and scheduling.

Reading Your Mail Using The Coordinator

The Coordinator organizes all communications on a particular subject and keeps them in sequential order as a "conversation."

Figure 9.2 illustrates the opening menu for The Coordinator. This menu can be customized so that a user's schedule for the day, unopened mail, uncompleted projects—or virtually any other material created with The Coordinator—will appear upon accessing the program. This entire process can be automated by including the MAIL command in a user's login script.

```
Read    Compose   Calendar   Organize   File   Edit   Tools   Exit   Help




       Note: You can customize startup windows so that you start the
       day with a display of your schedule and a list of your unopened
       mail.




Enter    Esc=Cancel    F1=Help    F10=Actions    End=OK    Mon 13-Jan 9:00am
```

Figure 9.2   Opening Menu of The Coordinator

The Coordinator organizes all communications on a particular subject, and keeps them in sequential order as a "conversation." Let's follow Carol Jackson for a couple of moments while she checks her mail. By pulling down the Read menu from the screen shown in Figure 9.2, she will see the Read options displayed in Figure 9.3. When she selects List unopened mail, she will see a screen similar to the one in Figure 9.4.

```
List unopened mail      F2
Open enclosure...
---------------------------
Read backward          F7
Read forward           F8
Read first        Shift+F7
Read latest       Shift+F8
```

Figure 9.3   The Read Menu

```
Read    Compose   Calendar   Organize   File   Edit   Tools   Exit   Help


                        Unopened Mail

                                   Subject

        New matters
        12-Jan   Joe     request    -> me      Expense report
        31-Dec   Terri   inform     -> me      Lead at ABC Corp

        Ongoing matters
        30-Dec   Phil    thankyou   -> me      Western region sales figures

        I am copied
        10-Jan   Joe     inform     -> sales   New expense report format




Enter    Esc=Cancel    F1=Help    F10=Actions    End=OK    Mon 13-Jan 9:00am
```

Figure 9.4   Carol Lists Her Unopened Mail

The Coordinator lists communications under four different categories:

- New matters includes open conversations in which Carol is a principal participant rather than an observer. This means it includes correspondence to and from her, but not correspondence in which she has merely received a copy (cc).

- Ongoing matters refers to new communications in ongoing conversations in which Carol is a principal participant.

- Completed matters lists communications that close a conversation and any communications that occur in that conversation after it closes. After a conversation is closed, participants can still send comments about it to each other.

- I am copied lists communications in which Carol is simply an observer (cc).

Since Joe is Carol's boss, she decides to open his message first. She moves her cursor to his item (listed under New matters), and presses Enter. Figure 9.5 illustrates a screen similar to what Carol will see.

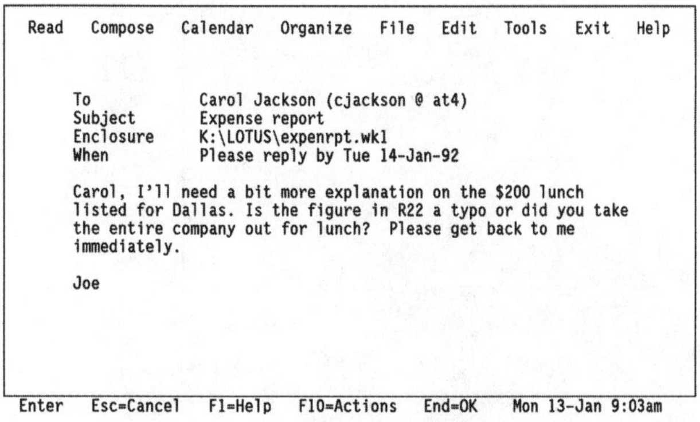

```
Read    Compose    Calendar    Organize    File    Edit    Tools    Exit    Help


        To            Carol Jackson (cjackson @ at4)
        Subject       Expense report
        Enclosure     K:\LOTUS\expenrpt.wk1
        When          Please reply by Tue 14-Jan-92

        Carol, I'll need a bit more explanation on the $200 lunch
        listed for Dallas. Is the figure in R22 a typo or did you take
        the entire company out for lunch?  Please get back to me
        immediately.

        Joe




Enter    Esc=Cancel    F1=Help    F10=Actions    End=OK    Mon 13-Jan 9:03am
```

Figure 9.5 Carol Reads Her Mail

Now that Carol has opened this correspondence, it will no longer be listed under "Unopened Mail." Under NetWare, Carol can select an Activate/Set Mail Alert option—which utilizes the memory-resident component of The Coordinator to check for new mail periodically, and to alert her when any mail arrives.

Carol could actually view the expense report she sent to Joe because it is attached to the message. Through the Open enclosure option she would be offered the opportunity to View, Edit, File, or Discard the enclosure. Only text files can actually be viewed. If Carol wanted a hard copy of her enclosure, she could select Edit and then select Print window from the Print menu under Tools.

Types of Communication Available with The Coordinator

The seven types of conversations available with The Coordinator are "Note," "Inform," "Question," "Offer," "Request," "Promise," and "What if."

Carol's day has not started very well. When she read Joe's note and then viewed the enclosure, she discovered that she made a serious mistake in her expense report. She needs to write Joe a note correcting this mistake. Her note will become part of the ongoing "conversation" The Coordinator will keep organized on this particular topic. To begin, Carol selects the Compose option from the Main menu. Figure 9.6 illustrates the Compose options available to Carol.

```
Note
Inform
Question
Offer
Request
Promise
What if
-------------------------
Envelope...
Reply...                F3
Forward...           Alt-F3
Send...                 F4
Utilities...
```

Figure 9.6   The Compose Menu

Notice that there are seven different types of conversations that can be composed:

- A *Note* is used to prepare a communication that opens a conversation and posts it for delivery. Use a Note when you don't need or want a response, and don't need a record of the conversation.

- The *Inform* type of conversation is used to convey information when you want an acknowledgement that your message has been received. When you send an important report or a memo that announces a new policy, you probably want an acknowledgement.

- The *Question* conversational type is used when you want to ask a simple question or make a simple request. Carol could use this option if she wanted to ask Joe for the address of the Tokyo sales office, or ask him if she could use some vacation time next Tuesday.

- Carol would use the *Offer* conversational type if she wanted to offer to teach a training class or offer to represent the company at an upcoming trade show. (If Joe accepts Carol's offer, then The Coordinator will treat it as a Promise, a conversational type we'll examine shortly.)

- The *Request* conversational type is used to ask one or more people to perform one or more actions. The Coordinator works more efficiently if you limit yourself to one request per conversation. The Request format can be used during any kind of negotiation, and The Coordinator will keep a running record of requests and counteroffers.

- Carol could select the *Promise* option if she wanted to promise to perform a specific action, or confirm that she had agreed to perform a specific action. The Coordinator will keep track of her progress on this particular project.

- The *What if* option is used to explore a possible course of action, or solicit suggestions and opinions about it. If Joe asked Carol to provide information on what effect a 10% cut would have on her budget, she would reply using this option.

The Coordinator requires the person opening a Question, Request, or What if conversation to close that conversation, since presumably that person has to decide whether requests have been fulfilled or questions answered. Similarly, only the person to whom an Offer or Promise has been made can close that conversation. The Coordinator considers all but Notes to be "managed conversations," and actually suggests the correct protocol or rules for ending the conversation. Table 9.2 illustrates the protocol acceptable for an Offer.

Table 9.2. The Protocol for Making an Offer

Standard format:

Starts with	The Exchange	Ends with
Offer	OK (accept)	
	[Do the work]	
	This is done	Thank you

Variants:

Starts with	The Exchange	Ends with
Offer	OK, except	
	Accept counteroffer	
	[Do this work]	
	This is done	Thank you
Offer	No, however	
	OK, except	
	Accept counteroffer	
	[Do the work]	
	This is done	Thank you
Offer	No, thank you	Acknowledge and close
Offer	Cancel offer	Acknowledge and close

Addressing Communications with The Coordinator

Carol composed a brief message to her boss, pointing out the mistake in her expense report and correcting it. She then needs to decide how to handle her communication. From the Compose menu, she can select from several options:

- The *Envelope* option is used to address an envelope for a communication that starts a conversation or establish reminder dates for a conversation so that your calendar will automatically be updated. It also is used if a file needs to be enclosed with a communication. Figure 9.7 illustrates the information required under the Envelope option.

```
                              Envelope
  Subject       [                              ]
  To...
  Cc...
  Categories...
  Enclosure...
  When...
  OK
```

Figure 9.7 Addressing an Envelope

- The *Cc* option includes the capability to send a courtesy copy, or blind courtesy copy ("bcc") that will go to a designated person without the knowledge of the person addressed in the communication.

- The *Categories* option allows Carol to include one or more categories associated with the topic on which she is composing a communication.

- The *When* option under the Envelope menu is used to set one or more reminders. Figure 9.8 illustrates that you may indicate a project's completion date and a "reply by" date. These two items are included in the headers of communications and distributed to all participants in a conversation.

Figure 9.8 Using the When Option

- The *Remind me* option sets a personal reminder; The Coordinator will remind you on a date you specify. You can use as many personal reminders as you wish—each with its own text—with a conversation. For example, Carol might want to include several personal reminders in conjunction with a memo she has drafted regarding a meeting she is planning. Figure 9.9 indicates how she would go about it.

Figure 9.9   The Coordinator Permits Personal Reminders

The Coordinator uses these categories to organize conversations. Several categories can be used with a single communication; for example, a memorandum explaining an unexpected telecommunications expense incurred during the XYZ project might contain the categories XYZ, BUDGET, and TELECOM. Up to 64 different categories may be defined at any time.

The Reply, Forward, and Send Options Using The Coordinator

The only possible reply to a Note under The Coordinator is with a Note. In other situations, though, this program will prompt you for the type of reply you wish to select. Figure 9.10 illustrates several different options regarding a request that has been received.

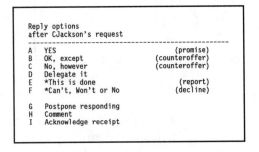

Figure 9.10   Reply Options

Choosing any of the first six options shown in Figure 9.10 will bring up a menu from which the user may choose to forward a reply to the Note.

The *Forward* option permits you to include the text of one communication in that of another. If, for example, you receive a request or question you need to delegate to another person, probably you would want to send that person a short memorandum—and forward the original request as part of the communication.

Once a communication has been written (and any envelope, reply, or forward information has been provided), it's time to post the mail. The *Send* option transfers the communication to MHS for routing and delivery.

The Coordinator's Calendar

The Coordinator's calendar feature provides the ability to make appointments for any date up to the year 2048, and keep detailed notes on each day's appointments.

What distinguishes The Coordinator from some other electronic mail programs is that it has the added dimensions of any good office coordinator: it keeps detailed calendars for all network users, provides reminders, and organizes all office files.

Figure 9.11 illustrates the options available under the Calendar menu. The program is capable of making appointments for any date up to the year 2048.

```
Show calendar...
Set appointment...
Set reminder...
------------------------
Repeat appt/rem...
Move reminders...
Change appointment...
```

Figure 9.11   The Calendar Menu

If you select Show Calendar, you'll see a screen similar to that in Figure 9.12—which provides a detailed listing of your day's schedule, including reminders, appointments, conversations that need replies, and any material you need to work on this day.

```
                  Calendar for Mon 13-Jan 1992

Appointments                        Subject
-9:00am--10:00am                    Discuss budget with Joe
10:00am---2:00pm                    Regional sales meeting
-4:00pm---5:00pm                    Interview new sales reps

Reminders                           Call for summer school schedule

Conversations
13 Jan  BJONES    to complete   request   Figures on trade show expenses

Carry forward
10 Jan  CJENN     to complete   request   PR release on widgets
-9 Jan  RWREN     to complete   request   Megawidget article
```

Figure 9.12   The Calendar Provides Details

The reminders listed are general reminders and not reminders specific to a particular conversation. The *Carry forward* category includes any unfinished actions, up to two weeks after their due dates. A *Print window* option in the Printing window enables you to print any daily calendar you wish.

One calendar feature that can make any executive more effective is the *Read appt/rem* option, which enables a repeat appointment to be scheduled daily, weekly, biweekly, monthly on a date, monthly on a day, yearly on a date, or yearly on a day. This makes it easy to set up standing appointments.

The Coordinator's Organizing Features

If you select Organize from The Coordinator's pull-down menu, you'll see a menu similar to that pictured in Figure 9.13. Figure 9.14 reveals the options you have when it comes to reviewing your communications and conversations, while Figure 9.15 shows your options under the "By type" submenu under the Review menu.

You could review all the promises you have made to your boss, all the conversations with a prospective customer, or even all the offers on a specific system that you have made to a prospective customer after July 1st. In other words, you can select all the options simultaneously if you need them to define a particular review.

Since many conversations specify future actions, you can use the Review option to identify and organize conversations with due dates (for actions you must carry out or for communications to which you must reply).

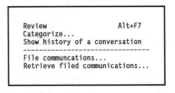

```
Review                        Alt+F7
Categorize...
Show history of a conversation
-----------------------------------
File communcations...
Retrieve filed communications...
```

Figure 9.13   The Organize Menu

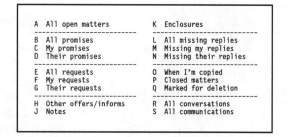

Figure 9.14 Options for Reviewing Communications

```
A  All open matters              K  Enclosures
   --------------------------        --------------------------
B  All promises                  L  All missing replies
C  My promises                   M  Missing my replies
D  Their promises                N  Missing their replies
   --------------------------        --------------------------
E  All requests                  O  When I'm copied
F  My requests                   P  Closed matters
G  Their requests                Q  Marked for deletion
   --------------------------        --------------------------
H  Other offers/informs          R  All conversations
J  Notes                         S  All communications
```

Figure 9.15 Reviewing Communications by Type

Some Other Valuable Features Found in The Coordinator

The Coordinator contains a word processing program, as well as a built-in gateway to other messaging systems—including those found on IBM, DEC, and Hewlett-Packard computers.

Under the Edit menu, The Coordinator contains a word processing program that produces standard ASCII text files. It permits text to be cut and pasted, moved in blocks, searched and replaced, and printed on most popular printers. The program's menus can be customized so that novices do not have to deal with so many different types of conversations.

The Coordinator can update both the sender's and recipient's calendars automatically, build distribution lists, enclose any type of file (such as a spreadsheet), and send conversations at certain dates you specify. This last feature is a characteristic of MHS's store-and-forward method of routing information. A memorandum can be written well ahead of time and not delivered until a certain date.

Because it uses MHS, The Coordinator has built-in gateways to other messaging systems—which include IBM's PROFS and DISOSS, DEC's All-in-1 and VMSmail, Wang Office, HP-DESK, CompuServe's InfoPlex, FAX, TELEX, and MCI Mail.

The cc:Mail Program

The *cc:Mail* program is the leading network E-mail program. It offers a number of major features—including the ability to attach files, send graphics, create distribution lists, and send copies to other network users.

Reading Your Mail with cc:Mail

Let's return to our example of Carol Jackson, who previously used The Coordinator to read and send mail. Let's assume that she now works for a company running cc:Mail on its LAN. Carol has logged in—which resulted in her login script executing a batch file that brought up the cc:Mail Main menu (illustrated in Figure 9.16).

```
┌─────────── MAIN MENU ───────────┐
│                                  │
│      Read inbox messages         │
│      Prepare new messages        │
│      reTrieve messages           │
│      Manage mailbox              │
│      eXit                        │
│                                  │
└──────────────────────────────────┘
```

Figure 9.16   The cc:Mail Main Menu

The *Inbox,* shown in Figure 9.17, is the place where you receive messages from other cc:Mail users. Carol currently has four messages in her Inbox; as she opens and reads each message, the "New" counter will decrease by one each time.

```
Inbox
4    Joe Blow        1/13/92      435t     Expense Report
3    Jack Smith      1/10/92     1044t     PR release
2    Mary Madrid     1/10/92     2400t     Product description
1    Bill Harris     1/09/92     12323     Market analysis




↑ ↓ and ENTER to display message.  F5 and F6 to select.  ESC to end
```

Figure 9.17   The cc:Mail Inbox Shows Messages from Other Users

As Carol files some of these messages, the folder count will adjust to include the new folders she creates. The program permits a user to have up to 200 folders at any time. If Carol simply does not want to deal with one of the new messages in her Inbox, she can leave it there, and it will remain as part of the "Msgs" total.

The cc:Mail program provides bulletin boards—accessible to all users—where they may read and post messages, but only the administrator may delete them. Carol could read a bulletin board message and then copy it to a personal folder for her own personal copy.

Joe Blow happens to be Carol's boss, so she'll select his message and press Enter. Figure 9.18 illustrates how cc:Mail displays a message. After Carol has read her message, she presses Enter to bring up an Action menu (Figure 9.19), which appears over the message text.

```
[4] From: Joe Blow  1/13/92  7:25PM (432 bytes: 10ln)
To: Carol Jackson
Subject: Expense Report

----------------------Message Contents----------------------

    Carol:

    I'm really concerned about the expense report
    you handed in for your Dallas trip. I realize
    that Consolidated Widgets is our biggest
    distributor in the southwest, but I can't imagine
    spending $200 on a lunch. Check that figure and
    please get back to me today.

    Joe


Window: 1-24   Lines:10   ↑ ↓ ← →  Help: F1   End:ENTER
```

Figure 9.18   Reading a Message in cc:Mail

```
================= ACTION MENU =================

display Next message          Move to folder
display Item                  Copy to folder
attach new iTems              Forward mesage
Return to main menu           replY to message
                              Print message
                              Write to ascii file
                              archiVe message
                              Delete message
```

Figure 9.19   The Action Menu

Replying to a Message with cc:Mail

We'll assume that Carol wants to reply immediately, and let Joe know that there's a mistake in her expense account report. She selects replY to message, and sees a screen similar to that displayed in Figure 9.20.

While replying, Carol can use the resources of cc:Mail's text editor. She can enter up to 20,000 characters in a text item, and use word processing features such as word wrap, reformatting, block movement of text, text finding and replacing, ASCII file creating, and printing to most standard printers.

```
From: Carol Jackson
To: Joe Blow
Subject: Correction to Expense Report

----------------------Message Contents--------------------

    Joe:

    I've looked over the expense report, and you're right,
    Consolidated Widget may be my bigget distributor,
    but the lunch in Dallas ran $20 and not $200. Believe
    it or not, $20 still buys a hamburger feast in Texas.

    Hope this clears up any questions or concerns you
    have about the report.



L:10  C:37  %Full:0  Highlight (   ): Alt+F1  Help:F1  END:F10
```

Figure 9.20   Writing a Quick Reply

Once Carol has completed her message, she can press the F10 key to bring up the *Send* menu (displayed in Figure 9.21).

```
================ SEND MENU ================

 Send message
 attach copy of dos File
 attach new iTems
 display Message
 edit sUbject
 Address message
 display Next message
 Return to main menu
```

Figure 9.21   The Send Menu

If Carol had wanted to send cc to another user, or even send a blind cc to another user, she could have selected the Address menu. Figure 9.22 illustrates the other options available here, including requesting a receipt.

Figure 9.22   The Address Menu

One of the options available under cc:Mail's Main menu is "Prepare new messages." The screen for writing new messages will look exactly like the screen displayed earlier for replying to messages. When Carol creates a new message, she has the option of including any kind of file with the message—as well as copying the message to a personal folder so she can keep the material on file with other related items. She also can send her communication to public mailing lists (available to all cc:Mail users), or to one of her own mailing lists.

Notice how practical this feature is for a department such as Human Resources; they might need to communicate with employees by position (all managers), by payroll designation (all nonexempt employees), or by sex and race.

Similarly, the *bulletin board option* under cc:Mail permits companies to post general announcements, job vacancies, and other company-wide information, without having to mail notices physically to everyone.

Attaching Files to Your Mail with cc:Mail

Virtually any kind of file can be attached to a cc:Mail communication.

Any type of DOS file may be attached to a cc:Mail communication—even an executable program (.COM or .EXE), as long as it is not copy-protected. By selecting the attach copy of DOS File option from the Send menu, Carol would see a screen similar to the one displayed in Figure 9.23.

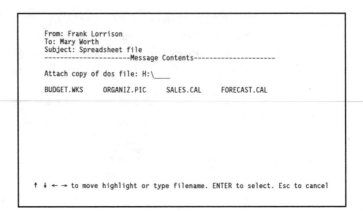

Figure 9.23   Attaching a DOS File

Notice that the directory shows a variety of different files, including electronic spreadsheets and picture files. By selecting "attach new iTems" from the Send menu, Carol would be provided with additional options for attaching material, as shown in Figure 9.24.

Figure 9.24   Attaching an Item to a Message

Up to 20 different items may be attached to a communication, and each item can be given a title—such as "Agenda for Annual Retreat" for a text item, or "Map showing directions to annual retreat" for a graphics item.

The Snapshot Utility Program with cc:Mail

The Snapshot utility program enables you to take "snapshots" of virtually any screen and then attach these pictures to any communication.

Using the *Snapshot* utility program (included at no additional cost), cc:Mail makes it possible to import information from other application programs and include it with mail communications. When you run the SNAPSHOT.COM program, a small resident kernel (around 20K) remains in RAM as a terminate-and-stay-resident (TSR) program. Since the

Snapshot program permits display of previous snapshots taken, it is possible to generate a "slide show" on any network workstation.

The Snapshot program permits you to select *hotkeys* to be used to take a snapshot, but it will default to the Alt-1 key combination. Figure 9.25 illustrates the Snapshot menu that will appear when you press the appropriate keys while running an application program.

```
┌─────────────── cc:Mail Snapshot ───────────────┐
│                                                 │
│  Take and store snapshot │ Display stored snapshot │
│                                                 │
└─────────────────────────────────────────────────┘
```

Figure 9.25   The Snapshot Menu

Figure 9.26 shows that if you select the Take and store snapshot option, you are given the opportunity to supply a file name for the picture.

```
┌─────────────── cc:Mail Snapshot ───────────────┐
│                                                 │
│  Take snapshot and store in file: C: ____       │
│                                                 │
└─────────────────────────────────────────────────┘
```

Figure 9.26   Taking and Storing a Snapshot

The procedure for taking a Snapshot of a graphics screen is slightly different from the procedure for a text screen. When you press the designated snapshot keys, the screen displayed is captured and then automatically given a file name and saved in the current drive and directory. The files are named "SNAP," followed by the letters "EGA," "CGA," or "HGC," depending upon the type of graphic adapter in use on the workstation.

These files are numbered consecutively so that the second EGA snapshot would carry the name "SNAPEGA.002."

Using cc:Mail to Create and Modify Graphics

The cc:Mail program contains a built-in graphics editor that can be used to create original graphics, or to modify graphics captured from other programs.

The cc:Mail program contains a built-in *graphics editor* so that original drawings can be created and incorporated into a message. It is also possible to use this graphics editor to modify graphics the Snapshot utility has captured from application programs. Let's examine, as an example, the way to create a graphic that will accompany a short Note.

After you have written your message, given it a subject, and addressed it, you can press the F10 key to bring up the Send menu (Figure 9.21).

When you select the attach new iTems option under this menu and press Enter, you will see the Attach menu (refer again to Figure 9.24). Selecting attach Graphics item will bring up the Graphics menu (displayed in Figure 9.27).

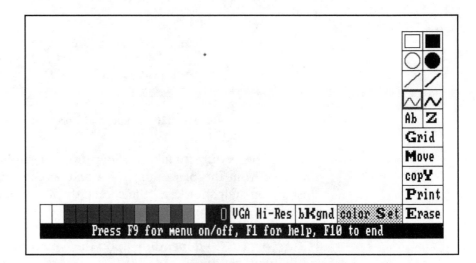

Figure 9.27 The Graphics Menu

With this Graphics menu, it is possible to select different color sets—as well as background colors, thick or thin free drawing lines, empty or solid circles, letters, and grids.

One very useful feature of cc:Mail is that you can share snapshots taken from selected application programs with users who may not have access to these programs. The cc:Mail program enables you to treat one of your snapshots as if it were a photocopy of a screen. You can also treat your snapshots like text, and simply add this text to whatever message you wish to send. Your recipient will see (for example) the database report or spreadsheet screen, without having to run the appropriate application program.

Viewing the Mail Directory of cc:Mail

One of the NetWare network supervisor's responsibilities under cc:Mail is to manage the *network mail directory* (see Figure 9.28). The network supervisor accesses the cc:Mail directory by typing `MAIL` and providing the correct password.

```
┌─── Name ──────── Loc ── Last Checked In ──────── Comments ───┐
│                                                              │
│   Albert, Charles      L    1/13/92    2:54PM     VP Sales   │
│   Bush, George         L    1/13/92    9:00AM     President  │
│   DeBaugh, Francis     R    1/13/92    7:01AM     Miami      │
│   Jackson, Andrew      r                          Phoenix    │
│   Peoples, Paul        L    1/13/92   10:09AM     Sales      │
│   TUCSONPOST           P    1/13/92    1:04PM     Tucson PO  │
│   Zaslow, Ziggy        L    1/10/92    3:45PM     Accounting │
│                                                              │
└──────────────────────────────────────────────────────────────┘
```

Figure 9.28   Network Mail Directory

Note: When we talk about E-mail programs running at different sites, familiar terms take on different meanings. The term *post office* will refer to a network mail hub, and not to a government postal facility; *mailbox* will refer to the computer storage used for E-mail, and not to a receptacle for letters.

As Figure 9.28 illustrates, the location status of a mailbox is identified as follows:

L local user

R remote (stand-alone) user

r remote network user on another post office

O (letter O, not zero) remote post office
that connects directly to yours

P remote post office that can be accessed through
another remote post office

Remote users have mailboxes in the network post office, just as local network users do; unfortunately, these remote users must access their mailboxes from outside the LAN. For direct access, they can use a stand-alone PC running *cc:Mail Remote* software, or they can access their post offices indirectly from another post office. These remote users can send and receive messages, but cannot use the local bulletin boards.

When a cc:Mail Remote user directly accesses a cc:Mail post office, the post office checks to see if the user has a mailbox at that particular post office. If the user is not listed in the mail directory, he or she can send messages to specific mailboxes but cannot receive mail.

Other post offices running the *cc:Mail Dialin* utility program can directly access a remote post office if it is running *cc:Mail Gateway*. The cc:Mail administrator must provide these remote users with a post office name, and a telephone number to which the cc:Mail Dialin utility program is connected.

Since you may need to see the mailbox address for remote users, you can use the right arrow key to move to the right of the "Comments" column, and see a screen that resembles Figure 9.29.

```
┌──── Name ────── Loc ══cc:Mail Address ───┐
│                                          │
│  Albert, Charles      L                  │
│  Bush, George         L                  │
│  DeBaugh, Francis      R    1-612-444-3232│
│  Jackson, Andrew       r    PHOENIXPOST   │
│  Peoples, Paul        L                  │
│  TUCSONPOST            P    1-602-443-4343│
│  Zaslow, Ziggy        L                  │
└──────────────────────────────────────────┘
```

Figure 9.29   Viewing cc:Mail Addresses

Compiling and Analyzing Mailbox Statistics

The Chkstat utility program provides the cc:Mail administrator with detailed statistics on individual mailbox usage, as well as total post office usage.

The cc:Mail program provides several vital utility programs to help the administrator manage a network's electronic mail efficiently. A directory function of the *cc:Mail Chkstat* program provides a listing of information on each individual mailbox, including the mailbox name, the location, the time the user last checked in, and any general comments. The list looks like this:

```
Mailbox Name        Locn    Last Checked In      Comments

Alpert, Harmon      L       01/13/92 2:15pm      Sales Mgr
Boris, Barbara      R       01/13/92 10:00am     LA Office
Smith, Sylvester    L       01/10/92 10:53am     Account Exec
```

A *Users* function of the Chkstat utility program provides detailed information on the mailbox users—including mailbox name, location, USR file number, and the number of bytes in the file. Since remote users and post offices have a remote post office as their cc:Mail address for indirect access, they do not have an individual user file number, hence no file bytes will appear when these users are listed. Chkstat provides a list that looks like this:

```
                            USR          File
Mailbox Name        Locn    File #       Bytes

Alpert, Harmon      L       00007        672
Boris, Barbara      R       00003
Smith, Sylvester    L       00010        1074
```

The *Messages* function of the cc:Mail Chkstat utility program provides the administrator with information (arranged by mailbox and by bulletin board) on how messages are dispersed on the mail system. It is possible to examine the total number of stored messages. The Messages function produces a report that looks like this:

```
             cc:Mail Post Office: LOCALPOST
               Message Statistics 01/13/92


        Number of stored messages        50
        Total bytes in messages       143356
        Total bytes remaining         272772
        Reclaimable bytes              16772
        Additional bytes              512000
```

The Messages function can also provide detailed statistics on the distribution of messages for individual mailboxes, including how many messages (in bytes) are shared, and how many are not shared (unique to a particular mailbox or bulletin board).

An administrator could also request reports regarding specific groups of messages—including (for example) information on the messages in Carol Jackson's mailbox, dated on or before January 10th, that have already been read.

Gateways from cc:Mail to the Rest of the World

The cc:Mail program provides gateways to IBM and DEC electronic mail users.

The cc:Mail program provides a number of *gateway connections* to other computer mail systems. *cc:Mail ProfsLINK* provides electronic mail exchange between the NetWare LAN running cc:Mail and any VM computer running IBM Professional Office System (PROFS). Users on this IBM mainframe system may also send mail to cc:Mail users on the local area network.

There is also a *cc:Mail DEClink* program to link a NetWare LAN to a DEC computer. Using this link, All-in-1 and VAXmail users can communicate directly with LAN users.

Other major cc:Mail gateways for interconnectivity of electronic mail include *cc:Mail for the Macintosh* and *cc:Mail FAXlink*. The cc:Mail for the Macintosh program provides a convenient way to transfer Macintosh and IBM PC files back and forth between networks: these files are placed in cc:Mail envelopes that use the same format on both computers. The cc:Mail FAXlink program permits PC and Macintosh users to create, send, receive, and view text and graphics messages electronically, to and from facsimile machines. Fax messages can be viewed prior to printing, replying, forwarding, or storing in electronic files. Only one facsimile board is required for each network.

Using the Network Courier

The Network Courier is a program that provides E-mail services, as well as additional features. It enables users to merge their E-mail in much the same way as they would their nonelectronic mail. The Network Courier comes with four major programs: the Administrator, the External Mail program, the Mail program, and the Mail Monitor program. The LAN supervisor serves as the Network Courier's administrator.

The Network Courier administrator is responsible for setting up a post office, providing mailbox names and privileges for users,

The *Administrator* program provides the supervisor with the ability to set up a post office, provide mailbox names and privileges for users, establish communications with other post offices, and define the times and frequency of calling other post offices.

establishing communications with other post offices, and defining the times and frequency of calling other post offices.

During installation, the administrator will use a Courier Administrator menu to specify network names and post office names associated with it, as well as network IDs. An External-Admin menu includes a Setup option, which lets the administrator specify such items as baud rate, parity, data bits, stop bits, dialing mode, and type of line (duplex, half-duplex). A *Config* option under Setup enables the administrator to specify hardware communications parameters for each external post office to be linked.

Before we look specifically at how a network administrator establishes network parameters for external communications, let's follow a network user and observe how he performs his routine daily work using this program.

Reading Your Mail with The Network Courier

We'll assume that John Smith is an average user on a Novell NetWare network running The Network Courier. John may have his login script written so that it automatically checks for new mail when he logs in and then lets him look at his mail. If he does not have a login script, John would type MAIL at the network prompt and see a screen similar to that in Figure 9.30.

```
Network Courier                         New mail: 6  Unread mail: 4

Alias Read Compose Delete Forward Storage Print Options Login Update
Read toggled items of mail, or all unread mail if nothing toggled


┌──────────────────────────────────────────────────────────────┐
│   FROM      SUBJECT              DATE      TIME    PRI          │
│  ─────────────────────────────────────────────────            │
│                                                                │
│                                                                │
│   VP Sales  Expense Report       01/13/92  15:57   4           │
│   KarenC    Upcoming Presentation 01/13/92 13:45   3           │
│   BillR     Questions on PO #33445 01/13/92 08:30  2           │
│   MaryCr    Printer Question      01/13/92  11:34   1           │
│   DickG     New Vacation Policy   01/10/92  10:34              │
│   PaulineC  List of References    01/09/92  12:34              │
│                                                                │
│                                                                │
│                                                                │
└──────────────────────────────────────────────────────────────┘
```

Figure 9.30 The Network Courier Mail Summary Screen

Notice that in this example, John's mail has been arranged automatically in order of priority—with the highest-priority item (priority 4) listed first. A network administrator may also provide certain users with the privilege of sending urgent mail (priority 5). Notice also that John can see the date and time each message was sent, as well as a corresponding subject. Messages that are unread are shown in bold or enhanced video on monochrome monitors, and in yellow on color monitors.

John has four new messages he has not read yet, and two items he has read. We'll assume that he wants to read his highest-priority message first, so John presses the R key (for the Read option), and uses his arrow keys to highlight the first item before pressing Enter. Figure 9.31 reveals the Read mail message screen John will see. (Notice that the mail in John's queue has decreased by one, since one less letter is left to read.)

```
Read                                           Mail in queue: 5

Delete  Hold  Forward  Print  Reply  Storage
Delete the current message

┌──────────────────────────────────────────────────────────────┐
│ FROM: VPSales                                                  │
│ TO: JohnG                            DATE: 01/13/92            │
│                                      TIME: 15:57               │
│ CC:                                                            │
│ SUBJECT: Expense Report                                        │
│ PRIORITY: 4                                                    │
│ ATTACHMENTS:                                                   │
│ ─────────────────────────────────────────────────────────     │
│ John,                                                          │
│                                                                │
│ A two hundred dollar "business lunch" in Dallas? Please check  │
│ your figures. Get back to me by 10AM tomorrow because I need to│
│ submit this ASAP.                                              │
│                                                                │
│ Fred Friendly                                                  │
└──────────────────────────────────────────────────────────────┘
```

Figure 9.31   Reading Mail with the Network Courier

If the message is lengthy, John could use his arrow keys (or even his PgUp and PgDn keys) to scroll through the document. At the top of the Read screen are several options, including Delete, Hold, Forward, Print, Reply, and Storage.

Replying to a Message with The Network Courier

We'll assume that John believes in the management principle that he should only deal with a piece of paper (or electronic message) once. He'll reply immediately to this first message, and thus clear up this problem before dealing with any other item. After John selects the Reply option and presses Enter, he should see a screen similar to the one pictured in Figure 9.32.

```
Reply                                      Mail in queue: 5

Edit  Print  Transmit  Storage
Press Enter to select names

┌─────────────────────────────────────────────────────────────┐
│ TO: VPSales                          DATE: 01/13/92           │
│                                      TIME: 16:03             │
│ CC:                                                          │
│ SUBJECT: Expense Report                                      │
│ PRIORITY: 4                                                  │
│ ATTACHMENTS:                                                 │
│                                                              │
│ _____ │
│                                                              │
│                                                              │
│                                                              │
│                                                              │
│                                                              │
│                                                              │
│                                                              │
└─────────────────────────────────────────────────────────────┘
```

Figure 9.32   Replying to a Message

The Reply screen comes pre-addressed to the sender of the current message, with the subject and priority fields of the current message copied automatically into the address section of the reply. John could use pop-up windows to display lists of mail users to determine whom he wanted to send copies to.

The Network Courier provides a simple text editor that has word wrap, overwrite, and insert modes. The F5 key gives John the option of including a DOS text file in his reply, wherever the cursor happens to be when he presses this key.

When John has completed his reply, he selects the Transmit option and presses Enter to send his reply. The program will give him the option *before* sending (Ok to transmit? Yes No) to save or print the reply before transmitting it. A document transmitted is like a letter dropped in a mailbox; once it has been mailed, it cannot be copied, taken back, or stored away.

After John has transmitted his reply, he'll be returned to the Read screen, where the original message is still displayed (refer back to Figure 9.31). John must decide at this point whether he wants to delete it, print it, store it, or simply hold it. A message that is *held* will be retained in the system, and appear in the future on John's Mail Summary screen—but it will not be prioritized or appear in boldface or yellow.

Composing a Message Using The Network Courier

Compose is one of the options under the Main menu we examined in Figure 9.30. The Compose screen looks exactly like the Reply screen, except it does not automatically fill in the TO: and SUBJECT: fields. With the cursor in the TO: field, John can press Enter and see a pull-down window that displays a list of all addresses available on the mail system. He may scroll through this list, select the desired person, and then press Enter.

The CC: field contains the very same pull-down window, listing possible addresses to be copied. The SUBJECT: field may be up to 40 characters in length, while the PRIORITY: field may be any number between 1 and 4 (or even 5, if John has been given the privilege of sending urgent messages).

The ATTACHMENTS: field can be used to attach virtually any kind of file. By placing his cursor over this field and pressing Enter, John is able to view the PATHNAME: prompt, as well as the current drive and path. If he presses Enter at this point, he'll see a files window where he can locate the file he needs to attach. John can attach files existing in different directories, and even files existing on different volumes. After he has selected all the files he wants to attach, he simply presses Enter.

One useful feature of The Network Courier's Attachments: function is that portions of files can be attached to a message that is being composed. If John had saved a spreadsheet as a print file, for example, he could use the *Storage/View* option to view the print file, mark the section of the spreadsheet needed, and copy the information from a paste area to wherever his cursor is located in the message he is composing. The marking (F6), pasting (F7), and copying (F8) functions are all performed with function keys.

Some Important Network Courier Options

Important Network Courier options include setting and changing passwords, dating and time-stamping communications, sorting communications a number of different ways, and establishing a "useful-life" for communications.

The *Options* menu (accessed from the Mail Summary screen) consists of five utilities: Password, Date/Time, Sortkey, Headers, and Useful-life. These utilities function as follows:

The *Password* option allows you to change your user password, and requires you to verify the new password before making the change.

The *Date/Time* utility lets you set the time and date, and stamp them on all mail you send. (You will not have to use this utility if your computer has a built-in clock/calendar.)

The *Sortkey* utility enables you to decide how you want your mail sorted. You might remember that John's mail was sorted according to priority, but there are four different sorting methods available:

- Date: in the order received
- From: by sender name
- Subject: by subject name
- Priority: by priority (top priority first)

The *Headers* utility is provided because normally The Network Courier is set to display only 50 notifications of mail (or headers) at a time. You can change this number to reflect your particular needs (let's say 200), and the new number will remain in the system until you decide to change it.

The *Useful-life* option lets you specify how long you want to continue attempting to deliver mail to another post office. This option's purpose is to cut the costs of external mail delivery after the mail's useful purpose has been eliminated. For the number of hours you set (from 0 to 101010), the program will keep trying to place mail successfully in an Inbox.

Note: Selecting zero as a Useful-life value means that the mail's life expectancy is unlimited; it will not be eliminated, even if undelivered. The Network Courier's publisher recommends that you leave the default value of zero (unlimited) for regular mail, but put a limit on urgent mail, since it will decline in value rapidly.

The Mail Monitor Program

The Network Courier's Mail Monitor program is memory-resident; it runs the mail program in the background while you are running an application program, and alerts you that mail has arrived.

The *Mail Monitor* program is memory-resident, permitting the mail program to run in the background while you are running an application program; it alerts you when mail arrives. Mail Monitor lets you interrupt the application program temporarily, read the message, store the message, or even reply to the message, and then return to your application program's screen.

The Mail Monitor program can be loaded by typing MONITOR at the M: prompt, followed by a space and your mailbox ID, followed by a space and P-YOURPASSWORD. For example, John might log in as follows:

```
M:MONITOR JOHNS P-PLAYBOY
```

John could then load and use any application program such as Lotus 1-2-3 or dBASE IV. Whenever he wants to use the Mail Monitor, John simply presses Alt-F1. These keys can be changed if the combination is needed by a specific application program.

The Mail Monitor program deals with incoming mail by offering the following options: Silent, Beep, and Notify. The options function in the following ways:

- The *Silent* option means the Mail Monitor will not inform you when mail arrives, but will store the message. You can still view the mail at any time by pressing the hotkeys.
- The *Beep* option will provide a beep when mail is delivered.
- The *Notify* option will beep to announce the arrival of mail, and also display a notice at the bottom left corner of your screen that resembles the following:

```
Message From: Frieda
Esc to Ignore, Enter to Read
```

Note: Since using the Notify option to display a notice will halt other I/O operations (such as printing), use care when specifying how many minutes you wish to have a notice displayed on your screen. Setting the value at 0 indicates that you wish the message to stay on the screen until you acknowledge it, no matter how long it takes.

The External Mail Program

The Network Courier's External Mail program is used to send and receive external mail (messages transferred between post offices).

As we indicated earlier in this chapter, The Network Courier's *External Mail* program is used to send and receive external mail—such as messages transferred between post offices. If a *Modem Mail* option is installed, external mail then includes mail sent to and received from modem mail users.

One of the mail administrator's responsibilities is to establish a *calling schedule* (under the Administrator program) to be used by the External Mail program. Figure 9.33 illustrates a typical calling schedule.

```
Times
_____

Regular  Intervals
Define/Modify intervals dial time


   Interval  From   To    First minute   Additional Minutes
                            (cents)           (cents)
     1:      00:01  07:59     20                45
     2:      12:00  12:59     35                65
     3:      13:00  17:00     35                50
     4:      17:01  23:59     20                50
```

Figure 9.33   A Network Courier Calling Schedule

If a specific time interval is not listed, only priority 5 calls (urgent) will be made during the unlisted time period. When mail is sent that requires the External Mail program to route it to another post office, the program checks the network clock to see if it is authorized to transmit at that time. If not, it holds the messages until it is running again at a time appropriate to begin transmitting them.

The program will track any costs listed in the calling schedule, and print these costs in report form. It is possible to dedicate a computer to running the External Mail program, and send and receive external mail 24 hours a day.

Running Higgins

Higgins is an E-mail program that is as helpful and thorough as an experienced butler. It offers substantial scheduling features in addition to messaging.

Reading Your Mail with Higgins

The Higgins program is invoked by typing HIGGINS from a directory immediately above the HIGGINS subdirectory. A NetWare supervisor can write a batch file or login script that will check for new mail upon login and then send the user directly to this program. The login script or batch file should be set up to access the appropriate monitor driver (monochrome or color) for the particular user.

A Higgins screen containing a greeting and copyright information will be displayed, and the user will be asked to type in identification: a user name (to allow access to your Higgins data) and an optional password (to restrict access to more sensitive information).

Let's assume that Mary Brown is the Sales Manager for Polytex General, a company that's using Higgins as its electronic messaging system on a NetWare network. Mary logs in with her ID and password, and sees a screen similar to the one in Figure 9.34.

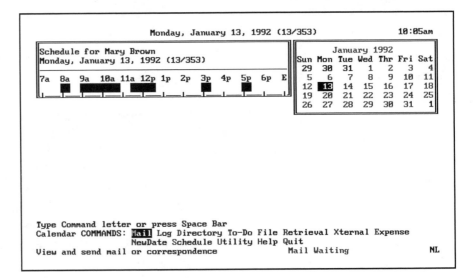

Figure 9.34 The Main Calendar Menu

Notice that she sees a calendar for the month, with today's date in boldface to indicate it is the current active date. To the left of the calendar is her appointment bar graph, with representation of her appointments and activity for today. Each 15-minute block within normal business hours is displayed.

Special Higgins functions include a scratchpad with which to take quick notes, a calculator, a stopwatch, and a Hide the Display option that will clear the main portion of a screen if an unexpected visitor enters your office.

Anytime while Mary is working, she may use any one of several interrupt keys to invoke special Higgins functions (scratchpad, calculator, stopwatch, and Hide the Display). The *Hide the Display* option is designed so that a user can hide confidential information (without having to exit the program currently running) when someone enters her office; it clears the main portion of Mary's display until she presses her space bar.

Notice that there are several options on the bottom of the screen available to Mary. She selects Mail by moving the cursor with her space bar and then pressing Enter; this command initiates the Higgins Electronic Mail System. It brings up a window titled "IN-BASKET," which lists all incoming memos (as well as memos Mary may be working on, or memos she may have copied to herself). Figure 9.35 illustrates the IN-BASKET window.

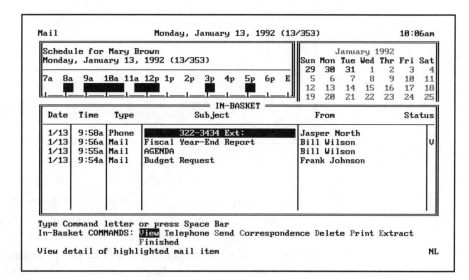

Figure 9.35 Examining Your In-Basket

Notice that phone messages are included in Mary's In-Basket list. The "V" status indicates a message has been viewed. Under "In-Basket COMMANDS," at the bottom of the screen, are the options to View a message: Telephone, Send Correspondence, Delete, Print, Extract, or Finished. If (for example) Mary selected Telephone with the phone message highlighted, Higgins would automatically call the number of the person who left this message. (Mary would have to have a modem and voice-card to do this.)

Mary selects a message she wants to View and presses Enter. The View command enables Mary to read and take action on her memos; she can answer them, forward them, file them, or delete them. The Higgins program differentiates between *attachments* (a memo sent, or a history built when a memo was first answered or routed) and *enclosures* (files—including text files and spreadsheet files—mailed along with the memo). Figure 9.36 illustrates the information available to Mary.

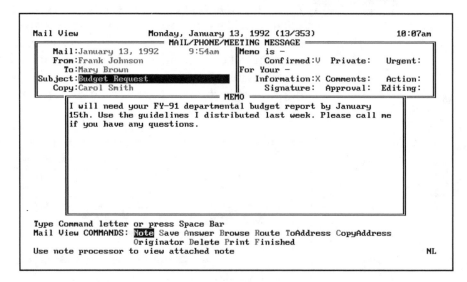

Figure 9.36 Viewing Your Mail

She can use the PgUp and PgDn keys to move through this message. Among her options at this point are Note (use her cursor keys to move through the memo), Save (save this memo), Route (forward the memo to other people), Answer (respond to the memo), and Delete (delete the memo from her In-Basket). Other options include Browse (view the next memo in the In-Basket), Enclosures (examine a list of the enclosures or view the files), History (a list of all attachments associated with viewing a memo that has been answered or routed at least once), and Originator (view the E-mail address of the person sending this memo).

Writing a Memo with Higgins

We'll assume that after reading her mail, Mary realizes she really needs to write a memo. She selects Send from her menu, and a "Mail Send" screen appears, similar to the one displayed in Figure 9.37.

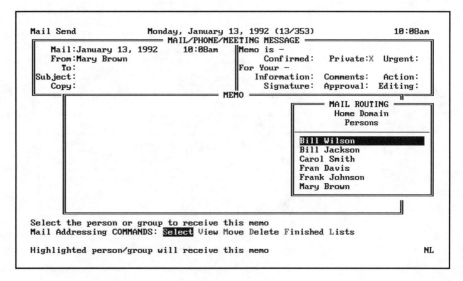

```
Mail Send                    Monday, January 13, 1992 (13/353)              10:08am
                         ═══════ MAIL/PHONE/MEETING MESSAGE ═══════
   ┌─ Mail:January 13, 1992      10:08am  ║Memo is -
   │ From:Mary Brown                      ║       Confirmed:    Private:X  Urgent:
   │   To:                                ║For Your -
   │Subject:                              ║       Information:  Comments:  Action:
   │ Copy:                                ║       Signature:    Approval:  Editing:
   │                              ═══════ MEMO ═══════╗
   │                                        ╔══════ MAIL ROUTING ══════╗
   │                                        ║          Home Domain     ║
   │                                        ║            Persons       ║
   │                                        ║ ▐▀▀▀▀▀▀▀▀▀▀▀▀▀▀▀▀▀▀▀▀▌   ║
   │                                        ║  Bill Wilson             ║
   │                                        ║  Bill Jackson            ║
   │                                        ║  Carol Smith             ║
   │                                        ║  Fran Davis              ║
   │                                        ║  Frank Johnson           ║
   │                                        ║  Mary Brown              ║
   │                                        ╚══════════════════════════╝
   │
   Select the person or group to receive this memo
   Mail Addressing COMMANDS: Select View Move Delete Finished Lists

   Highlighted person/group will receive this memo                          NL
```

Figure 9.37   Sending Mail

Pull-down windows are available (under the To: and Copy: fields) to display all users who may receive electronic mail. If the network also is running the *Higgins Exchange* program, then the list will contain names of people in other mail domains who can also receive electronic mail.

After filling in the memo's heading and writing her note, Mary has several options available to her, as indicated on the bottom of her screen. Mary's *blackbook* contains her own E-mail address list, while the *privatelist* contains specific individuals from different groups brought together to form a particular mailing or distribution list. The *Notlisted* option prints a hard copy of a memo from someone who is not listed in the mailing address list. By selecting Enclosures, Mary may add enclosures to her memo. An Enclosures window appears, requesting a file's name, directory, and description.

Using the Higgins Log Command

Now that Mary has read her mail and sent a memo, she returns to her main Higgins menu, shown earlier in Figure 9.34. The *Log* command displays Mary's appointment log window, shown in Figure 9.38.

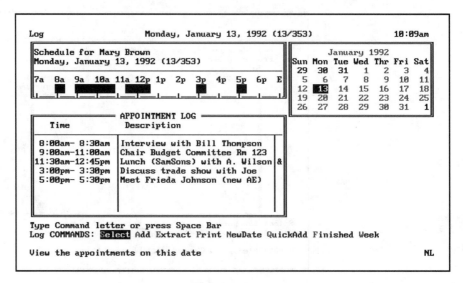

Figure 9.38　Using the Log Command

By choosing Select, Mary can view any item in her log. Other options permit Mary to *Add* an item to the log, *Extract* events from her schedule for a specific period of time (by using keywords and a data range), *Print* her log, move to a *NewDate*, quickly add a log entry (*QuickAdd*), or view her *Week* at a glance.

Higgins also provides a feature called *Appointment Call,* which, once installed in a batch file or activated by typing APPTCALL, permits Higgins to sound an alarm and remind you about an appointment, even while you are using another application program.

Using the Higgins Directory Command

The *Directory* command is one option under the Higgins Main menu. In Figure 9.39, Mary has selected the Directory option and now sees a summary window of names, companies, and telephone numbers.

```
Directory                Monday, January 13, 1992 (13/353)              10:13am
┌─────────────────────────────────────────┬────────────────────────────────┐
│Schedule for Mary Brown                    │           January 1992          │
│Monday, January 13, 1992 (13/353)          │Sun Mon Tue Wed Thr Fri Sat      │
│                                           │ 29  30  31   1   2   3   4       │
│7a  8a  9a  10a 11a 12p 1p  2p  3p  4p  5p  6p  E│  5   6   7   8   9  10  11  │
│                                           │ 12  13  14  15  16  17  18       │
│                                           │ 19  20  21  22  23  24  25       │
│                            ═══ DIRECTORY SUMMARY ═══          1              │
├──────────────────────┬──────────────────────┬─────────────────────────────┤
│        Name          │      Company         │        Telephone             │
├──────────────────────┼──────────────────────┼─────────────────────────────┤
│ Tom Allen            │ Citicorp             │  916-334-3322 X10            │
│ Mary Davis           │ PolyWidget           │  619-555-4343 X32            │
│ Higgins Group        │ Enable Software      │  (415)865-9805               │
│ Frank Larson         │ Pox Distributors     │  415-332-3434                │
│ Susan Martin         │ Polytex General      │  414-443-2555 Home           │
│ Patty Maryuma        │ Dreary Corporation   │  612-445-7890 Home           │
│ Sam Sanders          │ The Fountain         │  602-445-3411 Home           │
└──────────────────────┴──────────────────────┴─────────────────────────────┘

Type Command letter or press Space Bar
Directory COMMANDS: View Delete Add Extract Print Telephone Move Order Finished

View detail of highlighted entry                                      NL
```

Figure 9.39   Viewing the Directory

When she highlights a particular name and selects View, she'll see a screen like the one in Figure 9.40.

```
Directory View          Monday, January 13, 1992 (13/353)              10:15am
      Name:Susan Martin          * *  D I R E C T O R Y   E N T R Y  * *
     Title:Manufacturing Rep       City:San Diego
   Company:Polytex General        State:California        Zip:91232
Department:                      Business Phone:   619-443-3444 Ext:
 Address 1:1515 Widget Drive        Home Phone:   414-443-2555
 Address 2:                        Category:TELECOM        Private:No
                            ═══ NOTE ═══
        Susan usually can be reached early morning or very late
        afternoons. She doesn't like being called at home.

        Likes seafood. Will expedite any delivery if asked.


        Husband - Bob
        Kids - Mary (12/10/79) Billie (4/30/84)




Type Command letter or press Space Bar
Directory Entry COMMANDS: Note Attached Modify Delete Keywords Order BlackBook
                          Finished Calendar Telephone
Use note processor to modify the attached note                        NL
```

Figure 9.40   Viewing a Directory Entry Description

If Mary wants to write a note running several pages, she can select the Attached command and then the Add command, to add this material to her directory.

Using a To-Do List with Higgins

The *To-Do* command produces a To-Do List window similar to the one pictured in Figure 9.41. The list is organized as follows:

- According to project, alphabetically.
- Within a project, according to status, with Open before Done.
- Within status, according to priority, with priority one first.
- Within a priority, chronologically, from oldest date.

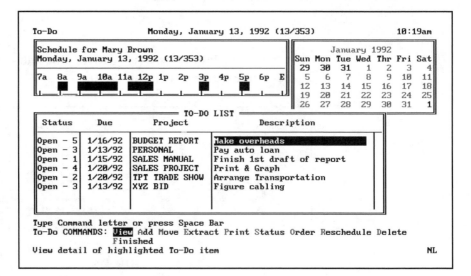

Figure 9.41 Viewing a To-Do List

If Mary wants to create a new item on her To-Do list, she selects the Add option. She'll have the opportunity to describe the item and categorize it by project name. The project name associated with the item is useful when searching by keywords. To-Do tasks may be designated as having *Open* or *Done* status, and may have priority levels between 1 and 5. A private field enables Mary to hide this item from someone else who might view her schedule in order to arrange a meeting.

Maintaining Expense Records with Higgins

One very useful Higgins feature is the *Expense* command, which maintains automated expense reports. Expense items may be entered in the log, where they are associated with an event and a directory entry. Higgins has two classifications for expenses: those already submitted on a report, and those not yet submitted on a report.

Higgins permits 12 different expense categories, which need only be named once (when the program is first installed). An *Assemble* command permits three activities: assembling new expenses for a new report, entering new expenses for a new report, or simply entering new expenses. Figure 9.42 illustrates an expense report being assembled.

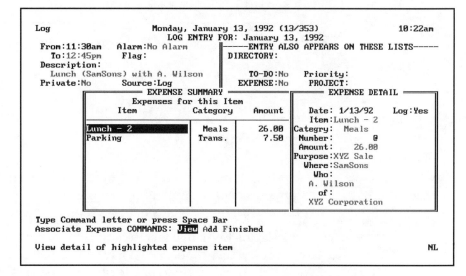

Figure 9.42   Keeping an Expense Log

Notice that for Mary's business lunch, Higgins provides details on the purpose of the meeting and the people entertained—precisely the facts needed in order to keep the IRS happy.

An *Expense Summary* window can provide a very effective expense report. Figure 9.43 illustrates such a typical report. (Notice that the report can be printed by selecting that particular option.)

```
Expense                 Monday, January 13, 1992 (13/353)           10:25am
                   ════════ EXPENSE SUMMARY ════════        ═══ EXPENSE DETAIL ═══
   Expense Report for Period Ending:  1/13/92
   Date      Item              Category    Amount      Date: 1/13/92    Log:Yes
                                                       Item:Airline Tickets
   1/13/92 Lunch - 2             Meals      26.00   Categry: Trans.
   1/13/92 Parking               Trans.      7.50   Number:         0
   1/13/92 Airline Tickets       Trans.    455.00   Amount:    455.00
   1/13/92 Hotel                 Lodging    56.00   Purpose:meet with Bill
   1/13/92 Taxi                  Trans.     26.00    Where:Washington D.C.
   1/13/92 Lunch                 Meals      18.00     Who:
                                                      Bill Thompson
                                                       of:
                                                    interviewee
                            ═══════ EXPENSE CATEGORIES ═══════
   Trans.   Lodging   Meals   Teleph   Incdntl      Auto        Travel Total
   488.50    56.00    44.00     .00       .00      0      .00       588.50

  Entrtain Shipping  Supplies Asoction Software      Other       REPORT TOTAL
     .00      .00      .00       .00      .00       0      .00       588.50

  Type Command letter or press Space Bar
  Expense Report COMMANDS: View Add Print Omit Finished

  View detail of highlighted expense item                              NL
```

Figure 9.43   An Expense Summary Report

Higgins Exchange and Higgins Gateways to Other E-mail Systems

Higgins Exchange provides routing between two networks running this program; Higgins Gateways provides connectivity with non-Higgins networks.

Each Higgins network requires only a single *Higgins Exchange* program to provide mail routing, and a single *Higgins Gateways* program to connect with non-Higgins mail systems.

Higgins Exchange takes responsibility for automatically distributing any directory changes that have taken place on another network. If copies of a memo have to be distributed to several people at a different location, the program sends one copy and a distribution list (to which the information is routed by the Higgins Exchange program running at the remote location).

Higgins Gateways provides connectivity with non-Higgins mail systems (including MHS, 3+Mail, SNADS, and PROFS). Higgins Exchange has a built-in asynchronous modem program, but it is also possible to utilize X.25 communications with the addition of appropriate software.

Enable Systems offers *Higgins To:FAX* software, designed to be used in conjunction with an Intel Connection CoProcessor board (which is installed on the workstation running Higgins Exchange). A special module of Higgins To:FAX software uses the Intel board in place of an existing standard modem, to provide 10,600 Bps mail transfer; to make the system even more efficient, file transfer takes place in the background.

Users of portable and stand-alone computers can send and receive Higgins electronic mail by using Higgins Remote and a modem, in conjunction with Higgins and Higgins Exchange. One very nice feature of this program is that it also supports direct peer-to-peer mail service between remote users.

DaVinci eMAIL

DaVinci Systems' eMAIL works under many network operating systems, but is optimized to work with NetWare.

DaVinci Systems' *DaVinci eMAIL* offers many features; these include establishing priorities and delivering certified mail. eMAIL can also send messages via fax, and via links to MCI Mail.

eMAIL is available for DOS, OS/2, Windows, and NewWave workstations. While it can be used by such network operating systems as Vines and LAN Manager, it is optimized to work with Novell's NetWare.

On a NetWare LAN, eMAIL provides automatic maintenance of its user list (from the Novell Bindery), as well as automatic management of NetWare privileges and directory access rights.

DaVinci's eMAIL features pop-up windows when run as a TSR program. A user-defined hotkey pulls in eMAIL at any time, and can be set to alert the user of all incoming messages while other applications continue to run. The program can also be run without the TSR option, to save memory.

Files can be attached to an eMAIL message and then saved onto the user's own workstation's hard disk drive. Files that can be attached include spreadsheets, executables, and graphics.

Users can take advantage of a number of eMAIL features, including the following:

- Security
- Context-sensitive on-line help
- Administrator- and user-maintained lists of names

- Carbon copies
- Certified mail
- Priority mail
- Forward and Reply

DaVinci's eMAIL can send messages to a number of different types of messaging systems, including the following:

- Fax machines
- MCI Mail
- QuickMail for the Macintosh
- DEC All-in-1 and VMSMail
- IBM's PROFS
- SYZYGY

Selecting the Right Electronic Messaging System for Your Netware Network

Selecting the right electronic messaging program requires considering many factors, including compatibility with the network.

We've examined six major electronic messaging programs in this chapter, all of which (except SMTP) are commonly used on NetWare networks. The programs range from those offering only electronic mail (cc:Mail and The Network Courier) to those offering a variety of extra scheduling and organizing functions (Higgins and The Coordinator). When selecting a program for your network, there are several issues that you must consider.

One major issue is compatibility. Does the program work on *all* the different networks you have? Does it work on the gateways to your company's minicomputers and mainframes? Some of these programs (Higgins, for example) do not offer Macintosh versions at this time, while others already have DEC gateways available (cc:Mail).

The gateways will not do you much good, however, if the electronic messaging system does not have the features your company needs. The material in this chapter was intended to make you aware of the major features these leading programs offer. The following list summarizes many of the features that may prove necessary if your company's electronic messaging is to be effective:

- Connects to other networks' electronic mail.
- Sends to distribution lists, or multiple distribution lists.
- Places restrictions on users' sending and receiving of mail.
- Auto-files messages that are sent or received.
- Provides on-line help.
- Automatically bills users who send mail.
- Uploads files to accompany messages sent.
- Prioritizes messages.
- Permits enclosures in the form of files.
- Permits attachment of related documents.

Facsimile Servers on a Network

Facsimile (fax) servers are used to receive and transmit network fax messages.

While electronic messaging software has become very popular, the link between these E-mail systems and facsimile machines is relatively new. A *facsimile (fax) server* can be used to transmit fax messages from different network workstations, as well as to receive messages and forward them to the appropriate workstation. One approach to using a fax server is to route messages to a *fax queue*: the fax server polls the file server, extracts a document from the queue (along with control information, such as the name and phone number of the destination user) and then transmits the fax message.

Some fax servers work in conjunction with E-mail systems. An E-mail user specifies that the message is to be sent to the receiver via fax transmission. This approach can be very efficient, because the fax server can take advantage of the E-mail's features (such as its global user directory). Messages can even be faxed to distribution lists created on the E-mail system.

What Have You Learned?

1. An electronic messaging system can encompass far more than just basic E-mail. It can include gateways to other networks and facsimile machines, as well as scheduling and organizing functions.

2. An X.400 message handling system includes user agents, message transfer agents, and a message transfer system.

3. Protocol P1 provides rules for routing information between two MTAs. Protocol P2 describes types of user services requested. Protocol P3 provides standards for changing existing mail parameters.

4. The CCITT X.400 recommendations cover electronic messaging, while the X.500 recommendations cover a worldwide common directory.

5. The Coordinator organizes all communications on a subject, and keeps them in sequential order as a "conversation."

6. The Coordinator offers seven types of conversations: Note, Inform, Question, Offer, Request, Promise, and What if.

7. One of cc:Mail's unique features is its ability to take snapshots of any screen and add them to any messages.

8. The cc:Mail program has a graphics editor that can be used to draw graphics or modify graphics taken from other programs.

9. The Network Courier permits the sorting of user mail by date, sender, subject, and priority.

10. Higgins provides many functions besides electronic mail, including sophisticated scheduling and organizing features.

11. Higgins Exchange connects two networks running this program, while Higgins Gateways is used to communicate with non-Higgins networks.

12. Fax servers work in conjunction with E-mail systems, so that E-mail messages can be transmitted via facsimile machines.

Quiz for Chapter 9

1. Electronic mail and the CCITT X.400 set of recommendations would be handled by which layer of the OSI model?

   a. Network

   b. Presentation

   c. Application

   d. Data Link

2. Which item is *not* part of an X.400 message handling system?

   a. A file server

   b. A user agent

   c. A message transfer agent

   d. A message transfer system

3. The basic approach of the MHS program is

   a. first-in-first-out.

   b. store-and-forward.

   c. list-in-first-out.

   d. transfer-and-process.

4. A request for an immediate reply to a message is described by which protocol under X.400?

   a. P1

   b. P2

   c. P3

   d. P4

5. Standards for a worldwide common directory are provided in

   a. X.300.

   b. X.400.

   c. X.500.

   d. X.600.

6. The electronic mail program once included with NetWare is
   a. The Coordinator.
   b. The Network Courier.
   c. cc:Mail.
   d. Higgins.

7. The program that organizes all communications into "conversa-tions" is
   a. Higgins.
   b. cc:Mail.
   c. The Coordinator.
   d. The Network Courier.

8. Which is *not* a type of conversation available under The Coordinator?
   a. Promise
   b. Request
   c. Memo
   d. What if

9. The Coordinator has a built-in gateway to other networks because it has
   a. LU 6.2.
   b. APPI.
   c. MS.
   d. MHS.

10. A special snapshot feature is available only on
    a. The Coordinator.
    b. The Network Courier.
    c. cc:Mail.
    d. Higgins.

11. Under which program do you receive information in your Inbox?
    a. The Coordinator
    b. The Network Courier
    c. cc:Mail
    d. Higgins

12. The electronic messaging program that permits graphics to be attached directly to a document is

    a. cc:Mail.

    b. The Coordinator.

    c. The Network Courier.

    d. Higgins.

13. The Chkstat utility program, providing detailed information on mailbox users, is available with

    a. The Coordinator.

    b. The Network Courier.

    c. cc:Mail.

    d. Higgins.

14. The Network Courier permits the sorting of users' mail by all these methods *except*

    a. by date.

    b. by sender's name.

    c. by subject name.

    d. by size.

15. The program that permits other users to see your To-Do list (but gives you the ability to hide certain items) is

    a. The Coordinator.

    b. Higgins.

    c. The Network Courier.

    d. cc:Mail.

16. The program providing a calculator, stopwatch, scratchpad, and a Hide the Display option is

    a. Higgins.

    b. The Network Courier.

    c. The Coordinator.

    d. cc:Mail.

17. The program that can utilize a coprocessor board to provide facsimile service is

    a. Higgins.

    b. The Network Courier.

    c. The Coordinator.

    d. cc:Mail.

18. The control information and date comprising an MHS message is enclosed in an

    a. MJB.

    b. MTC.

    c. MCB.

    d. MIT.

19. The External Mail program is a feature of

    a. Higgins.

    b. The Coordinator.

    c. cc:Mail.

    d. The Network Courier.

20. The NetWare command that permits users to connect with a different file server in order to access an external post office is

    a. ATTACH.

    b. LINK.

    c. CONNECT.

    d. MAIL.

10 | Network Management and Control

About This Chapter

The network manager is charged with responsibility for a local area network. In this chapter, we will examine many of the network manager's most important functions. Whenever possible, we will examine some of the actual management programs a network manager uses to manage and control a LAN. Finally, we will look at a protocol analyzer, one of the essential tools a network manager uses to analyze a network to determine why it is not running at maximum efficiency.

Five Functional Areas of LAN Management

The five key functional areas associated with LAN management are configuration, fault, performance, security, and accounting management.

The five functional areas of network management are configuration management, fault management, performance management, security management, and accounting management. Let's examine each of these key areas to see how a network manager spends a typical day.

Configuration Management

Configuration management consists of keeping track of what devices are attached to a network, and maintaining this information in a database for quick retrieval. The database can contain valuable information about the device, including any hardware attached and the type of software installed. This type of information is often produced by an automated *network inventory program;* the information such a program can retrieve and store about each workstation includes the following:

- The amount of RAM installed in this workstation.
- The microprocessor installed (Intel 80286, Intel 80386, etc.).
- The coprocessor (if any) installed.
- The type of network interface card installed.
- The type of video interface card installed (EGA, VGA, etc.).
- The operating system running and its version.

Among the more popular network inventory programs are Magee Enterprises' Network H.Q., Brightwork Development's LAN Automatic Inventory, and Horizons Technology's LAN Auditor. Some network inventory programs permit a network supervisor to add information and even create additional fields. Figure 10.1 illustrates a sample *hardware documentation sheet* created by a network manager who wanted to be able to retrieve this information.

```
                    Hardware Network Documentation


Type of Equipment:_____
Serial Number:_____
Location:_____
Date Purchased:_____
Warranty Expiration Date:_____
Vendor: _____ Contact:_____
Telephone:_____

Service Contract #:_____
Vendor:_____ Contact:_____
Telephone:_____

Problems:

Date    Problem           Solution
```

Figure 10.1 A Hardware Documentation Sheet

By using this format to keep vital information on all workstations, interface boards, printers, and other devices, the network supervisor will be able to organize network resources more efficiently. Figure 10.2 illustrates a *software documentation sheet,* a similar profile that can be maintained for all software installed on the network.

```
┌─────────────────────────────────────────────────────┐
│              Software Network Documentation           │
│                                                       │
│  Name of Program:_____ DOS Version:_____ │
│  Publisher:_____Tel:_____  │
│                                                       │
│  Purchased From:_____Tel:_____  │
│  Date Purchased:_____                      │
│  Warranty Expires:_____                       │
│                                                       │
│  System Requirements:                                 │
│    RAM Required: _____                        │
│    Hard Disk/Floppies:_____                      │
│                                                       │
│  Software Maintenance/Support:                        │
│    Vendor:_____                    │
│    Telephone:_____                     │
│                                                       │
│  Problems:                                            │
│                                                       │
│  Date    Problem         Solution                     │
└─────────────────────────────────────────────────────┘
```

Figure 10.2   A Software Documentation Sheet

An advantage of maintaining a network inventory in a database is that a manager can create network configuration reports for planning purposes. How many workstations, for example, are still using Intel 80286 microprocessors? These machines will not be able to take advantage of any Windows 3.1 packages that are purchased. How many machines only have 1 megabyte of RAM installed? These machines will have to be upgraded to at least 4 megabytes of RAM to take full advantage of Windows software. A network manager might also be interested in learning how many workstations are still running MS-DOS 3.3. What would it cost to upgrade these workstations to MS-DOS 5.0, in order to provide them with memory management capabilities?

Another important function of inventory software is to provide the information needed to solve network problems. In many companies with large local area networks, a network user who is having trouble running a particular program can call a *network help desk* and request help. The help desk specialist can use information provided by the network inventory software (in the *configuration database*) to examine the user's hardware and software configuration. The specialist might determine (for example) that a RAM shortage is causing the user's machine to lock up when a graphic file is loaded into a WordPerfect program.

Another user might be having a problem with a certain program because of its incompatibility with the version of MS-DOS running on the workstation. The network inventory program can help the supervisor isolate this problem.

LAN configuration programs can also provide a network manager with information about the status of all network devices, including bridges and routers. Some programs provide this information in a graphical format. (For example, the network supervisor's screen might show a device displayed in red to indicate that it is either turned off or malfunctioning.)

Fault Management

Fault management includes documenting and reporting network problems.

Fault management is the network management function concerned with documenting and reporting network errors. A network manager needs to know how many misformed packets are being produced, how many times packets must be retransmitted on an EtherNet network, whether a workstation is transmitting a beacon signal on a network, etc.

The Frye Utilities for Networks includes the *NetWare Early Warning System,* an example of how a network manager can use specialized software for fault management. A network manager might set the program's thresholds so that it will issue an alert under the following conditions:

- The file server does not respond.
- The file server's utilization reaches a certain percentage of capacity.
- Packets are discarded because they have crossed over 16 bridges.
- A printer is off-line.

The program can be instructed to notify the network manager in a number of different ways. One method would consist of displaying a 25th-line message on the network manager's monitor. A second method might transmit an electronic mail message automatically. If an electronic mail program with a *notify feature* (such as cc:Mail) is installed on the network, the network manager will hear a beep and see a message displayed—indicating that an E-mail message has just been received.

If a Hayes-compatible modem is available to the network, the Frye Utilities NetWare Early Warning System program can be instructed to transmit a pager message (for people who are rarely in their offices). The program can also be instructed to send a facsimile message (fax), but perhaps its most unusual option (assuming the proper hardware is installed) is to provide incoming voice notification and outgoing voice notification.

With these options installed, a network manager can call the LAN and receive a voice update concerning error conditions. The outgoing voice notification option enables the program to call a number and send a voice message. (Imagine the reaction of a network manager who receives a call at home at 3 a.m. from the LAN, and hears a digitized voice describe network error conditions.)

Performance Management

One of a network manager's major responsibilities is to ensure a network's *efficient performance,* and that its service is not deteriorating. Since new and occasional users may have trouble with such routine network functions as the login (for example), network supervisors must help them by establishing routines to follow. In the case of IBM's network software, such routines are customized batch files that need be written only once. Novell's NetWare includes login scripts; though these may take only a few minutes for a supervisor to write, they can save novices hours, and eliminate a good deal of frustration.

Another area of network efficiency that needs to be monitored by the network supervisor is *network traffic statistics.* By examining printer usage statistics, for example, the supervisor might determine that certain log reports need to be spooled and printed after peak hours. Heavy usage of certain accounting programs that place a premium on file server access can slow the entire network. The supervisor might decide to add a separate file server for the accounting department, in order to speed up the rest of the network.

Network General's *Watchdog* serves as an example of software (and hardware) that a network manager can use to ensure that a network performs efficiently. The workstation into which this software is loaded includes a network interface card which allows the workstation to capture real-time network data. The Watchdog provides detailed statistical information about network traffic patterns. This information can be displayed graphically, so that the network manager can view which workstations are generating the most traffic.

The Watchdog can report which workstations are generating packets with the most errors (a sign that the workstation might have a defective network interface card). The network manager can also monitor the traffic between a file server and print server—or between two workstations—to examine potential bottlenecks that might be causing network traffic congestion.

One advantage of gathering network traffic statistics when the network is performing efficiently is that it provides a benchmark which can be used to discover why a network suddenly begins to operate sluggishly. The Watchdog also has a *cable test function* that enables the network manager to check a network segment to see if there is a cabling problem.

Security Management

Security management includes protecting a network from unauthorized access, both from network and non-network users.

Another major network management function is *security*. A network manager must keep a network secure from unauthorized access, as well as from invasion by computer viruses. Protecting a network from unauthorized users means limiting the access of a company's own network users, as well as eliminating network access by noncompany employees.

Limiting a Company's Own Network Users

The access of network users can be limited by password protection, time restrictions, and restrictions on which workstations can be used to log into the network.

A network manager can use features found in most network operating systems (such as NetWare) to limit access by network users to the company's most important directories and files. A directory can be "hidden" so that it does not show up when a user issues a DIR command. Also, if the manager of a NetWare LAN does not give a user search-and-read rights to a particular network directory, the user will not see any files in that directory when issuing a DIR command. Similarly, a network manager can limit the rights of users to a specific file within a directory.

The network manager can require *passwords* for users when they log into a network and into a specific file server. This means that a user can be restricted from accessing a particular file server, while retaining access to a different file server. Some additional ways the network manager can enhance password protection when users log into the network are the following:

- Prevent users from placing their passwords in a batch file for automatic login. (Batch files can be viewed by unauthorized users.)

- Require the user's password to have a certain number of letters.

- Require the user to change a password at intervals (such as every 30 or 60 days).

- Prevent users from using the same password twice.

- Provide users with passwords containing random combinations of letters. (Passwords that represent the names of spouses, children, or pets are often too easy for outsiders to guess.)

- Prevent users from logging into the network from several different workstations concurrently.

- Restrict users from logging into the network during certain hours, and even during certain days of the week (Saturdays, Sundays, etc.).

- Some network operating systems (such as NetWare 3.x) *encrypt* passwords so that sophisticated users cannot examine the password file and learn users' passwords.

- Network managers must also be alert to prevent users from writing their passwords on scraps of paper and taping these notes to their computers or monitors because they are afraid they will forget them.

- Some users will log into the network and then leave their workstations unattended for extended periods of time. Unauthorized users can do enormous network damage if they take advantage of this situation.

- Network managers must be notified whenever an employee is terminated or voluntarily leaves a company, so that this person's network account can be eliminated.

- Temporary users should be assigned a network account with an expiration date, and with very limited access to sensitive network files.

Preventing Unauthorized Users from Dialing into a LAN

LAN security becomes even more difficult to maintain when users are permitted to log in from remote sites. Password protection provides one level of protection. This protection can be enhanced by limiting the number of unsuccessful login attempts before locking the user's account. After three (or perhaps five) unsuccessful login attempts, users might be required to contact the network manager to reset the account. This measure will prevent unauthorized users from dialing in repeatedly and using a random password generator to try to break into a network.

Another effective way to prevent unauthorized users from logging into a LAN from a remote site is to use a *call-back modem*—which receives a call, requires a password, and then calls the user back after a random number of seconds. The call-back modem is programmed with a table containing a list of authorized users, their passwords, and their phone numbers.

Protecting a Network from Computer Viruses

A network must be protected from computer viruses that attach themselves to other programs and then spread to additional programs, disrupting their operation.

Viruses are self-replicating bits of computer code that hide in computer programs (and often in RAM). They attach themselves to other programs, and accompany them when they are copied to other disks or onto a network. Once activated, these viruses can disrupt the programs to which they are attached. When they "hide" in RAM, viruses attach themselves to more and more programs as each one is executed.

A virus is particularly disruptive on a network; it can spread rapidly through a network's various directories and subdirectories until all traffic stops. The solution for many network managers is to install *preventive software* that checks for viruses before other software is executed—usually detecting a virus before it can do any damage. Many programs also destroy the virus once it is detected.

Central Point's *Anti-Virus* software serves as an example of how many of these programs function. It checks for viruses by verifying files' checksums, and checking for other file irregularities. A terminate-and-stay-resident (TSR) program loads into memory, and checks programs before they are executed. It notifies the user when a virus has been detected, names it, and then destroys it. The program is capable of removing viruses from infected files, boot sectors, and partition tables—without having to delete these files.

On many networks, only the LAN manager can load files onto the network. Often the network manager will test a program on a local workstation, and scan it for viruses before adding the program to the network. Users are prohibited from uploading files and programs directly from bulletin boards onto the network.

Accounting Management

Accounting management is the ability to allocate network costs to users and their departments.

Accounting management is the network function associated with allocating network costs to users and their departments. A network operating system such as NetWare provides the built-in capability to perform this task.

Under NetWare, a network manager can keep accurate track of when specific individuals use specific file servers. This means that users can be charged for using a print server, a file server, and even a gateway.

Users can be charged for how many blocks of information they read from a file server, and how many blocks they write to a file server. Network managers can even vary the charge rates for connections, so that it is less expensive for users who log into the network during off hours. A network manager can set charge rates for service requests so that users who want to print during prime time will pay considerably more than users who are willing to print during the late afternoon or evening.

Daily Network Management Chores for the Network Manager

We have examined some of the broad functional areas of network management associated with LAN management; now we will look at some of the day-to-day responsibilities associated with network management and control. These responsibilities include backing up file servers, maintaining the network user interface, troubleshooting network problems, and maintaining network hardware and software.

Backing Up File Servers

A major chore for all network supervisors is to develop a carefully planned schedule for *network backups.* Some network areas, such as accounting, might require backups twice a day. The entire system, of course, should be backed up on a daily basis. Most software will time-stamp files, requiring backup only of those files that have been modified since the last backup.

The supervisor should perform backups of all files every week and periodically place a backup in a safe off-site location.

Palodrome Corporation's *The Network Archivist (TNA)* serves as an example of specialized software that helps a network manager manage and control network backups. TNA enables a network manager to establish a backup schedule, indicate when tapes should be rotated, and schedule an unattended backup. The program maintains a backup history for each file, so that the network manager can restore a specific version of a file. This feature is useful when a user needs an earlier version of a file that has been overwritten. The network manager can restore an individual file, a directory, or the entire file server. For larger networks, the Network Archivist can be used in conjunction with a 2.2GB, 8mm tape drive.

Maintaining Network User Interfaces

The network manager must *maintain the LAN's user interface.* Often this means using a *menuing program* to create a common menu for network users, so that they will not need to know network commands to use the LAN.

The *Saber* menuing system serves as an excellent example of how a menuing program works. Each time the network manager adds an important program to the LAN, the new program can be added to the network's menu as well. A user who wants to use a word processing program, for example, can select the "Word Processing" menu option. A second menu is then displayed, offering WordPerfect 5.1, WordPerfect 5.0, and Word 5.0 as options. The user selects one of these programs, and presses Enter to load a copy of the chosen program from the network.

A network operating system lets you place users into groups, and the Saber menuing system can work with the operating system to display different menus to different groups. An Accounting Department employee might see a menu displayed that lets him load the Accounts Payable, Accounts Receivable, or Payroll programs. A Drafting Department employee might see an entirely different menu, which lets him load computer-assisted drawing and graphics programs. Finally, a temporary employee hired to perform word processing might see a menu that offers only the word processing option.

A menuing system can also be used to control network printing. A user can select the Print menu option and see several different printing options (Epson dot-matrix printer, Hewlett-Packard LaserJet III, etc.). The user then can load a program and select the print option, knowing the document will be sent to the selected printer.

A menuing system can also be customized for an individual user's hardware, so that a user with a monochrome monitor will load a monochrome menu. The Saber menuing system even permits users to customize their own menus. A user who frequently loads a word processing program might want to place this option in the Main menu to avoid going through two different menus to select this program.

A menuing program such as the Saber system can be used by a network manager to prevent users from issuing DOS-level commands. Because a user cannot break out of the menu to a DOS prompt, the user is unable to download files, load programs from a local hard disk, or perform any one of a host of tasks that could compromise a network's security.

A menuing system can also be used to monitor and control the number of users who can run a program concurrently. The Saber system, for example, lets the network manager control the number of users able to access a program at any given time. The network manager can purchase a license for 15 users, for example, and then establish this limit in the menuing program. The 16th user who attempts to access this program will be informed that the maximum number of users are currently running the program, and then will be provided with a list of these users. A user who desperately needs to access this program can check to see if someone on this list has forgotten to log out of the network.

Troubleshooting Network Problems

Many network managers spend a disproportionate amount of their time *troubleshooting network problems.* A user calls to report that she is unable to print, while a second user calls to complain that he is unable to use his mouse with a program. A third user might call to complain that he is unable to log into the network. The network manager diagnoses the user's problem by asking a series of questions—just as a doctor asks several questions to diagnose a patient's illness.

First, the network manager must determine whether the problem is *hardware-* or *software-related.* Is the problem limited to a single user's workstation, or is it a problem with the network program itself? Is the user's local network interface card defective, or is the network connector linking the workstation to the network loose?

Some network managers utilize a program such as *Closeup,* which enables them to "take over" a local workstation and view that workstation's screen from their own monitor. The network manager might take over the workstation of the user who complained about not being able to print, to see if the correct printer has been selected. The network manager might take over the workstation of the user unable to use his mouse so that the appropriate mouse can be installed (using the program's *install option*). In a later section, we will examine some of the network manager's major troubleshooting tools, including a protocol analyzer.

Maintaining Network Hardware and Software

Network maintenance includes updating software as new versions are released, creating and updating network documentation, replacing defective equipment, and periodically checking network cabling.

Network maintenance is a very important part of a network manager's daily responsibility. When a new release of a network application program appears, the network manager must install this software promptly, so that the software vendor can provide accurate technical support should it be needed.

Another major maintenance chore for the network manager is to create and maintain *network documentation.* If a user's network interface card becomes defective, the network manager must have documentation available that shows when the card was installed, the card's serial number, and the warranty expiration date. If a file server goes down, the network manager must know whether it is covered by a 24-hour service contract or an 8-5 contract. Similarly, the network manager must keep accurate documentation on other network equipment (such as printers, bridges, routers, gateways, and tape backup units).

This type of critical information often can be placed in a *network log book* to provide clear audit trails of all network changes. Password changes, alterations in user access, software updates that have been installed, and program additions or deletions can be noted and dated. Such a log book should be kept under lock and key when not being used. Without such an administrative tool, the network represents a disaster waiting to happen.

The network manager should be able to access this information rapidly, so that the equipment's manufacturer or vendor can be called quickly. Technical support departments usually require the equipment's serial number, warranty expiration date, and detailed information about the LAN's topology—including the version number of the network operating system.

In order to reduce the number of calls from frustrated users, the network manager must provide users with accurate and easy-to-read *network documentation.* How can users direct a document to a specific printer? How can a user copy several network files from one directory to another directory? How can a user customize a Saber menu? These are the types of questions that must be answered in user documentation.

Periodically, a network manager must "walk the network" to check the LAN's cabling. Checking the cabling can determine whether connectors are coming loose, cabling is cracking or pinched, or hubs are operating properly.

Some network managers report they have to reset network devices such as hubs at least a couple of times a week to keep them operating efficiently. Since so many network devices now have diagnostic lights to indicate how they are performing, a network manager can quickly determine whether traffic is flowing smoothly—or whether access collisions are taking place or a channel is not operating properly.

The Network Supervisor's Tools

A network supervisor would be well advised to have a number of tools and materials on hand—including both straight and Phillips screwdrivers, as well as needle-nose and diagonal-cutters pliers. A volt-ohm meter or digital voltmeter is useful for cable testing.

When workstations suffer hardware failure, often it is because of a bad interface board, a defective floppy disk drive, or some bad memory chips. While large companies will probably have in-house technicians to handle these problems, a network supervisor might find it expedient to keep some of these materials on-hand—as well as an ample supply of printer ribbons, printer paper, extra formatted tapes for file-server backups, toner cartridges for the network laser printer, and certainly a box (at least) of *formatted* floppy disks.

A Protocol Analyzer

A protocol analyzer analyzes the frames traveling across a network; it provides valuable information on the performance of the network's interface cards, file server, and software.

A *protocol analyzer* provides the key to understanding why a network is not running at top efficiency. Protocol analyzers analyze the packets of information flowing across a network and provide very valuable statistics. While there are several major protocol analyzers on the market, we'll focus on one of the major contenders: Network General Corporation's *The Sniffer*.

Attached to a network as if it were a workstation, the Sniffer listens to every transmission that goes by it. Although its major focus is the Data Link layer of the OSI model (discussed in Chapter 2), it displays information used by applications up to the Session layer.

The Sniffer is a self-contained computer—with its own network adapter card, hard disk, operating system, and software. If you exit from the Sniffer program, the machine becomes a standard DOS-based Compaq microcomputer. While running the Sniffer, however, the machine has two major functions: to *capture frames* and to *display information.*

Because of the amount of information passing through a protocol analyzer, it is usually *filtered* by establishing parameters. The user may want to select by station address, protocol, or particular frame pattern.

The Sniffer uses a bar graphic to display traffic density as kilobytes per second, as frames per second, or as a percentage of the network's available bandwidth. Information can be displayed in linear form or logarithmic scale.

The Sniffer also displays traffic statistics through the use of counters which reveal the number of frames seen, the number of frames accepted, and the percentage of the *capture buffer* (the area in the Sniffer's memory that holds captured packets) in use.

For each station that is contributing to network traffic, the Sniffer is able to display—in real time—a count of frames per second or kilobytes per second. The machine also displays *pair counts* for each pair of workstations communicating information.

Figure 10.3 illustrates both a summary and a detailed display of an exchange between two stations. Notice that the Sniffer identifies the two stations communicating from its own name table; apparently user Dan is communicating with the NetWare SERVER. The conversation we are eavesdropping on consists of a response from the NetWare file server regarding its LOGIN file.

Notice also that this protocol analyzer provides some detailed file directory information about the file being accessed. We are able to observe the file's length, its creation date, the last access date, and the last update date/time.

As this brief discussion of the Sniffer illustrates, protocol analyzers have proven to be invaluable tools for network managers. With some practice, a network manager can read and analyze their reports with relative ease—revealing a good deal of information regarding the network's general health.

```
- - - - - - - - - - Frame 31 - - - - - - - - - - - - - - - -

SUMMARY Rel Time NW Util Destination Source  Summary
    31   2.9825  1.43%  SERVER      User Dan LC 802.2 size=46 bytes
                                             NS NetWare Request N=89 C=4 T=1
                                             CP C Open file LOGIN
- - - - - - - - - - Frame 32 - - - - - - - - - - - - - - - -

SUMMARY Rel Time NW Util Destination Source  Summary
    32   2.9860  1.57%  User Dan    SERVER   DLC 802.2 size=74 bytes
                                             XLS NetWare Reply N=89 C=4 T=0
                                             NCP R F=08F1 OK Opened

DLC:  ---- DLC Header ----
DLC:
DLC:  Frame 32 arrived at  13:59:56.7703 ; frame size is 88 (0058 hex) bytes.
DLC:  Destination: Station 02608C119421, User Dan
DLC:  Source     : Station 02608C217692, SERVER
DLC:  802.2 LLC length = 74
DLC:
INS:  ---- INS Header ----
INS:
INS:  Checksum = FFFF
INS:  Length = 74
INS:  Transport control = 00
INS:      0000 .... = Reserved
INS:      .... 0000 = Hop count
INS:  Packet type = 17 (Novell NetWare)
INS:
INS:  Dest   net = 00217692, host = 02608C119421, socket = 4001 (16385)
INS:  Source net = 00217692, host = 02608C217692, socket = 1105 (NetWare Server)
INS:
INS:  ---- Novell Advanced NetWare ----
INS:
INS:  Request type = 3333 (Reply)
INS:  Seq no=89  Connection no=4   Task no=0
INS:
NCP:  ---- Open File Reply ----
NCP:
NCP:  Request code = 76 (reply to frame 31)
NCP:
NCP:  Completion code = 00 (OK)
NCP:  Connection status flags = 00 (OK)
NCP:  File handle = 0AF6 AC08 AE0F
NCP:  File name = "LOGIN"
NCP:  File attribute flags = 00
NCP:        0... .... = File is not sharable
NCP:        .0.. .... = Not defined
NCP:        ..0. .... = Not changed since last archive
NCP:        ...0 .... = Not a subdirectory
NCP:        .... 0... = Not execute-only file
NCP:        .... .0.. = Not a system file
NCP:        .... ..0. = Not a hidden file
NCP:        .... ...0 = Read and write allowed
NCP:  File execute type = 00
NCP:  File length = 16
NCP:  Creation date       = 2-Dec-86
NCP:  Last access date    = 13-Feb-87
NCP:  Last update date/time = 2-Dec-86 16:08:54
NCP:
NCP:  [Normal end of NetWare "Open File Reply" packet.]
NCP:
```

Summary view
of a request to open a file

Summary and detail views
of the server's reply

Low-level source and destination data
Stations identified from The Sniffer's
name table

High-level source and destination data

The Sniffer points back to the query
for which this frame is the response

File's name and handle

Attribute flags decoded

File directory data

Figure 10.3 A Report from The Sniffer (Reprinted with the Permission of Network General Corporation)

What Have You Learned?

1. The five functional areas of network management are configuration management, fault management, performance management, security management, and accounting management.

2. Automated inventory programs are useful tools for configuration management.

3. Fault management includes documenting and reporting network errors.

4. Monitoring network traffic patterns and generating network statistics are important parts of performance management.

5. Network users can be restricted from using key directories and files.

6. Call-back modems are a way of protecting a network from remote users' unauthorized access.

7. Network users can be limited to using the network certain days of the week and certain hours.

8. Viruses are self-replicating bits of computer code that hide in certain programs and then disrupt their operation.

9. A menuing program can provide an easy-to-use network user interface.

10. Protocol analyzers are excellent troubleshooting devices that examine the contents of network packets.

11. A network manager's primary responsibility is to keep the network running efficiently.

Quiz for Chapter 10

1. _____ is not a functional area of network management.
   a. Configuration management
   b. Documentation management
   c. Performance management
   d. Security management

2. Automated inventory programs are a part of
   a. configuration management.
   b. performance management.
   c. security management.
   d. accounting management.

3. Keeping track of the number of misformed packets is a function of
   a. performance management.
   b. fault management.
   c. security management.
   d. accounting management.

4. Network General's Watchdog is utilized by a network manager for
   a. accounting management.
   b. configuration management.
   c. security management.
   d. performance management.

5. Network security can be enhanced by all of the following except
   a. restricting users to certain days and hours.
   b. making users change their passwords at set intervals.
   c. letting users select their own passwords.
   d. preventing users from repeating the same passwords.

6. Remote users to a LAN can be restricted by

    a. dial-up modems.

    b. call-back modems.

    c. asynchronous modems.

    d. synchronous modems.

7. Computer viruses can be found in all but

    a. boot sectors.

    b. partition tables.

    c. RAM.

    d. video cards.

8. Network accounting bills everything except

    a. file server blocks read.

    b. file server blocks written.

    c. local workstation disk space used.

    d. network connections.

9. A menuing system can provide all the following benefits except

    a. making a network perform more efficiently.

    b. making it easier to use the network.

    c. preventing users from seeing certain menu options.

    d. preventing users from reaching a DOS-level prompt.

10. A protocol analyzer can

    a. display traffic patterns in graphic form.

    b. summarize traffic between two stations.

    c. provide detailed data on traffic between two stations.

    d. all of the above.

11 | A Guide to Networkable Software

About This Chapter

Many companies have found that installing a LAN also meant selecting new software written specifically for their network. Fortunately, MS-DOS and (more recently) OS/2 have provided some uniformity in network software. Since the network hardware and software offered by IBM, Artisoft, Novell, and AT&T all adhere to DOS standards, software publishers have found it fairly easy to write generic network editions of their products which will work on almost any DOS-based network.

In this chapter, we will examine how all versions of MS-DOS since 3.1 provide network features (such as record locking) and what options companies have if their single-user software cannot be upgraded to at least DOS 3.1 standards. We'll survey the most desirable features found in word processing programs, spreadsheets, database managers, and accounting programs, and see how they function in a network environment.

MS-DOS

MS-DOS has provided (in its versions since 3.1) true multiuser operations. Its SHARE program (which provides different levels of access) takes advantage of MS-DOS's record-locking and "byte-locking" functions.

As Figure 11.1 shows, MS-DOS resides in the Presentation layer of the OSI model, along with the Redirector program. It acts as an interface between the application programs and the NETBIOS (which resides between the Presentation and Session layers).

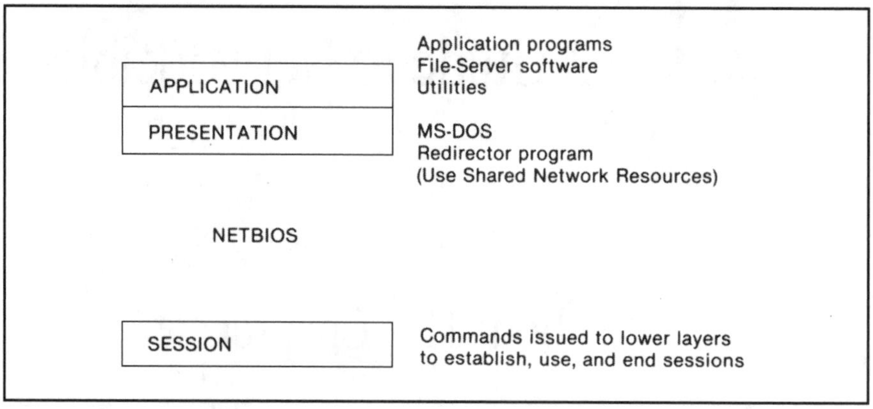

Figure 11.1 MS-DOS and the OSI Model

Under network conditions, MS-DOS provides multiuser access to files through its SHARE program. SHARE enables the programmer to specify that the first workstation to use a file has certain levels of access, while subsequent users have different levels of access.

A crucial accounting data file (for example), used by several different workstations, could be designated as read-write for the first user to request it. While this user continues to write to this file, other users (under SHARE's Read-Write with *deny-write sharing mode*) can only read the file.

MS-DOS versions 3.1 and above also have a *byte-locking* function—which enables a programmer to write a program so that a range of bytes is locked, and other users cannot write to this area until the first user "unlocks" the area. The result of the SHARE program's different access rights and MS-DOS's byte-locking is that a file will not be destroyed by two users simultaneously writing over each other's data.

Programs written prior to the release of MS-DOS version 3.1 are unable to utilize this multiuser feature. Although they can be installed on a network so that one user is allowed to write to a file while other users can only read it, such manipulation is of limited value in most office environments. This is because the only alternative with DOS 2.x versions is to write multiple copies of the file to different directories and have different people use different versions of the file (a cumbersome and confusing approach). With version 3.1's record locking, different users can take turns accessing the *same* record.

The Redirector program acts as a "traffic cop."

In addition to MS-DOS's multiuser capabilities, it allows use of the Redirector program, and programmers have begun to utilize this capability. The Redirector acts as a "traffic cop," directing requests for shared network resources, and it is used by many network programs.

Client/Server Applications Under OS/2

In Chapter 1 we examined some of the features that distinguish MS-OS/2, the operating system that IBM sees as the foundation of larger future LANs. Because of its true multitasking nature, OS/2 heralds a new level of distributed network computing.

Before OS/2, most LAN file servers handled a workstation's database query by sending the entire database file across the network to that workstation. When the workstation completed sorting the database (and making whatever changes it needed to make), it returned the information to the file server.

There are several problems associated with this traditional LAN approach to sharing a database program and its files. *Network congestion* increases as more and more workstations request that the program and its files be sent, and then send information back to the file server. *Network overhead* also can become a problem with this approach, since a database program may need to create several different processes to permit multiuser operations. With so many files traveling through the network, *data integrity* also may be an issue.

Microsoft and Ashton-Tate have developed a *structured query language (SQL)* server program called *SQL Server.* Running on a file server under OS/2, SQL Server can provide database management service to applications running on network workstations.

When a workstation queries an SQL database, SQL Server's "back-end" program receives the request, finds where the desired information resides on the database, then forwards only the specific information requested—not the entire database file—back to the workstation (which does its own processing). The end user's "front-end" application program uses APIs to make these queries and requests in a manner transparent to the user. It does not matter where the database is physically located. Figure 11.2 illustrates this process.

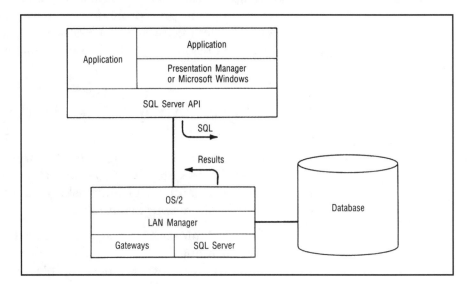

Figure 11.2 The Client/Server Model (Courtesy of Microsoft Corporation)

This type of distributed processing is called *client/server computing:* a "front-end" *client* application program accesses a "back-end" *server.* When this approach is used with a database, several different types of client "front-end" applications (spreadsheets, accounting programs, project management programs, etc.) can access the "back-end" server (in this case, the database server).

The "front-end" application program processes the information it requested and displays it on its screen. Meanwhile, the "back-end" server program maintains the database's integrity and ensures that the network will function with optimum efficiency.

Network Software and the Law

Most single-user software is licensed for one user and/or one machine. To use software on a network, it is necessary to buy a network version of the program, sign a site-licensing agreement, or negotiate a volume purchase from the software manufacturer.

Most *single-user* software packages specify that the program may only be used on a single machine and/or by one user at a time. *Using such programs under network conditions is clearly illegal.* Therefore, a major consideration in selecting network software is the software vendor's policy toward network use of its product.

Many companies have developed special *network versions* of their products; these are licensed for specific sizes of user groups. A network supervisor might select WordPerfect (for example) and then license a certain number of copies to run on the network. The customer pays for the initial package, and then a per-user fee. Beyond the basic program, WordPerfect Corporation supplies extra network features (such as some laser-printing utilities) that make it advantageous for a customer to purchase this edition.

For a negotiated fee, other companies provide a *site-licensing agreement* that specifies that the product may be used at that site by an unlimited number of users.

Unfortunately, many major software companies simply offer discounts if their single-user products are purchased in large volumes. This solution is not acceptable for most companies that use LANs; it is far too expensive, even with substantial discounts.

Word Processing Software

Word processing is probably the most common application that users require in their daily jobs. This section will discuss how word processing programs fit into the network picture.

Why Use a Network Version of a Word Processing Program?

Network versions of word processing programs provide some assurances of file compatibility, printer compatibility, and a standardized appearance for company documents.

Most network users have already developed a fondness for a particular word processing program, and prefer to continue using it. There are various problems, however, with everyone using his or her own word processing program—and then using the network file server for document storage:

- Not all word processing files are compatible with one another.
- Since different programs have varying formatting capabilities, it is difficult to achieve uniformity within a company. Bill's proposals might look completely different from Janet's, and when they work on a document together (and try to exchange data files), it might be impossible for either of them to determine what the final document will look like.
- Various program versions offer varying features. If two employees are using two versions of WordStar, only one of them might be able to perform a mail merge with a customer file to create customized form letters.
- Different versions of the same program also might contain slightly different printer drivers, and these could create some unpleasant printing surprises.
- Single-user word processing programs do not offer file-locking capabilities. This feature is extremely important on a network, because it means that several individuals can use the same word processing program without worrying about destroying a particular document file inadvertently.

Word Processing Features

While there are hundreds of word processing features available on some of the major network versions, we'll concentrate on those features of particular value to network users. We'll assume that a company with a LAN prints dozens of types of documents, including some material on pre-existing forms. Furthermore, the company has several hundred customers that it wishes to communicate with on a regular basis. To achieve these word processing objectives, a company would have to examine programs that offer certain formatting, editing, and file-managing features—and a number of utility programs. Let's look at some important formatting features.

Seeing Is Believing

A second major formatting feature that distinguishes some word processing programs is their ability to display information exactly as it will appear when printed. This *"what you see is what you get"* feature is particularly important in a network program, since network users frequently share laser printers as well as software.

For example, Microsoft Word has a network version that takes advantage of *Enhanced Graphics Adapter (EGA)* and *Video Graphics Adapter (VGA)* standards to display a number of fonts as they will appear when printed. The network version is specifically designed to work with a laser printer to produce typeset-like quality.

For those network users who need actual typesetting, Microsoft offers the Linoword interface between Word and the Linotron laser typesetting machine. While few programs can match Word's ability to display different fonts, the minimum acceptable functionality for most network users is the ability to see boldface, underlining, and strike-overs displayed on the screen. Word Perfect performs these features admirably.

Style Sheets

Style sheets enable word processing users to format documents after writing them, by linking the document to a particular set of style specifications.

Companies large enough to support a LAN usually require specific formats for their various types of documents. A company might stipulate, for example, that all top-level headings in its proposals be uppercase and boldface, and all subheadings be lowercase and underlined. Company policy might also dictate that all memos use a specific font, with the headings in boldface. Research reports might require still another company-dictated format, with footnotes placed at the bottom of the page.

Microsoft Word offers several *styles* for creating footnotes, headings, and subheadings. A network user writing a letter, memo, report, or proposal selects the appropriate *style sheet,* and Word automatically formats it correctly. This feature is especially valuable on a network, since it ensures that all company correspondence and reports are uniform in style and format.

Forms Processing

Certain word processing programs can design forms and then place information into these forms.

One frustrating aspect of using a word processing program instead of a typewriter is the difficulty of printing information precisely where a standard form requires it. This ability to define and print fields anywhere on a pre-existing form is known as *forms processing;* it is particularly valuable on a company network in which several different forms are used on a regular basis. Samna's Word program has this capability.

Editing Multiple Documents

A LAN user might need to view two documents simultaneously in order to compare certain passages. Some network word processing programs (such as WordStar and Word) enable users to view and edit different documents simultaneously as they are displayed in screen windows; Word enables the user to view up to eight windows at once. Other programs (such as WordPerfect) enable a user to load two documents and then switch back and forth between them; the Windows version of Word Perfect now offers simultaneous viewing of more than one document.

Mail Merge

Some word processing programs can merge information found in a database program (names, addresses, etc.) with a letter to produce individualized form letters.

One of the major word processing functions on a local area network is the *mail merge.* Companies frequently merge customer information (name, address, etc.) contained in database files with a form letter produced on the word processing program. Beyond that, the merge often permits important individualized information to be inserted within the letter if certain conditions are met. Widget Company might write a form letter to all its customers, for instance, but it might include a paragraph about an upcoming Megawidget Seminar only in those letters addressed to customers who recently purchased this product.

If mail merging is to be a major network function, the network administrator must address the critical question of what form the customer data will take—and how easily this information can be merged with a particular word processing program. Some word processing programs offer the capability to merge with several types of files, including dBASE, ASCII, and SYLK formats.

Word Processing Program File Formats

Effective mail merging requires complete compatibility between the word processing program and the database's customer files; if data communication is a major network concern, it is equally important to determine the file formats a word processor produces. A company might have its LAN connected through a gateway PC with its mainframe computer. It also might have its LAN connected with remote branch locations. Since PC communications programs are usually designed to transmit ASCII files without word processing control codes, it is important to consider which word processing file formats are available.

Most major word processing programs today can produce standard ASCII files, and can import the ASCII files produced by other word processing programs into the network. If network users wish to incorporate Lotus 1-2-3 worksheets within their word processing documents, WordStar 2000 can read Lotus files directly, as can several other word processing programs.

Printer Support

To utilize all the features of a laser printer, a word processing program should have a printer driver specifically written for that printer.

Since software programs require *printer drivers* in order to print documents, a company with incompatible printers offers a real challenge for a network administrator; proliferation of microcomputers and accessories in the company may have resulted in serious incompatibility problems. In such a case, a principal advantage that a LAN offers is the ability to share valuable resources such as laser printers. Perhaps the administrator's most basic question, when selecting a word processing program for the network, is: "Does the program support *all* our printers?"

Programs such as WordPerfect and Word are particularly strong in this area. Because network programs normally are installed to run with a specific printer, the administrator usually writes batch files under DOS that enable a user to access the word processing program along with the specific printer driver needed. When a novice network user accesses the network version of Word or WordPerfect (for example), normally the word processing program is already configured for the printer that it needs; the user will not have to specify the printer.

Laser printers have assumed a major role on most LANs, which is a major consideration in the selection of a word processing program for a network. Does the program support the laser printer's proportionally spaced fonts? *Proportional spacing* eliminates those gaping spaces found in most documents when a word processing program justifies the left and right margins.

For international companies with LANs, a second criterion for word processing programs is whether or not users must write in other languages. WordPerfect offers editions in French, German, Spanish, Finnish, Swedish, Norwegian, Dutch, and Danish.

Perhaps the most specialized foreign-language-oriented word processing program is Arabic/English/French Interword from Computers Anyware. The program comes with an EPROM chip; when installed in the motherboard of a PC, this chip permits the use of multiple languages. Interword also includes keyboard overlays that identify the letters in each language. The program permits simultaneous display of the three languages, in multiple side-by-side columns. Computers Anyware also offers word processing programs in several other languages—including Russian, Dutch, and Icelandic.

If network users need to print in any foreign language, it is imperative that the administrator select a laser printer which can use downloaded fonts (such as the Hewlett-Packard LaserJet III). The network printer will also need this capability if its users want to print special mathematical symbols and other specific characters.

Other Desirable Word Processing Features

Among the more advanced word processing features are macros, mathematical functions, multiple columns, and graphics capabilities.

All the major networkable word processing programs offer the standard, expected features—such as the capabilities to search and replace text, move and replace block paragraphs, and format text. Other word processing features are not standard, but might be desirable on a LAN; these include macros, glossaries, mathematical functions, dictionaries, and searches of documents by keywords.

Some programs (such as WordPerfect) can produce *macros*—lists of instructions the program will perform when a specific combination of keys is pressed. For example, if a company required documents to be formatted in a way that involved several complicated steps, a network administrator could write a macro that executed these steps with a single keystroke—enabling the novice user to accomplish the formatting without having to learn the entire procedure.

Many companies use what are called "boilerplate" letters—series of form paragraphs that are organized around a customer's individual request. For example, a customer who wanted to know about the availability of a Superwidget and the training classes offered might receive a letter with paragraphs describing the company, the Superwidget, and the training classes available, as well as a standard concluding paragraph offering immediate service. Some programs (such as Microsoft Word) provide glossaries that can be written and then stored. A network user who needs to insert a paragraph about the Superwidget's specifications checks the list of glossaries, and selects the appropriate Superwidget glossary entry. This material—which can range from one paragraph to several pages—would then be inserted into the letter at the desired location.

Using mathematical functions can also save network users valuable time. A salesperson can draw up a contract, have the word processing program line up the numbers in appropriate columns, and perform all the mathematical operations before providing the final cost to the customer on the appropriate contract line.

Also valuable is the inclusion of a dictionary, and even a thesaurus. Programs such as Microsoft Word and WordPerfect offer sophisticated dictionaries that help guide spelling accuracy. If a word processing program does not offer an internal dictionary, the administrator should determine whether the program's files can be read by one of the major dictionary/thesaurus programs on the market (such as those from Random House and American Heritage).

Because of the sheer number of document files found on many LANs, the capability of identifying documents by certain keywords can be an advantageous feature. A company routinely uses its word processing *document summary screen* to list the document's recipient (ABC

Supply Company), the type of correspondence (sales order confirmation), and the salesperson involved (Frank Wilson). With a program such as Ashton-Tate's network version of MultiMate Advantage, it is possible to create a *document library* and search it for a list of correspondence that matches specified criteria. This particular program also offers other special network features; these include enabling each user to create a customized dictionary, as well as public and private document files.

We have not discussed other significant word processing features; these capabilities—which include producing columns side-by-side and incorporating text and graphics on the same page—are related more closely to desktop publishing, which will be discussed shortly. The network administrator should, however, become familiar with these particular features of word processing, because desktop publishing is becoming a major network function for many companies.

Desktop Publishing

Desktop publishing refers primarily to the ability to perform a series of closely related functions, which include combining text and graphics on a single page, and designing a page with multiple columns and multiple typefaces. With programs such as Ventura Publisher and Aldus PageMaker, users can construct a newsletter with graphics and multiple columns and then produce typeset-quality copies.

Spreadsheet Features for Network Use

Spreadsheet programs are ideal for creating and maintaining budgets, performing financial analyses, forecasting sales, and thousands of other jobs involving mathematical calculations. For network use, network administrators often provide services to make the spreadsheet program easier to use.

Many network administrators will create *spreadsheet templates* for different types of users; salespeople might have a bid form, while financial analysts might have a budget form. These templates can be in a public area of the file server, so that everyone can use them. Network users who need to share the information in their completed spreadsheet generally with the network can place a copy of their data in the public area.

Macros for Spreadsheets

Because network users' levels of sophistication vary so widely, network administrators can enable novices to use complicated spreadsheets (such as Excel, Lotus 1-2-3, or SuperCalc) by writing macros—mini-programs which execute specific commands within a spreadsheet, so that a user can perform very complex operations by pressing two keys.

Special Financial/Mathematical Considerations

Some companies select a spreadsheet because of particular financial or mathematical functions. One such feature is *goal seeking*—which allows a user to name a *target value* and have the program calculate the *variable value* required to reach that goal. If a company wants to achieve a certain profit level, for example, the spreadsheet will indicate the sales volume necessary to achieve this level. SuperCalc offers this highly desirable feature. Some programs have built-in functions to handle amortization and depreciation. A network of financial analysts would want to use a program that offered various built-in functions, including those for net present value, internal rate of return, payment, future value, present value, and others.

Database Management

Database programs on a network must have record-locking as well as the ability to provide customized reports to meet the network users' range of needs.

While word processing might be the function used most often on a LAN, the LAN's very heart—and cost justification—is likely to be its *database management program.* An insurance office (for example) might have several agents accessing a central database to identify customers whose policies are about to come due. Similarly, a mail-order business might have several people processing phone orders, checking current inventory, and determining customer credit history—all dependent upon a central database program on a LAN.

Because many network users will need to use the database program simultaneously, it is essential to select a program that has a network version. Network versions will provide *record locking*—which permits several people to use the same file (such as a list of customers), as long as they don't try to view the same record (a customer's history) simultaneously. The program permits only one user to revise a specific record at a time.

Most of the major network programs are *relational database programs.* This means that it is possible to create a number of files or tables and then produce reports that reveal the *relationships* among various fields. Borland's dBASE IV is an example of this type of program. While today's database management programs have hundreds of features, we'll examine only those few which are essential for a network.

Customized Reports

Since a network must serve many different user needs, it is essential that the database management program have a sophisticated *report generator* that can create customized reports. Network administrators with unusual reporting needs might want to consider programs that can perform these functions:

- Create column-oriented or row-oriented reports
- Stamp reports with the time and date
- Provide custom borders and footers

Record and Field Limitations

Because of the scope of many network database management files, it is imperative that the network administrator determine the maximum number of records and fields that might be needed, and determine unusual field requirements so the company will not outgrow the program. For example, a salesperson who wants to keep detailed records of conversations with each customer might want a memo field capable of holding an entire page of comments.

Procedural, Programming, and Query Languages

Some companies might find that even the most sophisticated database program cannot meet their needs. In such cases, it is essential that the program offer *programming interfaces;* then database information can be manipulated by a customized program.

Some programs permit data tables to be manipulated from C programs. In their network versions, many of these programs offer *procedural language* capabilities. This means they permit the writing of short programs within the database itself.

Many network users do not need a programming or procedural language so much as they need the ability to *query* the database—to ask complicated questions based upon data relationships. A police department with a network database program (containing the characteristics of thousands of criminals) might ask to see a list of all the male burglars between 20 and 35 who are left-handed, have red hair, and walk with a limp. A *query language* would permit the user to phrase this question in English.

IBM has made it clear that it supports its Structured Query Language (SQL) as the future standard for relational database programs. Companies that wish to install network software consistent with this language—and want their future minicomputer and microcomputer network software to have file compatibility—would be wise to look at programs that support SQL.

File Formats for Databases

Because a network might be linked to a mainframe computer or another LAN, it is advantageous to have a database program capable of importing and exporting data files in a variety of formats. In addition to the dBASE format (which has become a standard at some companies), other formats such as ASCII, DIF, and SYLK are useful.

A second major consideration is whether the company already has a multiuser computer system, and wishes to move database information back and forth between the network and the operating system. Informix-SQL—a powerful database management program available under both

DOS and UNIX—is an example of how this need can be met. Since the file structure is identical under both operating systems, data can be imported and exported quickly.

Network Accounting Software

Network accounting programs must have record-locking capabilities, as well as a set of integrated modules that provide adequate network security.

Just as a database program would lose most of its value on a network without record-locking capability, an *accounting program* must also enable several users to access the same module simultaneously. A large company—with hundreds of payments arriving the first week of each month—might need several Accounts Receivable clerks to update its accounting program. While not all these clerks would need to examine the same customer record at the same time, they all would need to be able to use the Accounts Receivable module. Similarly, a computerized retail store must have an accounting program that enables several clerks to perform order entry (or point-of-sale processing) as the program instantly updates the store's inventory information.

In addition to record-locking capabilities, the network administrator and company accountant should consider a number of other accounting program features. We'll examine some of the more pressing issues that must be addressed.

The Scope of Integrated Accounting Modules

Network accounting programs offer a variety of *integrated modules.* This means that a customer chooses whether such program modules as Order Entry, Point-of-Sale, Fixed Assets, and Job Costing are needed to supplement the standard General Ledger, Accounts Receivable, Accounts Payable, and Payroll modules.

Many network programs offer integrated modules for specific industries. PROLOGIC, for example, links its financial modules and its distribution modules through Accounts Receivable and Accounts Payable. Figure 11.3 shows the relationships between integrated modules.

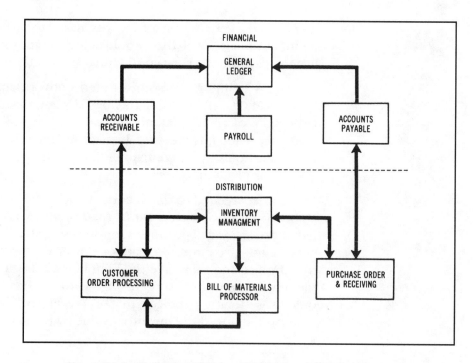

Figure 11.3 Data Flow Within a Financial and Distribution System
(Courtesy of PROLOGIC Management Systems, Inc.)

As the figure shows, this relationship can be quite complex. A wholesale distributor might have several different prices for various customers. The Customer Order Processing module creates an invoice (using information from the Bill of Materials and Inventory modules) and sends the invoice to the Accounts Receivable module (where a record of the customer's invoice amount is maintained, along with any payments made).

A network administrator who needs specialized accounting modules may have to compromise some basic accounting program features in order to enjoy the advantages of integrating specialized information into the General Ledger.

Program Security

Because of the nature of accounting, simple network security (such as a login password) is not sufficient. Most accounting departments need different security levels within a module. A payroll clerk (for example) might need a certain level of security access to produce a payroll—but definitely not a level that would allow unauthorized personnel to change pay rates or view confidential salary information.

Many of the more sophisticated network accounting packages (such as PROLOGIC) enable the network administrator to limit access to portions of a particular module. An employee might be able to enter inventory when it is received, but not see the screen listing the actual cost of the items; some companies don't want their employees to know what their profit margin is.

Closely related to this security issue is the accounting program's ability to produce a clear *audit trail* of all transactions. Most of the better programs will produce a report listing all inventory transactions, for example. An employee cannot simply reduce an item's inventory total by one and then take the item home. The audit trail report will identify the employee from the password used when he or she logged onto the system, and indicate that on a certain date at a certain time, the employee reduced the inventory value by the specified amount.

Specific Accounting Requirements

While many companies keep track of their inventories using a *FIFO* approach (first in, first out) or a *LIFO* approach (last in, first out), most accounting programs don't compute inventory in this fashion. Instead, they use a *weighted average* approach; the value of inventory is totaled and then divided by the number of items, with some items "counting heavier" than others. Some powerful programs (such as Solomon) let the network administrator and accountant specify which type of cost method to use: LIFO, FIFO, average cost, specific identification, standard, or a user-defined approach.

Companies often have specific field requirements. They may need a 12-digit general ledger account number, for example, or inventory part numbers of 14 digits. The network administrator and accountant should use their present accounting reports as a model, and ask prospective software vendors to provide a demonstration that proves their programs can meet such requirements. The demonstration should also provide evidence of how easy it is to enter information and move from one menu screen to another. Figure 11.4 illustrates the amount of information provided on typical menu screens in the Solomon accounting program.

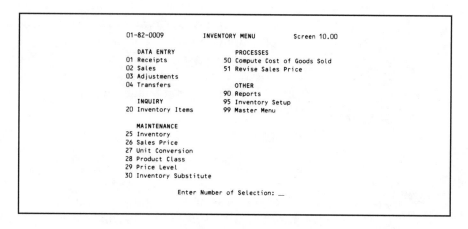

Figure 11.4   Typical Inventory Screens (Portions of this work have been copyrighted by TLB, Inc., and have been used in this work with the consent of TLB, Inc.)

Accounting Report Capabilities

Many accounting programs offer dozens of standard reports, but what happens if a company needs a certain report that doesn't follow the conventional pattern? Some companies, such as MBA, offer built-in *financial report writers* that permit some choice in selecting which lines will be printed in a balance sheet.

What if a company needs a report comprised of information from two or three modules? There are two possible solutions to this dilemma. One solution is to pay thousands of dollars for a customized program.

Or, if the accounting program is written in COBOL, then Snow Software's qPLEX IV might be a viable solution. This program can generate reports from various files, and then perform mathematical operations within the reports. The program works with accounting programs such as Real World, and database management programs such as DataFlex and dBASE IV.

Customizing Accounting Programs

It's unlikely that one program will satisfy all the accounting needs of a company. Some programs permit *user customization,* while others require the purchase of a source code, or provide a customizing service to users at standard programming rates. Open Systems Accounting Software permits its users to customize menus (which can include rewriting menu entries and changing the order of a menu). If more elaborate programming changes are needed, Open Systems makes the source code available. The company also publishes a list of software developers familiar with its source code.

Other Major Accounting Features Worth Considering

Since the implementation of an accounting program on a network is supposed to make the accounting more efficient, a number of program features that can help achieve this goal are worth considering:

- Automatic (rather than manual) handling of recurring entries can help reduce errors.
- Since a network frequently adds users, a feature that provides on-line help screens can reduce training time and make new users more productive.
- Since networks are as prone to power failure as single-user systems, some accounting programs provide frequent backups, and even update their master file with each transaction. This approach ensures accurate on-line data queries, and minimizes data loss in the event of power failure.

Network Groupware Software

One major new type of network software is known as *groupware:* software that permits several users to work on the same document and observe each other's suggestions. Computer Associates' ForComment, for example, enables authors to supply annotations and suggested revisions to a document. These notes are collated automatically, on a line-by-line basis; the original author can view each suggested revision, and then accept it with a single keystroke. The software maintains an *audit log* that records all suggestions and changes.

Group Technologies' Aspect is a program that permits several authors to work simultaneously on the same document. Whenever one user makes a change, all users' copies of this document change to reflect the emendation.

While groupware lends itself very easily to word processing applications, it can be used with a variety of different types of programs. SoftSolutions Technology Corporation, for example, publishes a program called SoftSolutions Global—which enables users of a LAN or a *WAN (wide area network)* to access, manage, and combine spreadsheets or documents produced with other applications, across several LANs or WANs.

One vital requirement for many groupware packages is the ability to share information across a distributed platform that includes several different network operating systems. Some users of a company's UNIX network might need to exchange or replicate information from a document found on a LAN Manager or NetWare network. Lotus' Notes program enables users to work on the same document on several different platforms.

The Notes program illustrates how groupware programs replicate a document so it can be edited and revised simultaneously on several different platforms. A *Notes domain* consists of up to 10,000 network users. Each domain has its own Name and Address Book, which defines the domain's structure. Each Notes server communicates with another Notes server by creating a Connection Document (which handles replication of a document by prioritizing when a particular database should be replicated).

A network manager can determine whether Notes replication takes place in a bidirectional or unidirectional way. When two servers exchange information in a *bidirectional replication mode,* both servers' databases are updated to reflect changes to the same document made by users on both networks. The Notes program uses a time-stamp feature to determine the latest version of a document that has been undergoing a number of changes.

What Have You Learned?

1. MS-DOS versions 3.1 and above permit multiuser operations on a LAN because they permit byte-locking.

2. Single-user software lacks the record-locking feature desirable on a LAN. Using such a program on a network also violates its licensing agreement.

3. Document-oriented word processing programs offer many advantages over page-oriented programs.

4. A query language can make it much easier to use a powerful database management program.

5. Network accounting programs often consist of a number of sophisticated integrated modules.

6. Some software vendors encourage customers to customize their packages to meet individual needs.

7. Groupware software enables several users to work on the same project at the same time, and see one another's comments.

Quiz for Chapter 11

1. For multiuser operations, use a version of MS-DOS that is at least

    a. 3.0.

    b. 2.1.

    c. 3.1.

    d. 1.1.

2. The program that acts as a "traffic cop" to direct requests for shared network resources is called

    a. Master Manager.

    b. IBM PC Traffic Manager.

    c. the Director.

    d. the Redirector.

3. A single Notes domain can handle

    a. 10,000 users.

    b. 100 users.

    c. 1,000 users.

    d. 1 million users.

4. Writing a customized form letter using a list of names and addresses is a function known as

    a. the "Dear John" letter.

    b. boilerplate.

    c. mail merge.

    d. "shopping list" processing.

5. A series of form paragraphs linked together is a word processing function known as

    a. mail merge.

    b. boilerplate.

    c. mail link.

    d. paragraph meld.

6. A feature that enables an electronic spreadsheet user to program several spreadsheet functions so that they may be performed with a couple of keystrokes is known as a

   a. micro.

   b. macro.

   c. BASIC interface.

   d. firmware chip.

7. A spreadsheet feature that allows a user to name a target value and have the program calculate the variable value required to reach that goal is known as

   a. circular reasoning.

   b. target variables.

   c. micro justification.

   d. goal seeking.

8. As a query language, IBM supports

   a. Clout.

   b. SQL.

   c. ADL.

   d. QUESTION.

12 | Local Area Network Selection

About This Chapter

A company must make many decisions before it purchases a LAN. We'll examine how a company can do its initial needs analysis—factoring in company information needs, existing resources, and plans for future growth. While most companies will still need to talk with data communications and telecommunications consultants, such early analysis provides a basis for discussion and prevents the consultants from selecting a system that may meet *their* needs, but does not solve the company's major problems.

In this chapter, we'll look at the steps necessary to develop a request for proposal (RFP) and follow-up procedures. We will also consider the problems posed by multiple vendors, and by maintenance and training considerations for both hardware and software.

Solving Problems with Local Area Networks

Once problems are identified, the question to ask is, "Will a LAN help solve these problems?"

When assessing their LAN needs, companies that already have data communication and telecommunication equipment will generally ask this question first: "What problems do we have that might be solved if we implement a network?" When interviewing employees from several departments, you will often hear similar problems described. These might include:

- Too much duplication of effort (several salespeople typing form letters, for example).
- Too much paperwork. (Why can't we eliminate most of the memos and use electronic mail?)
- Loss of data integrity because people working on the same project need to swap disks frequently.
- Mounting hardware and software expenses, since departments don't share resources but build "kingdoms."
- Inability to obtain data from other departments.
- Security concerns over use of computerized information.
- Growing hardware and line expenses for departments that need to use public information networks.

Problems such as these suggest a need for a LAN. The next step is to inventory existing hardware and software resources, to determine whether they are compatible with a LAN's solution.

The information gathered could result in a *request for proposals (RFP)*. By analyzing a company's current equipment, it is possible to determine what additional equipment is needed to enable the company to operate more efficiently—as well as what additional functions need to be performed. As we will see later in this chapter, vendors reply to an RFP with specific lists of equipment and software to address the company's needs.

Surveying Your Data Communications and Telecommunications Resources

Telecommunications Equipment

Surveying your company's data communications and telecommunications capabilities can improve the flow of information.

In order to learn the most effective way to improve the flow of information, companies need to survey their data communications and telecommunications equipment. In some small companies, for example, a survey might take one minute—and consist of looking around the office—to conclude that the company has a simple telephone system (with four lines and eight telephones), and two IBM PS/2 workstations (used for word processing and accounting, respectively).

In larger companies—with much more equipment—the survey must be formalized, and an instrument developed to ensure standardized answers. Assuming the company has a PBX telephone system, some of the questions that should be asked include:

• Has a traffic study been done to determine peak periods of phone system usage?

• If the PBX were to be used for data as well as telecommunications, how much surplus capacity does the system have at present?

> **Note:** People are used to a brief delay when accessing a computer, but they expect instant telephone response. It is necessary to estimate the *degree of degradation* that would result if telecommunications and data communications were combined. Since some older PBX systems require two *dedicated data lines* for a single voice terminal, it is essential to estimate the number of terminals (and lines) the company will need for the future.

• Would some of the PBX functions—such as its *call accounting system* (which records each call, keeping track of the resulting expense)—be cost-effective if the company's data communications were linked to these functions? In other words, if the company currently uses modems to transmit data over telephone lines, would it save money if these transactions could be tracked, and perhaps recharged to the departments using these services?

• Is there significant interest in integrating voice and data communications? Is there a proportional need for it?

• If the PBX represents a possible LAN, is there any *redundancy* (backup hardware) built into this proposed switch? What happens if the PBX fails?

• Is a mainframe computer located at the same location? Is it feasible (or even desirable) for the microcomputers that comprise a LAN to communicate with the mainframe computer through the PBX?

• What kinds of private networks must be accessed by the LAN? Do these networks require speeds that are possible with a PBX?

- Does the company need to tie a number of asynchronous PC terminals to its synchronous mainframe? (Since a PBX is an excellent way of linking synchronous and asynchronous devices—and providing protocol conversion—a company that already has a PBX should consider this question very carefully.)

- Perhaps the most critical question of all—*what kind of information* needs to be shared and transmitted through a network? If the information consists of lengthy files, it might well be that the PBX isn't fast enough to accommodate the network.

In most cases, a PBX will prove inadequate to handle all data communications, because its speed cannot approach that of a dedicated computer system with data-grade cabling. Most major PBX companies (such as AT&T and Northern Telecom) offer LAN interfaces to their digital PBX systems; a company with a PBX might consider using it primarily for features like modem pooling and automatic route selection—while handling heavy data communication over a computer-based LAN.

Surveying Present Hardware/Software and Targeting Desirable Additions

Before investing in any new system, it is important to take inventory of any existing hardware and software that could be put to use on the LAN. The Marketing Department's inventory of current hardware and software might look like this:

　　1 IBM PS/80 with 4 megabytes of RAM

　　2 IBM ATs with 640K of RAM and 40-MB hard drives

　　1 Compaq 386 with an 80-MB hard disk

　　1 Dell 12-MHz 286 model with dual floppy drives

　　1 HP Vectra 286 model with a 40-MB hard drive

　　1 Hewlett-Packard LaserJet III printer

　　3 Epson LQ model 24-pin dot-matrix printers

The department currently uses a word processor, a spreadsheet, and a database manager program. Its list of present computer activity—as well as what it would like to be able to do in the future with a LAN—might look like this:

Lotus 1-2-3 worksheets for forecasting future sales

dBASE IV customer list that everyone could access

dBASE IV customer sales histories

WordPerfect sales form letter

Ability to merge form letters with customer lists

Ability to print sales contracts

Lotus 1-2-3 commission worksheets

Ability to access MRP manufacturing information (from mainframe)

Electronic mail

Remote ability to inquire on product availability

Ability to input an order on-line

Ability to track salespeople's phone expenses

Ability to switch salespeople to the least expensive long-distance carrier

Ability to share resources such as laser printer and dot-matrix printers

Ability to print envelopes as well as letters

Ability to track salespeople's performance, and produce graphs available only to the salesperson involved

After having each department make a "wish list" that includes present activity as well as these future capabilities, you need to decide whether the present software can be networked. This assessment involves evaluating present capabilities and estimating what problems a LAN might pose.

For example, if the Accounting Department has a single-user program that cannot be upgraded to a networkable version with record locking, then a new program might be needed—and buying it might be prohibitively expensive. (Even if the present accounting program uses ASCII data files, extensive programming would be needed to format this data so that it corresponds to a new program's field-and-record parameters. And this assumes it is possible to obtain the new accounting program's source code.)

The Marketing Department's desire to have remote access to the LAN is understandable. Salespeople would like to be able to view current inventory levels, and perhaps even place their orders over phone lines. If the company decides this capability is essential in its LAN implementation, it must include this requirement in its RFP.

Not all major LAN software can support remote entry. Even those networks that do may have their own requirements (such as a dedicated gateway workstation), and these can add to the expense.

The Marketing Department also expressed an interest in being able to access (or at least view) manufacturing data currently residing on a mainframe computer. Before deciding that a micro-mainframe network connection is desirable, the network administrator must determine whether or not this mainframe information is important enough to Marketing's performance to justify its access.

A complementary question can be applied to the departments using the LAN. What programming would be necessary to download the information directly from the mainframe into one of the network's programs? Of the departments that will be linked by the LAN, which ones have sufficient reason to view mainframe information to warrant the security problems that could result from establishing the link?

A major concern in many companies is the variety of computer models within departments. Not all IBM-compatibles are actually compatible *enough* to use network adapter circuit cards. As we will see shortly, the RFP needs to address this issue—and place the burden of proof on the network vendor to guarantee its network will work with all present equipment.

The Nature of Data Transmission

When contemplating installing a LAN, a company must consider what type of data will be transmitted, and must address geographic and security concerns.

Before selecting the media and network hardware and software, you need to analyze the work that will be done on the network. We just saw what the Marketing Department has in mind, but we need to know how large the dBASE IV customer lists and Lotus 1-2-3 worksheets are. Very large dBASE IV file transfers will consume valuable network time; the company may have to eliminate from consideration some of the slower LANs (1–2 Mbs) in favor of a faster network (6–20 Mbs).

Once this determination has been made, the company can look at related issues—such as geographic considerations and security requirements.

Geographic Considerations

Once a company has an idea of the software it plans in its network, and a clear picture of its present resources, the next step is to determine the geographic parameters of the network. Will it encompass several departments, a single building, or multiple buildings? Since many of the LANs use a bus topology that is limited to 1,000 feet (300 meters), a network administrator might have to look at another architecture (such as a token ring) for a larger building.

Media Selection

The network medium might be directly related to the company's geographic requirements. If the network will be installed in an environment where there is a good deal of interference, fiber optics might be required. If the building already has twisted-pair unshielded telephone wire installed, it might be cost-effective to determine whether a network could handle the data transmission requirements using this medium. If the company wants simultaneous voice and data transmission, then a medium capable of such transmission must be selected.

Security Considerations

LANs vary in the degree of security they offer. As a rule, star topology networks offer the means to *monitor all workstations,* and record the files and programs they access. (Software such as Novell's NetWare, for example, establishes several levels of network security beyond simple password protection—including the ability to set file attributes.)

It is also important to consider whether it is possible to *change user access* quickly. (Novell's concept of user groups is beneficial in situations where people's assignments change frequently, requiring changes in network access.)

There needs to be some concern for the *security and integrity of data.* What happens if a user turns off the workstation without properly closing his or her files? Sophisticated network software will prevent files from being damaged in such situations.

Another security concern is the ease with which the network topology and media allow *unauthorized entry.* It is relatively easy to connect a tap via a small isolation transformer hidden behind a termination panel. It is then child's play to connect this transformer to another line, and dial in from another location to access the network. Fiber-optic cabling offers the best protection against such intrusions.

If security is a great concern, the network administrator should consider incorporating additional security measures in the RFP. One such measure is the purchase of *terminal locks* to protect unattended workstations from unauthorized entry.

Another safeguard is the use of *callback modems.* In this system, a remote user must provide a password, which the network checks against its list of authorized passwords. If there is a match, the network hangs up and calls the remote user back, using a telephone number that is stored next to the authorized password. This practice ensures that only authorized users can access sensitive network files, and—with the use of inexpensive WATS lines—offers substantial savings. Unhappily, not all networks permit this security measure. IBM's Asynchronous Communications Server, for example, is not designed to handle callback modems.

Backing Up the File Server

The RFP should require a *backup system* so that the file server is backed up on a regular basis. Will backup software permit unattended backups? Can the network administrator flag certain files that will be backed up at specified intervals or whenever they change? Can files be restored easily if the version running on the file server is damaged?

The RFP should also require an *uninterruptible power source (UPS)* for the file server. If power is lost abruptly, the UPS (and appropriate software running on the file server) should shut down the file server quickly and efficiently, so that no files are damaged.

Developing a Request for Proposals (RFP)

A request for proposals to implement a LAN must solicit vendor information on network hardware, software, and applications programs.

We have seen that a company must conduct a thorough needs analysis before it can begin the process of inviting vendor proposals. In our example, the company first determined which software was currently being used, and then which software it planned to use under network conditions. To ensure complete compatibility, the company also surveyed its present computer workstations and printers.

Because of the limitations inherent in many networks, the company also determined the maximum size of the network, the potential for expansion, and the type of information and size of files that it wanted to transmit over a network. It also examined the security measures it might want to require to ensure only authorized access. Now the company can develop a formal RFP.

In order to receive viable vendor proposals, we must provide information in a logical order. Here is a basic outline for the heart of the RFP—to which we will add several important sections (with explanations) shortly:

I. Hardware

   A. Microcomputers

      1. What is currently on hand (brand, configuration)?

      2. Additional workstations required for network:

         a. IBM compatibility to be able to run which programs?

         b. How much RAM is required?

         c. Number of disk drives required:

            i. For security reasons, do you prefer no disk drives and an autoboot ROM chip?

            ii. If disk drives are required, what size and capacity? (360K, 720K, 1.2M, 1.44M)

         d. If a hard disk is required:

            i. Size (megabytes)

            ii. Mounted in what kind of microcomputer?

            iii. Formatted in which version of DOS?

e. Monitors and monitor adapter cards required?

    i. Color or monochrome?

    ii. Capable of what resolution?

    iii. What size?

    iv. Dual mode?

    v. Capable of running certain graphics programs?

    vi. Other features required?

f. Other I/O cards required?

    i. Parallel or serial cards and cables

    ii. Additional RAM cards

    iii. Multifunction cards

    iv. Accelerator cards

    v. Others

B. File Servers

1. Size required

2. Processing speed of file server

3. System fault tolerance (if required)

4. Number of tape backup units

5. Other features required

C. Bridges to other networks

1. Other networks to be connected

2. Adapter cards and cabling required

3. Software required

D. Backbone networks required to connect multiple bridges

1. Description of bridges to be connected

2. Processing speed required

E. Gateways to mini/mainframe environments

1. Local or remote connections

2. Protocols required

3. Number of concurrent sessions required

4. Terminal emulation required

    5. Local printer emulation required

    6. Amount of activity to be handled

F. Minicomputers

    1. Currently on hand (brand, configuration)

    2. Need to integrate information with LAN

G. Mainframe computer

    1. Currently installed (brand, configuration)

    2. Need to integrate information with LAN

H. Printers

    1. Currently on hand (brands, buffers, accessories)

    2. Additional printers needed for the LAN

        a. Speed required

        b. Type (laser, dot-matrix, etc.)

        c. Compatibility with which major printer drivers?

        d. Type of connection (parallel, serial)

        e. Length of distance from workstations

        f. Other special printer features

            i. Special language fonts or downloadable fonts

           ii. Near-letter-quality and fast dot-matrix modes

          iii. Which workstations/areas will need to access which printers?

          iv. Any unusual printing requirements (color, multiple copy, specific accounting forms, etc.)?

           v. Do any software packages that will be on the network require a specific printer?

I. Modems

    1. Currently on hand (brand, speed, special features, etc.)

    2. Needs for additional units with the LAN

    3. Transmission mode required (simplex, half duplex, full duplex)

    4. Interconnections required (point-to-point, multiple drops)

5. Special features needed

   a. Auto-dial

   b. Auto-logon

   c. Auto-answer

   d. Other

J. Plotters

   1. Presently on hand (brands, configuration)

   2. Additional units required

      a. Speed

      b. Number of colors

      c. Compatibility with which major brand?

      d. Programs to drive plotters?

K. Optical scanners

   1. Currently on hand

   2. Additional units required

      a. Speed

      b. Which fonts will be scanned?

      c. Which programs will need access to this data?

L. Other hardware required

   1. Cash registers (for retail environment)

      a. Type of connection (serial, parallel)

      b. Compatibility with which point-of-sale accounting program?

   2. Badge readers (for manufacturing environment)

      a. Will employees clock in and out of several jobs for the same day?

      b. Does this information have to be interfaced with an accounting program's payroll module?

   3. Multiplexers

      a. Devices to be attached

      b. Location of these devices

       c. Type of transmission required

       d. Speed required

   4. Protocol converters

       a. Devices to be attached

       b. Protocols involved (SNA, BSC, ASCII, etc.)?

   5. Power protection required

       a. Voltage regulation

       b. Limits sags, surges

       c. Prevents common-mode noise

       d. Provides battery backup

II. Software

  A. Operating system and utility programs

   1. DOS

       a. Which version for the root directory?

       b. Are there multiple versions on the network?

   2. Electronic mail

       a. Menu-driven

       b. Help screens available to users

       c. Display messages

       d. Distribution lists possible

       e. Notification when a message arrives

       f. Ability to forward messages

       g. Ability to define multiple user groups

       h. Ability to print and file messages

       i. Ability to attach files including graphics

       j. Other features desirable

   3. Network calendar

       a. All workstations allowed access to calendar features

       b. Ability to schedule rooms and hardware resources

B. Network management

1. Ability to perform diagnostics
2. Ability to add and delete user groups
3. Password protection
4. Maintain user statistics
5. Ability to handle remote dial-in users
6. Ability to handle multiple operating systems
7. Ability to handle bridges to other networks
8. Ability to add and delete printers easily
9. Security provided

   a. Log-in level (password required)
   b. Directory level
   c. File level
   d. File attributes

10. Menu-driven, but allowing sophisticated users to bypass the menu and use commands
11. Log-in scripts or other facilities (such as batch files) permitted to make it easier for novice users to log in
12. Printer server software

    a. Number of printers permitted on the network
    b. Number of share devices
    c. Printer queues

       i. Size
       ii. Ability to change printing priority

    d. Commands available to network users

       i. For setting parameters for specific printing jobs
       ii. For disabling printers for routine servicing

    e. Print spooling software
    f. Types of printers supported

       i. Parallel
       ii. Serial
       iii. Laser
       iv. Line printers

13. File server software

    a. Size of volumes permitted

    b. Access speed

    c. Network drives (logical drives) permitted

    d. Virtual drives (transparent to users)

    e. Restore tape to disk capability

    f. Directory hashing

14. Network communications server software

    a. Protocols supported

        i. ASCII asynchronous

        ii. 3270 BSC

        iii. 3270 SNA

        iv. X.25

    b. Speed supported

    c. Ability to handle call-back modems

    d. Automatic dial-out

    e. User statistics provided

C. Current software that the network must support

    1. Word processing

    2. Spreadsheets

    3. Database management

    4. Accounting

    5. Other application software

When the company has gathered information for its RFP up to this point, it is in a better position to determine the extent to which the prospective LAN requires a networkable upgrade (or replacement) of existing software.

Trying to Avoid Starting Over

Usually it is unlikely a new LAN will support a company's current software. Your request for proposals should detail which programs are currently being used, and the nature of their current file structure. If the word processing program permits files to be saved in ASCII format, it probably will be possible to use the data files with the new network program. Many of the most popular programs (WordPerfect, for example) have network versions of their programs. Selecting a networkable upgrade would ensure that there would be no training necessary for this portion of network activity.

Accounting is a far more complex area. Some programs have networkable upgrades. A company fortunate enough to be using a single-user version of such a program can upgrade to a network version without having to worry about file transfers or training. In most cases, however, as we saw earlier, moving from a single-user accounting program to a network accounting program means starting over.

In such a case, the company probably will choose to run the single-user program until the fiscal year's accounting cycle is complete, while gradually adding more and more customer information to the network software. After running both programs concurrently for at least a couple of months (to ensure the accuracy of the new program), the company can switch to the new system.

Software Licenses

Virtually all software packages restrict their usage—sometimes to one user, and sometimes to one machine. The RFP should provide for *site licensing* (software licensing for the network site), or specify a network version licensed for a specific number of users. This consideration leads us to add another section to our RFP outline:

D. New application software required

    1. Word processing

        a. Compatibility with current software

        b. Features required

        c. Training to be provided

    2. Spreadsheet/financial analysis

        a. Compatibility with current software

        b. Features required

        c. Training to be provided

3. Database management

    a. Compatibility with current software
    b. Features required
    c. Training to be provided

4. Accounting

    a. Compatibility with current software
    b. Features required
    c. Training to be provided

5. Custom software required

    a. Compatibility with current software
    b. Features required
    c. Training to be provided

Vendor Requirements

Vendors replying to an RFP must match benchmarks for hardware and software.

In order to complete this outline of information in our RFP, we need to examine the relationship between the company and the prospective LAN vendors. A number of questions need to be asked of vendors before a network is purchased and installed. It is an excellent idea, for example, to require that a vendor demonstrates its network's ability to run the software your company plans to install. Often companies will require a "benchmark showdown" of sorts, in which competing vendors are asked to perform under similar conditions.

Even if a vendor's equipment is capable of providing a LAN that meets your company's speed and compatibility requirements at a reasonable cost, the equipment may not prove to be sufficiently reliable. As shown in our outline for an RFP, it is imperative to request references to vendors' customers who have installations similar to the one you are considering. It is also essential to secure information about the equipment's reliability—including a *mean time between failures (MTBF),* maintenance contracts, and response time.

Frequently network vendors will offer a variety of maintenance options—including a guaranteed response time, a repair-or-replace designation, or even a guarantee to provide a "loaner" file server if the vendor is unable to repair the network within a given length of time. Before issuing an RFP, your company must determine how long it can afford to be without network services—and then require vendors to meet a response-time requirement that suits your needs.

Because a LAN includes computer hardware, network hardware and software, and third-party software, it is common for vendors to "pass the buck," and not to accept responsibility when a network problem arises. Part of the RFP should require the principal vendor to take overall responsibility for the network's maintenance. If a software problem suddenly develops, for example, the principal vendor should act as a liaison with the software company to solve your problem.

Often you may discover (to your horror) that none of the vendors have practical installation experience with the precise network configuration your company requires. At that point, you may insist on serving as a *beta site* for the vendor (and perhaps the manufacturer). A beta-site user tests the new product in a real-world work environment. Usually many bugs are discovered that require working with the vendor to fix these problems. In exchange for the experience you provide the vendor by serving as a beta site (and the referral you may later provide), you should receive a substantial discount in price.

Your company might want to insist on other safeguards as well. These can include a *performance bond* to be posted by the vendor, and a payment schedule phased to correspond to the completion level of the network (including software and hardware).

Your safeguards should be linked to the minimum level of performance you specify in your RFP. If you fear serious degradation in response time with heavy activity, you might require a minimum response time for each of a certain number of workstations when all are involved simultaneously in a certain procedure. Several major network software companies (including Novell and 3Com) make *benchmark test reports* available; these provide excellent "tests" that you can require your vendors to duplicate.

Since LANs' topology and media have a direct effect on their maximum distance, be sure the RFP includes a diagram indicating where workstations will be placed, and their approximate distances from each other. Also—and this is essential—*indicate where future growth will take place*, and whether these future workstations will require additional file servers and other peripherals.

III. Vendor Requirements

A. Experience

1. Company history: how long at present location?

2. Customer references for similar installations?

B. Service

1. Number of factory-trained service technicians

2. Ability to provide on-site service:

   a. Repair-or-replace service within 24 hours?

   b. Responds 24 hours a day?

   c. Ability to respond within two hours?

   d. Maintains a sufficient inventory of parts to provide adequate service?

C. Ability to provide a LAN demonstration

1. Software to be identical with ordered software

2. Hardware to be identical with ordered hardware

3. Benchmark tests to be conducted

D. Training

1. Can the supplier provide basic user training?

2. Can the supplier provide training on all purchased software?

3. How much training is provided with installation?

4. What is the charge for additional training?

5. Is phone support included in purchase price?

6. What kind of training does the network administrator receive? How many people may take this training?

E. If multiple vendors are required for this network, who will assume responsibility for:

1. Hardware training and network familiarization?

2. Hardware service?

3. Software training?

4. Software service?

Evaluating an RFP

Evaluating an RFP is not difficult—assuming that all key decision makers within a company agree on the criteria to be used for evaluation and (most importantly) agree on the weight each item in the evaluation should have. Table 12.1 shows sample list of criteria, and the weight associated with each one, for a company issuing an RFP.

Table 12.1. Sample Criteria List and Suggested Weight

Evaluation Item	Weight (%)
1. Cost (hardware & software)	20
2. Quality of hardware & software	10
3. Database management system	5
4. Accounting software	15
5. Productivity software	5
6. Flexibility of report generation	12
7. Response time	5
8. Vendor hardware/software support	10
9. Rapid implementation by July 1	8
10. Previous implementation record	5
11. Company's references & stability	5
	100%

What Have You Learned?

1. The first step in developing an RFP is to analyze the company's needs.

2. The geography of a company's proposed LAN will determine what kind of network topology and media are feasible.

3. In order to ensure network security, some network workstations use auto-boot ROM chips, and do not have any floppy disk drives.

4. Most software generally is licensed for one user. Network applications require special network versions (designated for a certain number of users) or software "site licensing."

5. A beta-site user tests a product under real-world conditions.

6. Vendors need to be evaluated on far more criteria than just the price they charge for equipment and services.

Quiz for Chapter 12

1. The first step in an analysis of company LAN needs is to

   a. examine the problems that currently exist that could be solved with a LAN.

   b. inventory all current software.

   c. inventory all current computer hardware.

   d. write a request for proposal (RFP).

2. The variety of microcomputers found in most companies creates a potential LAN problem because of

   a. different costs for different components.

   b. service needs.

   c. NETBIOS incompatibility.

   d. different disk drive speed.

3. If a needs analysis reveals that several programs on the network will include large databases, this could mean

   a. you will need a disk server rather than a file server.

   b. there might be a problem with file server access speed.

   c. the database software had better be able to handle long field names.

   d. the operating system cannot be DOS.

4. The geography of the company's building (including where it will need workstations) has a direct effect on

   a. the network topology.

   b. the network's medium.

   c. the network's cost.

   d. all of the above.

5. For security purposes, a network workstation might include

   a. a lock.

   b. an auto-boot ROM.

   c. no disk drives.

   d. all of the above.

6. In order to have the entire network use a specific software program, the company must obtain permission from the software company. This is known as

   a. site licensing.
   b. software permission.
   c. multiple network copies (MNC).
   d. workstation access to software help (WASH).

7. The major problem with multiple vendors in a network environment is

   a. the expense.
   b. the lack of quality.
   c. the lack of clear responsibility.
   d. network efficiency.

8. Once company officials agree on RFP criteria, these criteria should be

   a. changed.
   b. kept secret.
   c. suggestions that the vendors can change.
   d. weighted.

9. In case of a power failure, the RFP should require a(n)

   a. UPS.
   b. SQL.
   c. XCOM.
   d. Kermit.

10. In order to be able to restore damaged files, the RFP should provide for a(n)

    a. file server backup software program.
    b. UPS.
    c. asynchronous communications server.
    d. modem.

A | Directory of Local Area Network Vendors

Apple Computer Inc.
20525 Mariani Avenue
Cupertino, California 95014

Artisoft Inc.
575 East River Road
Tucson, Arizona 85704

AT&T Information Systems
1 Speedway Avenue
Morristown, New Jersey 07960

Banyan Systems, Inc.
135 Flanders Road
Westboro, Massachusetts 01581

Datapoint Corporation
9725 Datapoint Drive
San Antonio, Texas 78784

DCA (10Net)
(Digital Communications Associates, Inc.)
1000 Aldermann Drive
Alpharetta, Georgia 30201

IBM
(International Business Machines Corporation)
Post Office Box 1328
Boca Raton, Florida 33429-1328

IEEE
(Institute of Electrical and Electronics Engineers, Inc.)*
10662 Los Vaqueros Circle
Los Alamitos, California 90720

Novell, Inc.
122 East 1700 South
Provo, Utah 84601

Sitka
(formerly TOPS, now a subsidiary of Sun Microsystems, Inc.)
950 Marina Village Parkway
Alameda, California 94501

Source of information on IEEE standards

B | Glossary

Active Token Monitor: The workstation that assumes responsibility for network management in IBM's Token Ring Network.

Apple File Protocol: The suite of protocols associated with Apple's local area network.

AppleShare: Apple's file server software for its local area networks.

Application Layer: The layer of the OSI model concerned with application programs such as electronic mail, database managers, and file server software.

ARCnet: A local area network featuring a physical bus and logical star.

ARM: Asynchronous Response Mode. Stations send messages whenever they desire to transmit, without waiting for a poll bit.

ASCII: American Standard Code for Information Interchange. A character code used by microcomputers.

Asynchronous Communications Server: Provides the capability for network workstations to access ASCII applications via switched communications lines.

Automatic Rollback: Under TTS, when a system fails, the database is reconstructed at the point just prior to the transaction during which the failure took place.

Backbone: A high-speed link joining together several network bridges.

Background Tasks: The tasks performed by other network users under PC Network.

Baseband: Single-channel coaxial cable.

Batch File: A file containing commands that can cause several different programs to execute automatically.

Beacon: A special network signal indicating the address of a node immediately upstream from a defective node.

BIOS: Basic Input/Output System. ROM software.

Bit Stuffing: The insertion of a 0-bit to ensure that no data contains more than five straight zeros.

BRI: Basic Rate Interface. Under ISDN, used to service small-capacity devices such as terminals.

Bridge: A connection between two networks that takes place at the Data Link layer.

Broadband: Coaxial cable capable of carrying several signals simultaneously on different channels.

Broadcast Messages: Messages sent to all computers on a network.

BSC: Binary Synchronous Communication. A synchronous protocol used on many older IBM mainframe computers.

Bus: A data highway. This term is also used to designate a simple linear-shaped local area network.

Call-Back Modem: Modems designed to call back a remote caller to verify identity for security purposes.

CCITT: Consultative Committee for International Telephony and Telegraphy.

CCITT X.3: Protocol for the packet assembly/disassembly facility in a public data network.

CCITT X.25: A standard for data packets sent to public switched networks. This standard corresponds to the OSI model's first three layers.

CCITT X.28: Protocol governing the interface between a DTE and a DCE, when a DTE in start-stop mode accesses the packet assembly/disassembly facility (PAD) on a public data network situated in the same country.

CCITT X.75: Protocol governing control procedures for terminals, transmitted calls, and the data transfer system on international circuits between packet-switched networks.

CCITT X.400: A set of protocols governing electronic mail.

CCITT X.500: A set of protocols governing worldwide directories for electronic mail.

Centralized File Server: A single file server that serves a local area network.

Cladding: A layer of glass that surrounds optic fibers in fiber-optic cables.

Client/Server: A type of network relationship in which a node runs "front-end" (client) software to access the software running on a "server."

Contention Network: Workstations competing for the right to send a message over the network.

CSMA/CD: Carrier Sense Multiple Access with Collision Detection. A method of avoiding data collisions on a local area network.

DCE: Data Communication Equipment; generally refers to modems.

Dedicated File Server: A file server that performs only that function, and performs no computing functions.

Directory Hashing: File server software that maps all directory files and keeps this information in RAM.

Disk Caching: File server keeps often-requested files in RAM for rapid response in workstation requests.

Disk Server: A hard disk used to share files with several users. Usually programs are single-user (only one user may use them at a time).

Distributed File Serving: Distributed data processing to several computers rather than one central computer.

Domain Controller: A file server controlling security for a set of resources under the Extended Services option of the IBM PC LAN Program.

DTE: Data Terminal Equipment; generally consists of terminals or computers.

Duplexed Drives: A system fault tolerant technique in which virtually all hardware is duplicated, including disk controller, interface, and power supply.

EBCDIC: The Extended Binary Coded Decimal Interchange Code. A character code used by IBM's larger computers.

Elevator Seeking: A file server determines in which order to execute file requests, based upon the current location of the disk drive heads.

FAT: File Allocation Table. A table that helps a disk server or file server keep track of where particular files are located.

FDDI: The Fiber Data Distributed Interface of fiber-optic cabling. A standard for 100-Mbs network transmission speed.

File Locking: Software that locks a file so that only one user may use it at a time.

File Server: A PC that maintains its own FAT and provides files to nodes.

Foreground Task: A task a user performs on his or her own machine while using IBM PC LAN Program.

FSK: Frequency Shift Keying. A technique of shifting between two close frequencies to modulate ones and zeroes and speed up transmission.

Gateway PC: A PC containing gateway hardware and software, used as a LAN gateway to another machine (often a mainframe computer).

Headend: That portion of a broadband network that serves as the communications center for transmission and reception of signals.

HDLC: High-Level Data Link Control procedures. This protocol defines standards for linking a DTE and a DCE.

IEEE: The Institute of Electrical and Electronics Engineers.

IEEE 802.3: The industry standard for a bus local area network using CSMA/CD.

IEEE 802.4: The industry standard for a token bus local area network.

IEEE 802.5: The industry standard for a token ring local area network.

IEEE 802.6: The industry standard for metropolitan area networks.

Inbound Band: Carries data from a LAN node to the headend.

ISDN: Integrated Services Digital Network. A CCITT model for the eventual integration of voice and data and a universal interface for networks.

ISN: Information Systems Network. AT&T's high-speed network that features integrated voice and data transmission.

ISO: International Standards Organization.

Jam: A signal sent through a network to indicate a data collision has occurred.

LAN Manager: OS/2's network operating system.

LLC: The Logical Link sublayer of the OSI model's Data Link layer.

Local Printer: A printer attached to a microcomputer that prints this computer's documents only, and performs no network printing functions.

LocalTalk: The hardware associated with Apple's local area network.

Login Script: A predetermined set of steps performed to customize a network environment whenever a user logs in.

LU: Logical Units. These can represent end users, application programs, or other devices. Communication under SNA is among LUs.

LU 6.2: A protocol that will make it possible to have peer-to-peer communications under SNA.

MAC: The Media Access Control sublayer of the OSI model's Data Link layer.

Mirrored Drives: Two hard drives onto which data is simultaneously written.

MAU: Multistation Access Unit. A wiring concentrator linking several network workstations to an IBM Token Ring Network.

MTBF: Mean Time Between Failures. A standard used to evaluate a product's reliability.

Multimode Fiber: Fiber-optic cabling consisting of several fibers.

NAK: A Negative AcKnowledgement signal.

NAU: Network Addressable Unit; under SNA, logical units, physical units, and system services control points.

Network Adapter Card: Circuit card required in the expansion bus of a workstation under most popular LAN operating systems.

Network Layer: The layer of the OSI LAN model that establishes protocols for packets, message priorities, and network traffic control.

Node: An individual workstation on a local area network. Generally includes a monitor, keyboard, and its own microprocessor, as well as a network interface card; it may or may not have its own disk drives.

Nondedicated File Server: A file server that also functions as an independent microcomputer.

NRM: Normal Response Mode. When a central computer receives a message that a station wishes to send, it sends a poll bit to the requesting station.

OSI Model: Open Systems Interconnection protocols for establishing a local area network.

Outbound Band: Carries data from the headend to the LAN nodes.

Partitioning: Dividing a hard disk into several user volumes or areas.

Path Control Network: Responsible under SNA for identifying addresses of devices that wish to converse, and then establishing a network path for them.

PBX: Private Branch Exchange. A sophisticated telephone system.

Peer-to-Peer Network: A network in which nodes share their resources (such as printers or hard disk drives) with other network users.

Physical Layer: The layer of the OSI LAN model that establishes protocols for voltage, data transmission timing, and rules for "handshaking."

PMD: The Physical Media-Dependent layer of the fiber data distributed interface found in fiber-optic cabling.

Presentation Layer: The layer of the OSI model concerned with protocols for network security, file transfers, and format functions.

PRI: Primary Rate Interface. Used under ISDN to service large-capacity devices such as PBXs.

Print Spooler: Software that creates a buffer where files to be printed can be stored while they wait their turn.

Protocol: A set of rules or procedures commonly agreed upon by industry-wide committees (such as IEEE and ANSI).

PU: Physical Unit. This represents a tangible part of the system (such as a terminal or intelligent controller) under SNA.

Public Volume: An area of a hard disk containing information that may be shared by several users.

Read-Only: Files that can be read but cannot be changed.

Record Locking: Software feature that locks a record so that several users can share the same file, but cannot share the same record.

Repeaters: Devices on local area networks that rebroadcast a signal to prevent its degradation.

RFP: Request For Proposals.

RJE: Remote Job Entry. The sending of information in batch form, from a remote site (often unattended by a user) to an IBM mainframe.

Roll-Forward Recovery: Under TTS, keeping a complete log of all transactions in order to ensure that everything can be recovered.

Router: A device that links two networks that are running different protocols.

SCSI: Small Computer Systems Interface. An interface used to connect additional disk drives, tape backup units, or other SCSI-based peripherals to a PC.

SDLC: Synchronous Data Link Control. A subset of the HDLC protocol used by IBM computers running under SNA.

Semaphore: A flag that is set in order to make a file local; this procedure prevents two users from using the file simultaneously, which would destroy it.

Session: Under SNA, a logical and physical path connecting two NAUs for data transmission.

Session Layer: The layer of the OSI model concerned with network management functions (including passwords, network monitoring, and reporting).

Site Licensing: Procedure in which software is licensed to be used only at a particular location.

SMDR: Station Message Detail Reporting. This type of report uses a computer to analyze telephone calls to determine cost patterns.

SNA: Systems Network Architecture. The architecture used by IBM's minicomputers and mainframe computers.

Spanning Tree: A type of bridge where networks with multiple bridges ensure that the traffic transmitted on a bridge flows in one direction only.

Split Seeks: A system with duplexed drives checks to see which disk system can respond more quickly.

Splitter: A device that divides a signal into two different paths.

SRPI: Under SNA, the Server/Requester Programming Interface that allows PC applications to request services from IBM mainframes.

SSCP: System Services Control Point. An SNA network manager for a single SNA domain.

Star: A network topology physically resembling a star. This network, built around a central computer, fails completely if the main computer fails.

StreetTalk: The distributed database serving as a network-naming service for the Vines local area network.

Synchronous Transmission: The continuous sending of information in packet form, rather than one byte at a time.

System Fault Tolerant: Duplication of hardware and data to ensure that failure of part of a network (a system fault) will not result in network downtime.

10BaseT: A new IEEE standard for a 10-Mbs twisted-pair transmission network.

Token: A data packet used to transmit information on a Token Ring Network.

Topology: The physical arrangement or shape of a network.

Transient Error: A "soft" network transmission error, often intermittent and easily corrected by retransmission.

Transport Layer: The layer of the OSI model concerned with protocols for error recognition and recovery, as well as with regulation of information flow.

TSI: Time Slice Intervals. The way a file server divides its time.

TTS: Transaction Tracking System. A way to ensure data integrity on multiuser databases.

Twisted-Pair Wire: Two insulated wires twisted together so that each wire faces the same amount of interference from the environment.

Wire Center: Connections that enable network administrators to add and remove network workstations without disrupting network operations.

Workstation: A network node. Often such nodes do not contain disk drives.

APPENDIX

C | Bibliography

American Telephone and Telegraph Company. *Introduction to Information Systems Network (ISN)*. AT&T Information Systems Publication 999-740-101IS.

American Telephone and Telegraph Company. *STARLAN Network Application Programmer's Reference Manual*. AT&T Information Systems Publication 999-802-215IS.

American Telephone and Telegraph Company. *AT&T STARLAN Network Custom Guide*. AT&T Information Systems Publication 999-350-00115.

American Telephone and Telegraph Company. *STARLAN Network Design Guide*. AT&T Information Systems Publication 999-809-101IS.

American Telephone and Telegraph Company. *STARLAN Network Introduction*. AT&T Information Systems Publication 999-809-100IS.

American Telephone and Telegraph Company. *STARLAN Network Technical Reference Manual*. AT&T Information Systems Publication 999-300-208IS.

Apple Computer Corporation. *AppleTalk Network System Overview*. Addison-Wesley Publishing Company, 1989.

Banyan Systems, Inc. *Vines Administrator's Reference*. Banyan Systems Publication 092047-000.

Banyan Systems, Inc. *Vines User's Guide.* Banyan Systems Publication 092002-002.

Bartee, Thomas C., ed. *Data Communications, Networks, and Systems.* Howard W. Sams, 1985.

Digital Communications Association, Inc. *10Net Software Reference Manual.* 10Net Communications (DCA) Publication 001908.

Dixon, R.C., Strole, N.C. and Markov, J.D. "A Token Ring Network for Local Data Communications." *IBM Systems Journal* 22 (1983): 47-62.

International Business Machines Corporation. *An Introduction to Local Area Networks.* IBM Publication GC 20-8203-1.

International Business Machines Corporation. *IBM PC Network Program User's Guide.* IBM Publication 6361559.

International Business Machines Corporation. *IBM Token Ring Network: A Functional Perspective.* IBM Publication G520-6062-1.

International Business Machines Corporation. *IBM Token Ring Network Decision.* IBM Publication G320-9438-1.

International Business Machines Corporation. *IBM Token Ring Network PC Products Description and Installation.* IBM Publication GG 24-173900.

Novell, Inc. *Menu Utilities.* Novell Publication 100-000323-001.

Novell, Inc. *Supervisor's Guide.* Novell Publication 100-000425-001.

O'Brien, Bill. "Network Management: Tips, & Traps." *PC World* (September 1986): 228-237.

Schatt, Stan. *Linking LANs.* Tab/McGraw-Hill, 1991.

Schatt, Stan. *Microcomputers in Business & Society.* Charles Merrill Publishing Company, 1989.

Schatt, Stan. *Understanding NetWare.* Howard W. Sams, 1989.

Stamper, David. *Business Data Communications.* Benjamin/ Cummings, 1986.

Strole, Normal C. "A Local Communications Network Based on Interconnected Token-Access Rings: A Tutorial." *IBM Journal of Research Development* 27 (September 1983): 481-496.

Sun Microsystems, Inc. *TOPS DOS Version 2.1.* Sun Microsystems, TOPS Division (now Sitka Division), 1988.

3Com Corporation. *3+ Administrator Guide for Macintosh.* 3Com Publication 3283-8145.

D | Answers to Quizzes

Chapter 1:

1. a
2. b
3. a
4. b
5. d
6. a
7. c
8. b

Chapter 2:

1. c
2. c
3. b
4. b
5. b
6. b
7. d
8. a
9. b
10. c
11. a
12. c
13. a
14. b
15. c
16. b
17. b
18. b
19. d
20. a

Chapter 3:	Chapter 4:
1. b	1. b
2. b	2. b
3. d	3. b
4. c	4. a
5. b	5. b
6. c	6. b
7. a	7. a
8. c	8. c
9. d	9. a
10. c	10. b
11. c	11. c
12. b	12. c
13. b	13. b
14. c	14. a
15. b	15. c
16. b	16. b
17. d	17. a
18. a	18. c
19. a	
20. a	

Chapter 5:

1. c
2. b
3. d
4. a
5. b
6. a
7. a
8. b
9. b
10. c
11. a
12. c
13. b
14. d
15. b
16. b
17. d
18. d

Chapter 6:

1. d
2. b
3. c
4. d
5. a
6. b
7. c
8. d
9. b
10. b
11. a
12. b
13. b
14. d
15. b
16. a
17. b
18. c
19. a
20. d

Chapter 7:

1. b
2. c
3. a
4. b
5. a
6. d
7. c
8. d
9. a
10. b
11. b
12. a
13. a
14. b
15. c
16. b
17. a
18. a
19. b
20. b

Chapter 8:

1. a
2. b
3. d
4. c
5. a
6. b
7. b
8. c
9. c
10. b
11. a
12. c
13. d
14. c
15. a

Chapter 9:

1. c
2. a
3. b
4. b
5. c
6. a
7. c
8. c
9. d
10. c
11. c
12. a
13. c
14. d
15. b
16. a
17. a
18. c
19. d
20. a

Chapter 10:

1. b
2. a
3. b
4. d
5. c
6. b
7. d
8. c
9. a
10. d

Chapter 11:

1. c
2. d
3. a
4. c
5. b
6. b
7. d
8. b

Chapter 12:

1. a
2. c
3. b
4. d
5. d
6. a
7. c
8. d
9. a
10. a

Index

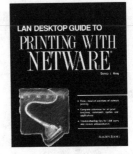

Sams Guarantees Your Success In 10 Minutes!

The *10 Minute Guides* provide a new approach to learning computer programs. Each book teaches you the most often used features of a particular program in 15 to 20 short lessons—all of which can be completed in 10 minutes or less. What's more, the *10 Minute Guides* are simple to use. You won't find any "computer-ese" or technical jargon— just plain English explanations. With straightforward instructions, easy-to-follow steps, and special margin icons to call attention to important tips and definitions, the *10 Minute Guides* make learning a new software program easy and fun!

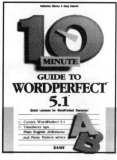

10 Minute Guide to WordPerfect 5.1
Katherine Murray & Doug Sabotin
160 pages, 51/2 x 81/2, $9.95 USA
0-672-22808-4

10 Minute Guide to MS-DOS 5
Jack Nimersheim
160 pages, 5 1/2 x 81/2, $9.95 USA
0-672-22807-6

10 Minute Guide to Windows 3
Katherine Murray & Doug Sabotin
160 pages, 5 1/2 x 81/2, $9.95 USA
0-672-22812-2

10 Minute Guide to PC Tools 7
Joe Kraynak
160 pages, 5 1/2 x 81/2, $9.95 USA
0-672-30021-4

10 Minute Guide to Lotus 1-2-3
Katherine Murray & Doug Sabotin
160 pages, 51/2 x 8 1/2, $9.95 USA
0-672-22809-2

10 Minute Guide to Q&A 4, Revised Edition
Arlene Azzarello
160 pages, 51/2 x 81/2, $9.95 USA
0-672-30035-4

10 Minute Guide to Harvard Graphics 2.3
Lisa Bucki
160 pages, 51/2 x 81/2, $9.95 USA
0-672-22837-8

See your local retailer or call 1-800-428-5331.